# UNDERSTANDING WESTERN TOURISTS IN DEVELOPING COUNTRIES

# Understanding Western Tourists in Developing Countries

**Ton van Egmond**
*NHTV Breda University of Applied Sciences, the Netherlands*

www.cabi.org

**CABI is a trading name of CAB International**

CABI Head Office
Nosworthy Way
Wallingford
Oxfordshire OX10 8DE
UK

CABI North American Office
875 Massachusetts Avenue
7th Floor
Cambridge, MA 02139
USA

Tel: +44 (0)1491 832111
Fax: +44 (0)1491 833508
E-mail: cabi@cabi.org
Website: www.cabi.org

Tel: +1 617 395 4056
Fax: +1 617 354 6875
E-mail: cabi-nao@cabi.org

A catalogue record for this book is available from the British Library, London, UK.

A catalogue record for this book is available from the Library of Congress, Washington, DC.

ISBN-13: 978 1 84593 195 7

Typeset by AMA DataSet Ltd, UK.
Printed and bound in the UK by Biddles Ltd, King's Lynn, Norfolk.

# Contents

# The Great Unknown

Tourists are a poorly explored part of the tourism business despite the fact that within a few decades tourism has grown from a marginal to one of the world's dominant economic sectors. Leading umbrella organizations such as the World Tourism Organization (WTO) and the World Travel and Tourism Council (WTTC) believe that, from a global perspective, the full expansion of tourism growth has yet to come. In spite of its present importance virtually all parties involved lack sufficient knowledge of the tourism consumer, in particular in relation to sustainable tourism development. 'Most tourism executives, managers, planners and developers pay respect to the adage "know thy consumer". Little consistent effort has been directed in research and in academia towards a basic understanding of the consumer' (Taylor, 1998, p. 267). Failing to understand the complexity and dynamics of the tourist phenomenon, many policy papers and development plans related to tourism are unable to adequately analyse the tourism potential or competitive position of destination areas. Consequently, both in the fields of product development and visitor management, as well as in the field of communication with the consumer, countless initiatives and interventions by either public or private sector or non-governmental organizations have had limited results or even overreached their goals.

Understanding tourists is an urgent need particularly in relation to developing countries. With a few exceptions only, developing countries exert themselves to develop tourism in order to increase foreign exchange earnings, to generate income and employment and to diversify the economy. The World Tourism Organization strongly advocates tourism as a tool for the alleviation of poverty in poor countries. All over Latin America, Africa and parts of Asia numerous tourism projects are initiated by local authorities, communities or non-governmental organizations to contribute to local and regional economic development. Many projects, however, fail to reach their economic goals. They either have problems in attracting the required volume of visitors, so as to pass the break-even point, or host the 'wrong' (i.e. non-lucrative and/or harmful) visitors. Most projects are inward-oriented rather than market-oriented, that is, they are not set up to meet an apparent demand but rather to reduce local needs. Knowledge of potential markets is commonly lacking, as are the tools to enter and exploit these markets. An additional complication for most developing countries is that long-haul markets, in particular European and North American markets, are more interesting, from an income and employment point of view, than domestic or regional markets. Last but not least, many local tourism projects, community-based projects in particular, are by their very nature dependent upon specific niches in the international long-haul markets.

Understanding the tourist phenomenon, as well as the ability to employ specific marketing tools, are critical success factors for tourism development in local and regional destination areas in developing countries.

In a similar way, understanding tourists is a critical success factor in using tourism as a tool for nature protection. Non-governmental organizations involved in nature conservation and national authorities in quite a few developing countries are increasingly aware of the potential of tourism to contribute to the protection and conservation of nature areas, of wildlife and biological diversity. The opening of nature areas to tourists creates a cash flow that might be used for effective conservation and management of nature. When using the attraction of natural areas brings along additional employment and income for inhabitants of the nature areas, support for conservation will increase. In developing countries nature protection and poverty alleviation might go hand in hand this way. Attracting both the 'right' tourists and the desired number of tourists is one of the critical issues. Most conservation projects, however, are resource-oriented rather than market-oriented, that is, managers – often conservationists – think more in terms of nature protection than of attracting and serving specific target groups. A better understanding of tourists is an essential condition for effective marketing and management of nature.

Besides nature, many developing countries offer culture to tourists, in terms of heritage sites, local folklore or community life. To maximize economic benefits and minimize undesired social and cultural impacts, adequate product development and visitor management is essential. However, the examination of the cultural tourism market is typified by descriptive and unsophisticated analysis. Most research is focused upon documenting the size of the consumer base, without considering that different types of cultural tourists may seek qualitatively different experiences or may be capable of appreciating attractions at different levels (McKercher, 2002, p. 29). So, a better understanding of tourists is an essential condition for effective marketing and management of culture.

An issue that is not specific to developing countries concerns the nature of tourists themselves. Many discourses on sustainable tourism development refer to lack of awareness of environmental and social-cultural impacts among tourists. Tourist attitudes and behaviour are presumed to be critical factors in successfully developing tourism in a sustainable way. However, research focusing upon tourists' attitudes and behaviour in relation to sustainability issues is still largely in its infancy. Consequently, strategies have yet to be developed that adequately address the contribution of tourists to sustainable development of tourism, or reduce unsustainable impacts.

## 1.1 The Study of Tourists

Recent years have shown a flood of literature about tourism and tourists, in more than a dozen tourism-related journals and in an abundance of textbooks. Disciplines such as sociology, (social) psychology and anthropology have joined economics and geography, which were the first to discover tourism. Although many authors argue that tourism should be the subject of multidisciplinary (e.g. Wang, 2000; Mowforth and Munt, 2003), interdisciplinary or even extradisciplinary studies (Tribe, 1997), there is still a lack of comprehensive studies that take into account the heterogeneity, complexity and dynamics of the phenomenon.

Textbooks on consumer behaviour generally do not take the social or cultural context of this behaviour into account (e.g. Kardes, 2001; Solomon, 2001; Solomon *et al.*, 2002; Schiffman and Kanuk, 2004). They all devote a chapter to *Consumer Motivation* but motivation is about human needs. It is seen as a psychological force, as is demonstrated by chapters such as 'The motivation process: a psychological perspective' (Solomon *et al.*, 2002, p. 93). Needs are taken for granted as something universal, not culture-bound, and are either seen as biological (innate) or learned. Learning processes are approached as individual learning processes, rather than collective or group processes. This book takes the position that learning, including learning of needs and preferences, finds place in a social and cultural context. Only by specifying this context can one understand individual learning processes and motivation (see Appendix A). Innate biological needs do not have a great relevance for understanding tourist behaviour. If we have innate needs, as is presumed by Maslow

(1970), among others, these needs cannot explain the specific choices consumers make. Undoubtedly, a certain explorative instinct is part of our biological equipment: not long after having been born, we start to explore the world around us, showing an innate tendency. A need for exploration, however, cannot explain tourist behaviour. If an innate *Ulysses factor* should exist (a discoverer's gene, an inborn tendency to sail the seven seas, named after Odysseus or Ulysses), most of us are extremely skilful in hiding it.

Understanding tourist behaviour (including motivation, learning processes and the development of tastes and preferences) in a social and cultural context requires linking up psychological and anthropological micro-level studies with historical, sociological and economic macro-level studies. Most tourism related studies, however, are disciplinary in character and are not able to link these levels. Studies that explicitly attempt to show the interrelationships between the micro-level psychological and the macro-level sociological aspects of tourist behaviour are almost entirely missing (Jamal and Lee, 2003, p. 48). Starting from sociological, psychological, economic or anthropological disciplines, most studies have not been able to meet Cohen's (1988, p. 45) plea in favour of theoretically complex and sophisticated research that would simultaneously take account of, and compare, the tourist's psychological needs and experiences, the socio-structural features of tourist settings, and the cultural symbols expressed in the touristic process.

Unfortunately, lack of comprehensive studies is only one of several inadequacies in tourism literature. Among the other inadequacies – which the present study aspires to overcome – are:

- Both academic authors on the tourist phenomenon and travel writers show middle class and/or elitist pre-occupations with mass tourism, as opposed to travelling, 'real holidays' or 'serious holidays', and, consequently, are evaluative rather than analytical in their approaches to tourism issues.
- This holds particularly true for tourism impact studies, which often divide up tourists as either belonging to the masses or the travellers, with the implication that good behaviour tends to reside in the latter rather than the former. Mowforth and Munt (2003, p. 26) refer to a highly polarized and simplified debate, equating to 'tourists = mass tourism = bad' and 'travellers = appropriate travelling = good'.
- Many textbooks and articles fail to take the complexity and dynamics of the tourist phenomenon into account by reducing it to something simple and static and treating it as a unitary type. Textbooks easily refer to THE cultural tourist, THE ecotourist, THE backpacker, THE senior tourist, or even THE tourist. These terms mask a plenitude of social and cultural distinctions.

- Examination of tourist markets is generally descriptive. Most research is focused upon documenting the size of loosely defined markets, without considering differences in motivations, behaviour and experiences of participants in these markets.

- Tourism literature has a strong bias towards 'travelling', as opposed to stationary mass tourism. Conventional beach tourism, for example, has always been – and still is – the biggest segment in tourism but it has neither generated serious interest and attention from the academic world, nor from travel writers. The vast majority of issues discussed in academic literature relates to travelling around, visiting cultural and natural sites, avoiding the crowds, the search for authenticity, interaction with local communities, etc. An additional bias found in the literature on international tourism is that studies of tourism in developing countries, or 'North–South tourism', tend to be over-represented (Wyllie, 2000, p. 3).

- Cross-cultural tourist studies are almost entirely missing. Tourism literature is dominated by academics working essentially to, on the one hand North American, and on the other Australian/New Zealand/British discourses (Prentice, 2004, p. 276). There is no understanding of differences in motivation, preferences, behaviour and experiences across cultures. Most textbooks do not refer to Northern European and North American bias in international tourism, or, in other terms, do not give account of the fact that the vast majority of the world's population does not travel at all. The motivations of many South American, Arab, African, Indian, or non-English-speaking Europeans are hardly known at all internationally (Prentice, 2004, p. 276). Understanding class differences as well as differences between nationalities or ethnic groups may enhance both efficiency and effectiveness in international tourism management.

- Historical accounts of change in the tourism industry or in tourists' motivations, preferences, behaviour and experiences commonly refer to concepts like 'post-tourism', 'post-modern tourism', 'new tourism', as opposed to 'traditional tourism', 'modern tourism', 'old tourism', suggesting a dichotomy between past and present. It will be argued in this study that reality does not simply meet 'either-or' criteria but constitutes a complex of diffuse and often contradictory and conflicting trends.

## 1.2  West–South Tourism

As will be explained shortly, the focus of this book is upon tourists from the West who travel in the South for holiday purposes, that is, upon round trips rather than stationary beach holidays.

For the sake of convenience, the terms 'developing countries', or the South, refer to Latin America, Africa and Asia.

The West consists of West, North and Central Europe and – to a lesser extent – North America and Australia/New Zealand. The European tourists are citizens from the historically Protestant countries of Europe. These are Germany, Great Britain, the Netherlands, Scandinavia (Denmark, Finland, Iceland, Norway, Sweden) and Switzerland. According to Inglehart *et al.* (1998) and Hofstede (1991), there are tremendous cultural differences between Protestant and non-Protestant (including Catholic) societies. Having inherited a Protestant ethic, consumers in these countries are presumed to exhibit tourist motivation and behaviour that is different from other countries. To a lesser extent, the focus is also upon the countries in the New World that were influenced by migrants and their Protestant ethic from these parts of Europe. Besides the USA these are Australia, Canada and New Zealand. Together with Europe they constitute the West or the 'Western' world. In terms of GNP per capita, the Protestant countries, including the migrant countries, are the most prosperous countries of the world, with the exception of Japan as the only non-Protestant country among the top-ten (Inglehart *et al.*, 1998, p. 3). Moreover, the European countries mentioned have a long holiday tradition and are the biggest spenders per capita in international tourism (WTO). They constitute the most important target countries for many areas in the developing world. Finally, the Protestant countries value 'environment' and 'sustainable development' much higher than other countries (Inglehart *et al.*, 1998; Miller, 2002). Wherever relevant and possible, comparisons will be made to other countries (e.g. Southern Europe, Eastern Asia). These comparisons will be brief and casual. It's up to future research to conduct more in-depth cross-cultural tourist studies.

The reasons for the focus upon developing countries are twofold:

**1.**   The author is involved in sustainable development of tourism in developing countries, in particular in the promotion of tourism as a tool for both poverty alleviation and preservation of nature and culture. Countless initiatives are taken by local entrepreneurs, authorities, communities or NGOs – even in the most remote areas of the world – to generate additional income and jobs by means of tourism. One of the main issues has to do with lack of knowledge of the tourist markets among local stakeholders in many destination areas. Lack of knowledge of the markets means difficulties in assessing tourism potential for any destination area or tourism product, identifying the competitive position of a destination, defining the 'right' markets and addressing them effectively.
**2.**   In less than two decades – having started after the economic recession of the early 1980s – tourism from the West to the South has grown exponentially. Although it is clear that we do not travel to discover the

world but because the world has already been discovered, the question why people from the developed world travel to developing countries has not yet been answered. Whereas individual travellers, backpackers in particular, have been given more and more academic attention in recent years, organized travelling is still an unexplored domain. Consequently, much attention will be paid to organized cultural and natural round trips, besides backpackers and other individual travellers, as well as volunteers.

## 1.3   Size of West–South Tourism

The World Tourism Organization (WTO) employs definitions that were recommended by the United Nations Conference on International Travel and Tourism in 1963, and that have generally been accepted, ever since, as the foundation for tourism statistics. The WTO distinguishes (*international*) *visitors, tourists* and *excursionists*.

An international visitor is any person visiting a place that is not his usual country of residence. The purposes of visit can be many. Excluded from the definition are visitors who enjoy some kind of salary or payment in the country visited, as well as commuters, immigrants, refugees, nomads, travellers passing through, military men and diplomats. A tourist is a visitor who remains in the visited country for a minimum period of 24 hours to a maximum of 1 year. Consequently, a tourist spends at least one night in the destination country. Visitors staying less than 24 hours, i.e. same-day visitors, are excursionists.

Although there has been significant progress in reaching consensus on what constitutes *international* tourism, there is no such consensus in *domestic* tourism terminology (Theobald, 1998, p. 19). Still, it is estimated that domestic tourist arrivals exceed international ones by a ratio of 10 to 1. Domestic tourists' expenditures exceed those of international tourists by a ratio of 7 to 1 (Wyllie, 2000, p. 2). According to the WTO's definition of international tourism, the number of international arrivals has increased from 25 million in 1950 to over 800 million in 2005. In the early 2000s the number of arrivals has been fluctuating, for several reasons, among which are insecure economic conditions in the main generating countries, terrorist attacks, SARS and the Iraq War. The WTO nevertheless forecasts an increase to over one billion arrivals in the decade to come.

'Western' countries dominate international tourism. Countries in West, North and Central Europe and North America plus Australia/New Zealand represent less than 8 per cent of the world's population but generate more than 50 per cent of all international arrivals. The share of the South (Africa, Asia, Latin America) in international tourist arrivals and receipts was almost 27 per cent in 2003 (WTO, 2004a). In absolute numbers this equals some 190 million arrivals. A big proportion of arrivals to the South can be characterized as 'small trade' or VFR, 'visiting friends and relatives' of persons living in neighbouring countries or working elsewhere, who go back to their country of origin for informal visits. Most of these visits do not generate substantial income for the destination countries.

Comparatively, expenditures by European or American tourists generally contribute much more to tourism receipts in the destination.

The countries in the South that are most frequently visited by Europeans (West, North, Central) and North Americans are shown in Table 1.1.

Some comments must be given on these statistics. The vast majority (over 90 per cent) of tourist arrivals to Mexico generated by the USA (18.5 million) is either related to VFR or conventional stationary beach

**Table 1.1**   Top-20 destinations in the South for Europeans from West, North and Central Europe and North Americans (number of arrivals, 2002).

|                    | Total (000s) | Europe (000s) | North America (000s) |
|--------------------|-------------:|--------------:|---------------------:|
| Mexico             | 19,340       | 479           | 18,861[a]            |
| China              | 2,368        | 956           | 1,412                |
| Thailand           | 2,344        | 1,733         | 611                  |
| Tunisia            | 1,646        | 1,618         | 28                   |
| Egypt              | 1,626        | 1,477         | 149                  |
| Dominican Republic | 1,499        | 474           | 1,025                |
| Bahamas            | 1,440        | 60            | 1,380                |
| Brazil             | 1,357        | 653           | 704                  |
| South Africa       | 1,254        | 931           | 323                  |
| Singapore          | 1,240        | 844           | 396                  |
| India              | 1,033        | 615           | 418                  |
| Indonesia          | 794          | 585           | 209                  |
| Cuba               | 765          | 340           | 425[b]               |
| Philippines        | 594          | 144           | 450                  |
| Malaysia           | 571          | 408           | 163                  |
| Costa Rica         | 560          | 83            | 477[a]               |
| Kenya              | 523          | 439           | 84                   |
| Morocco            | 497          | 395           | 102                  |
| Vietnam            | 481          | 177           | 304                  |
| Argentina          | 477          | 324           | 153                  |

Source: estimates by the author, based on WTO data.
[a]USA mainly.
[b]Canada mainly.

tourism, not to round trips. Many arrivals to China are VFR trips of ethnic Chinese Americans. Most European tourism to Tunisia and North American tourism to the Bahamas and Dominican Republic is beach tourism.

WTO's technical definition does not capture the essential features of a 'tourist' or 'tourist experiences'. Nor is it helpful in providing a focus for social and cultural study of tourists. In this book, travelling for instrumental purposes, such as business, conferences, pilgrimages, educational trips, missions, development projects, exchange projects, etc., will be left aside. Adopting and adapting Wang's definition (2000, p. 6), it will treat a tourist as:

> A person from 'Western' countries who voluntarily travels to the South for non-instrumental purposes such as recreation, pleasure or interesting experiences.

A rough estimation of the number of West–South tourists who match this definition is some 20 million arrivals.

## 1.4  Sustainable Tourism Development

This study will not review the recent abundance of literature on sustainable tourism and sustainable tourism development. Selected existing criteria and indicators for sustainable tourism development will be adapted and made operational to provide destinations with tools to develop sustainable products and sustainable visitor management strategies. Sustainable tourism should not be associated with small-scale tourism, although many sources in literature show this bias. If planned and managed well, mass facilities and mass tourism are not unsustainable by definition. Although tourists from the historically Protestant countries of Europe value 'environment' and 'sustainable development' much higher than other countries, sustainable tourism development should not be dependent upon the environmental awareness and attitudes of the consumer. The position taken here is that sustainable tourism products can be successfully sold to tourists who are not specifically seeking it. If expectations and preferences of tourists are met through the provision of a quality experience, with the needs of the local environment and community taken into account, there is no specific need for a 'sustainable tourism product' to be labelled and sold as such. In the words of Sharpley and Sharpley (1997, p. 241), 'whilst this might require a "re-definition" of the form and objectives of sustainable tourism, there is no doubt that its future lies in a broad approach, the fundamental basis of which must be the satisfaction of consumer needs.'

In brief, this book endeavours to bring about a basic understanding of Western tourists who travel in the South, in order to provide suppliers with tools to meet these interests and preferences and develop sustainable products and practices concurrently.

# Towards Understanding Western Tourists: Theoretical Perspectives

**2**

## 2.1 Modernity

Western tourism must be regarded as an integral element of modern life, that is, it can only be understood in the context of *modernity*. According to Giddens, 'modernity' refers to modes of social life or organization which emerged in Europe from about the 17th century onwards and which subsequently became more or less worldwide in their influence (1990, p. 1). To define modernity is difficult. It is a controversial concept, reflected in diverse and competing definitions. It is highly ambivalent, as will be discussed shortly. Moreover, today, it is argued by many, we stand at the opening of a new era, which is taking us beyond modernity itself. A dazzling variety of terms has been suggested to refer to this new era, a few of which refer positively to the emergence of a new type of social system (such as the 'information society' or the 'consumer society') but most of which suggest rather that a preceding state of affairs is drawing to a close ('post-modernity', 'post-modernism', 'post-industrial society', 'post-capitalism' and so forth) (Giddens, 1990, p. 2).

The ambivalence of modernity is mirrored in several contrasting concepts such as Modernity 1 versus Modernity 2 versus Postmodernism (Rojek, 1995), First versus Second Modernity versus Global Information Culture (Lash, 1999), Logos Modernity versus Eros Modernity (Wang, 2000), Solid versus Liquid Modernity (Bauman, 2000). Understanding tourism in the context of modernity implies understanding both historical roots and present manifestations of tourism as reflections of the structure and contradiction of modernity. This chapter will follow several lines of thought about modernity, each of which leads to specific views and explanations of the tourism phenomenon.

## Rationalization

The first line is the line of Reason, corresponding with Rojek's Modernity 1 ('The Roots of Order') and Wang's Logos-modernity. Most versions of early modernity seem to mirror the discourse of the Enlightenment. According to Giddens, Enlightenment thought, and Western culture in general, emerged from a religious context, which emphasized teleology and the achievement of God's grace. Divine providence had long been a guiding idea of Christian thought (Giddens, 1990, p. 48). At the core of Enlightenment thinking are the principles of *reason* and *rationality*. For Enlightenment thinkers, to be modern is to be rational and, rather than trust in divine providence, avoid irrational factors.

The discourse of the Enlightenment holds to a tradition of Logos that can be traced back to ancient Greek philosophy, particularly to Aristotle. According to this tradition, the essence of humankind is Logos (reason and rationality), and the ideal person is one whose soul is governed and informed by Logos (Wang, 2000, p. 28).

The 'march of the mind' in the 'age of reason' (Porter, 2003) sought to control both nature and society. So, its impacts were to be found in all aspects of life. *Rationalization*, as described by Weber (1978), is the key word. The rational part of modernity comprises an institutional order (most clearly expressed in capitalism, industrialism and bureaucracy), an intellectual order (which is at the basis of science and technology), a temporal order (schedulization, synchronization, routinization, or accelerating tempo and rhythm) and a socio-spatial order (urbanization, globalization) (Wang, 2000, p. 15).

As for the institutional order, according to Weber (1978), both capitalism, industrialism and bureaucracy are the results of rationalization processes. Capitalism has thrived, because it is technically a superior form of social organization. At least in the West, capitalistic activity has become associated with the rational organization of formally free labour. By 'rational organization' Weber means its routinized, calculated administration within continuously functioning enterprises. A rationalized capitalistic enterprise implies a disciplined labour force and the regularized investment of capital (Giddens, in Weber, 1976, p. 3). Thus, rationalization is also the rationale behind industrialism, culminating in Taylor's *scientific management* in the early 20th century, which Charles Chaplin memorably satirized in his classic film *Modern Times*. Moreover, bureaucracy is, again according to Weber (1970), the most efficient form of organization known in human society. It involves precision, speed, impersonality, unambiguity,

methodical training, specialization and agreed rules of conduct. The aim
of bureaucracy is to produce co-ordinated, calculable action. By standard-
izing the basic elements of interaction, predictability and efficiency are
increased.

The intellectual order celebrates the victory of human reason over
irrationality and prejudice. Both empiricism and rationalism, although
virtually contrasting concepts, made triumphal progress as products of
enlightened human thinking, from Bacon and Locke to Kant. All matter,
including human body and mind, became subject of analysis. That's why
Harvey could discover the blood circulation in the human body (1628),
that's why Descartes could publish his *Discours de la méthode* (1637). Time
and space were separated. Time became measurable. Huygens consequently invented the pendulum clock (1656). The clock expresses a uni-
form dimension of 'empty' time, quantified in such a way as to permit the
precise designation of 'zones' of the day (e.g. the 'working day') (Giddens,
1990, p. 17).

The first phases of the industrial revolution took place in the 18th and
19th centuries, and a recent phase after the second World War. The first
brought about a new social class, the working class. Where farmers and
farm workers were bound by their agricultural lands before, the newly
emerged working class was confined to the location of the factory, mine or
distribution centre. Working-class houses and facilities that mushroomed
around these locations, caused a vast sprawl of urbanization.

Early industrial life was characterized by long, strictly scheduled
working days, poor working conditions, little leisure time and little recreation. While the 19th century was dominated by the struggles of workers
to compel their employers to improve the basic working environment and
living conditions, the first half of the 20th century was marked by the
battle in several Western countries between labour unions and employers
for – among other things – paid leave arrangements and holiday
entitlements. After the Second World War, this battle had ended in most
countries, and holiday entitlements (a series of continuous days off) were
an acquired right for all employees (Hessels, 1973; Pimlott, 1976).

Although the system was opposed to Western European capitalism,
a similar development took place in Eastern Europe during the 20th
century, in the sense that – during the peak of communism – holiday
entitlements for labourers were developed on a large scale within the
Eastern bloc countries. The complete shift after 1989 heralded the decay of
these arrangements. In rapidly industrializing countries in East Asia,
holiday entitlements had already become an acquired right at an early
stage, although they encompassed fewer days than in Europe (van
Egmond, 2005, p. 50).

According to this line of thought, the development in the early 20th
century, of the holiday phenomenon should be sought in compensation

motives: deficiencies in our daily existence induce us to travel at fixed intervals, in order to compensate for these deficiencies, to re-energize, refill the batteries, re-create. A period of diversion, recuperating and refreshing is needed so that workers are able to return to the wear and tear of 'serious' living. In the words of Rojek: Modernity 1 treated the subject of organizing leisure with the same sober spirit of rationalism that it applied to every other part of life (1995, p. 57). 'Push-motives' are concerned here, in the sense that it is the deficiencies in daily life which induce us and not factors beyond our own life world which attract us ('pull-motives'). Destinations can essentially be anywhere, but (domestic) seaside and spa resorts were dominant in the early days of 20th century tourism.

This is the mode of tourism which a structural-functionalist analysis of society would lead us to expect as typical for modern man (Hessels, 1973; Cohen, 1979a). The line of Reason, through rationalization and the institutional, intellectual, temporal and socio-spatial order leads to rational temporary breaks, in nature akin to other forms of entertainment such as the cinema, theatre or day-trips. Not only the individual enjoys the holiday but also society as a whole, because it restores the individual's physical and mental powers and endows him or her with a general sense of well-being. Having re-created these powers and recharged the batteries, workers are able to contribute fully again to a rational functioning of industrial society.

## Alienation

The victory of reason and rationality, however, has other sides, as expressed in a different line of thought: alienation. Discomfort about rationalized society turned out to be a key element in many discourses about modern civilization (Freud, Fromm, Marcuse, to mention a few). In the words of Wang (2000, p. 29), the Logos version of modernity has celebrated the marvellous material, intellectual and organizational miracles of Logos found in civilization. However, it is interesting to note that adherents of the Logos version of modernity have also assumed a critical orientation towards it. For example, while Marx, Weber and Durkheim celebrated the progress of modernization, they also delivered verbal attacks on the limitations of Logos-modernity. Thus, Marx criticized the *alienation* conditions of capitalism, Weber complained of the 'Iron Cage' of bureaucratic state, and Durkheim revealed the prevalence of anomie in industrial society (Wang, 2000, pp. 29–30).

Alienation is of course one of the most enduring concepts produced by Marx. He used it to denote the estrangement of individuals from themselves and from others (Rojek, 1995, p. 14).

'Although Marx's discussion of alienation seems to be narrowly focused upon work experience there are in fact clear implications for leisure experience. Marx understood labour to be the key to human fulfillment and happiness. What happens in work experience therefore affects the whole of human life. Thus, the experience of labour as external or self-denying finds its parallel in the experience of the consumption of leisure experience as external, coerced and manipulated. The spontaneous activity of human imagination seems to be sacrificed to the world of produced commodities and packaged experiences. Our leisure does not seem to be our own. Instead, it is constructed for us by the captains of the leisure industry. We are reduced to the state of passive consumption – a state which Marx explicitly identifies with animal functions'
(Rojek, 1995, p. 16).

Weber's 'Iron Cage' refers to an increasingly bureaucratic order from which 'spontaneous enjoyment of life' is ruthlessly expunged. It is a heritage from the Protestant work ethic of the Puritans, which will be dealt with shortly.

Anomie is the opposite to order, structure and rationality of modern life as reflected in the Logos version of modernity or Modernity 1. It refers to the structurelessness of relationships in industrial and bureaucratic organizations. Division and specialization of labour make workers mutually dependent. Rationally this should lead to social solidarity. Everyday practice, however, shows, according to Durkheim, little solidarity between workers, and between employers and employees. In the words of Rojek:

Industrialization may have vastly increased productivity but it also atomized the worker, commodified work activity, alienated work from leisure and fetishized 'labour' as the key to existence. It wrecked the traditional balance between personal development and the cohesion of the community. It magnified the tendencies in society towards chronic *anomie*, fragmentation and restlessness.
(Rojek, 1995, pp. 183–184)

It was MacCannell (1973, 1976) who argued that alienation is at the very basis of contemporary tourism.

Everyday life and its grinding familiarity stand in opposition to the many versions of the 'high life' in the modern world. Everyday life threatens the solidarity of modernity by atomizing individuals and families into isolated local groupings which are not functionally or ideologically interrelated. But everyday life is composed of souvenirs of life elsewhere. In this way, modernity and the modern consciousness infiltrate everyday existence and, at the same time, subordinate it to life elsewhere. . . .. The more the individual sinks into everyday life, the more he is reminded of reality and authenticity elsewhere.
(1976, pp. 159–160)

Somewhere else there is a *genuine* society. So, in 'this most depersonalized epoch' (p. 160), we are looking for meaning in the life of others. Authentic experiences are believed to be available only to those moderns who try to break the bonds of their everyday existence and begin to 'live'. The search for authentic experiences is essentially a religious quest: 'tourism absorbs some of the social functions in the modern world' (MacCannell, 1973, p. 589). MacCannell draws on Goffman's (1959) discussion of front and back regions in destination countries. 'The front is the meeting place of hosts and guests or customers and service persons, and the back is the place where members of the home team retire between performances to relax and prepare' (1976, p. 92). In their search for authentic experiences, tourists like to visit the back region, i.e. go 'backstage'.

Cohen (1979a) also takes modern man's alienation from his society as a starting point, because the assumption that modern man will generally adhere to the centre of 'his' society is simplistic in his view. What about the 'spiritual' centre of such alienated people? Several alternatives can be discerned: (i) some may be so completely alienated as not to look for any centre at all, i.e. not to seek any ultimate locus of meaning; (ii) some, aware of what to them looks an irretrievable loss of their centre, seek to experience vicariously the authentic participation in the centres of others, who are as yet less modern and less 'disinherited'. Here Cohen and MacCannell meet; (iii) some possess a 'decentralized personality' and equivocate between different centres, almost turning the quest into the purpose of their life; (iv) finally, some may find that their spiritual centre lies somewhere else, in another society or culture other than their own (1996, p. 92). The phenomenology of distinct modes of touristic experiences that is based on these four alternatives will be discussed later.


## Romanticism

Romanticism was a cultural movement against the dominance of reason and rationality of the Enlightenment. Whereas the Enlightenment has its roots in the 17th century, Romanticism is a product of the late 18th and early 19th centuries and continued until the early 20th century. The First World War brought along the end of Romanticism. Although it generated intense and continuous interest, especially among young intellectuals, it was secondary to the rationalist outlook. Romantic philosophers, poets, painters and composers focused upon emotions, sensations, aestheticism, mysticism, sentimentalism, irrationality, disorder and *Sturm-und-Drang*, rather than reason, order, controllability and intellectual clarity.

A taste and passion for landscapes and nature was one of the original characteristics of Romanticism. Through the ages, nature had always been a source of threat rather than a source of interest and aestheticism. Seas, mountains, forests and swamps were 'home of evil spirits', areas to be avoided, unless going there was necessary for survival. In 1657 a dictionary still describes 'forest' as 'awful', 'gloomy', 'desolate', 'inhospitable'

(Lemaire, 1988, p. 62). The Enlightenment brought about a shift in attitude. Nature became object of rational analysis and control. Paradoxically, this new attitude towards nature as something controllable rather than magical or mystical allowed the Romanticists to celebrate nature as object of intense emotion. One could feel emotional about landscapes and scenery, without fear. Nature became a source of individual aesthetic enjoyment. 'Individual pleasures were to be derived from an appreciation of impressive physical sights' (Urry, 2002, p. 20). Rousseau's *Julie ou la Nouvelle Heloïse* (1761) is commonly seen as the precursor of emotional appreciation of nature. The great Romanticists in Britain were Byron, Coleridge, Shelley and Wordsworth, in Germany Goethe and Schlegel, in France Chateaubriand, Hugo and Lamartine, most of whom lived in the first half of the 19th century.

Throughout history an archetypical version of an idyllic landscape has been part of the collective memory of different peoples. The *Garden of Eden*, *Arcadia* in Vergilius' *Bucolica*, landscapes in Homer's *Iliad* and *Odyssey* all represent charming, idyllic landscapes with a few scattered (fruit) trees, meadows, a well, flowers, shadow, soft winds, etc. (Lemaire, 1988, p. 60). The Romanticists turned to untamed nature and wilderness rather than idyllic Arcadia. According to Lemaire, the search for untamed nature is a metaphor of discomfort with existing civilization. It is an escape to nature of 18th-citizens from rationalized life. The new interest in nature didn't start among nature-dwellers but is a fruit of the city. This was most prominent in Germany and England. Young citizens who made up for the 'back-to-nature' movement in Germany are referred to as *Wandervögel*. Lemaire speculates that in Germany and England – in the remote corners of Europe – archaic nature awareness never completely disappeared during Roman and Christian times and was revitalized by Romanticism (p. 63). Moreover, the wilderness, in particular the wild forest, became associated for many Romanticists with the experience of God's Creation and as such turned out to be the centre of spiritual and religious regeneration.

Nature tourism in Western societies can be linked to Romanticism in two senses (Wang, 2000, p. 82). First, landscape or nature tourism originated from the 'turn of mind' and the emergence of a romantic taste for natural landscapes amongst the intellectual élite in the later stages of the 18th century. Second, famous romantics such as Wordsworth, through their poetic or romantic discourses on the taste and love of nature, in turn shaped nature tourism. The romantic feelings, emotions and experiences of nature which were finely described and recorded in such discourses have become what many travellers and tourists seek now when they visit nature.

Romanticism as a concrete doctrine is perhaps transcended today, but romanticism as a general taste and regard for nature is never outdated. Rather it is spread throughout society as a whole, and constitutes the cultural foundation of contemporary nature, green, or rural tourism (Wang,

2000, p. 86). It is also at the basis of Urry's 'Romantic Gaze'. Urry (1990) introduced the Romantic Gaze (as opposed to a 'Collective Gaze') to describe contemporary ways of looking at nature. In tourism we 'gaze' at what we encounter, we visually consume places, but there is no single tourist gaze as such. 'Undisturbed natural beauty' constitutes the typical object of the Romantic Gaze. Characteristic of the Collective Gaze is that it is thoroughly based on popular pleasures and on an anti-elitism. The Romantic Gaze is much more obviously auratic, concerned with the more elitist – and solitary – appreciation of magnificent scenery, an appreciation which requires considerable cultural capital (2002, p. 78). It implies solitude, privacy and a personal, semi-spiritual relationship with the object of the gaze.

Together with the revaluation of the wilderness the image of the inhabitants of wilderness changed during Romanticism. In ancient Greek and Roman times 'wild' people were irrational barbarians who lived without law and were, like animals, subdued to their instincts and passions. They symbolized what civilized citizens did *not* want to be. During Romanticism their image shifted from 'demons of the dark' to symbols of simplicity, freedom and naturalness (Lemaire, 1988, p. 66). The myth of the 'Noble Savage' became widespread, in particular in France (*le Bon Sauvage*), as a metaphor of 'real and authentic life out-there'. The rehabilitation of the 'Wild Man' is an index of discomfort with 18th century's civilization. Here we arrive at a striking similarity with MacCannell's pilgrimage in search of authenticity.

Perceptions of indigenous peoples have changed over time. The colonization of the world by European powers, including slave trade, was definitely not inspired by romantic images of Noble Savages. Neither did 19th and 20th centuries' missionaries have a romantic image in mind when they tried to convert primitive and undeveloped tribes to the 'right' religion. The second half of the 20th century, the final decades in particular, witnessed the emergence of a new romanticism in terms of interest in 'unspoilt' communities, not contaminated by the achievements of the modern consumer state. Living in and with nature, simplicity, 'non-modernism' of indigenous communities have become major selling points for tour operators all over the modern world. Although Urry confines the Romantic Gaze mainly to 'undisturbed natural beauty', it is easily transferred to 'unspoilt local life'. 'The romantic gaze is an important mechanism which is helping to spread tourism on a global scale' (Urry, 2002, p. 44).

## The Protestant Ethic

The Reformation was a period of religious and political upheaval in Western Europe during the 16th century, opposing both the doctrines and the political position of the dominant Roman Catholic Church. During that century it resulted in Protestantism (the term was coined in 1529), referring to the reactionary character, and the Protestant churches. Two key religious leaders who influenced the development of Western culture during this period were Martin Luther (1483–1546) and John Calvin (1509–1564).

Although Protestantism is a pre-Enlightenment phenomenon in its origin, it had tremenedous influence on modernity and modern behaviour in the Protestant countries. On one hand it produced a work-ethic that, according to Weber (1976) and many of his followers, was at the basis of economic growth in Protestant countries. On the other hand it brought along a certain asceticism, which was most prominent among the Puritans of the 16th and 17th century in England, but is still influencing present-day behaviour of many. Weber made a distinction between salvation religions turning towards the world and those turning away from the world (Whimster and Lash, 1987, p. 112). In contrast to, for example, Hinduism and Buddhism, Protestantism has turned towards the world from the very beginning. The Protestant asceticism was active in that its basic attitude to the world was one of 'mastery' rather than passively accepting one's fate in the world. It was and still is a 'this-worldly asceticism'. Calvinism in particular supplies the moral energy and drive of the capitalist entrepreneur, as long as the accumulation of wealth was combined with a sober, industrious career; wealth was condemned only if employed to support a life of idle luxury or self-indulgence (see the section 'Modern consumer culture'). An important part of 'world-mastery' was getting methodical control over the whole man. To lead an alert, intelligent life, the most urgent task was the destruction of spontaneous, impulsive enjoyment, 'the most important means was to bring order into the conduct of its adherents' (Weber, 1976, p. 119). Although Puritanism lost its rigid character after the 17th century, it has deeply influenced the contemporary value systems of Protestant European countries and the countries in the New World that were influenced by migrants from these parts of Europe (Inglehart *et al.*, 1998). These Protestant countries are Denmark, Finland, Germany, Iceland, the Netherlands, Norway, Sweden, Switzerland and, to a certain extent, Great Britain and Austria. Migrant countries are Australia, Canada, New Zealand and the USA. There are tremendous cultural differences between Protestant and Catholic societies. Although church attendance has fallen drastically in most of the historically Protestant countries – to the point where many observers now speak of the Nordic countries as post-Christian societies – religious traditions helped shape enduring *national* cultures that persist today (id: 17). This is quite consistent with the research of Hofstede (1991), who found that the Protestant countries of Europe have many patterns of thinking, feeling and acting in common. In his terms they have similar mental programmes, or 'software of the mind'. Though geographically located next door to Belgium and sharing a common language with half of that country, the Netherlands are culturally much closer to Nordic countries than to Belgium. Historically, the Netherlands have been shaped by Protestantism; even the Dutch Catholics today are remarkably Calvinist (Inglehart *et al.*, 1998, p. 17). Vogel (2001, pp. 27–30) gives a clear overview of the main characteristics of Protestant mental programmes, that are 'a direct legacy of Calvinism' (p. 27).

1.   The Protestant view of the world is relatively pessimistic or even apocalyptic. If we continue in our present behaviours and values we are doomed. We live in a depraved world filled with sinners bent on their own destruction.

2.   Within Protestantism there is a deep suspicion of self-indulgence and excessive consumption and a strong bias in favour of self-discipline.

3.   Protestantism is a morally rigorous religion, one which places a high value on consistency: thus if something is morally wrong, one should not do it.

4.   For Protestantism, the ordinary person bears some individual moral responsibility for the fate of the world, mirrored in the concept of 'stewardship'. We are responsible for 'our common future', the future we share with the coming generations.

5.   Protestantism is a relatively egalitarian religion, one based on the relationship between God and each individual. This theological egalitarianism in part explains the strong historical links between Protestantism and democracy. The core democratic concept of the rights of man can be readily expanded to encompass the concept of the rights of nature.

6.   Protestantism, precisely because it tends to be relatively devoid of rituals and symbols, may be especially conducive to the notion that nature can, or should, have spiritual significance. Nature can be a source of spiritual rebirth. In the words of one Jonathan Edwards (cited in Vogel, 2001, p. 30), 'God's excellency, his wisdom, his purity and love . . . appear in everything, in the sun, moon, and stars; in the clouds and blue sky; in the grass, flowers, trees; in the water, and all nature . . .'. Historically Protestant countries like the United States, Germany and England, share a strong cultural tradition of viewing 'nature' as a source of spiritual value as well as a counterpart to the ills of industrial capitalism (p. 30).

Rigorous morality, combined with individual moral responsibility, is a source of guilt. Protestant societies can be described as guilt cultures: persons who infringe upon the rules of society will often feel guilty, ridden by an individually developed conscience which functions as a private inner pilot (Hofstede, 1991, p. 60). Guilt is different from shame. According to Hofstede, shame is social in nature, characteristic of collectivist (see next paragraph) societies, guilt is individual. Whether shame is felt depends on whether the infringement has become known by others. This becoming known is more a source of shame than the infringement itself (id). Guilt is private.

To the list of characteristics of Protestant mental programmes can be added the concept of solitude. In the Bible prophets from Moses to Jesus experienced their spiritual enlightenment at remote, lonesome locations – and always under ascetic conditions (Welk, 2004, p. 81). For Western, Protestant societies, the concepts of remoteness and solitude have special meaning through being rooted in the Bible (p. 81). These concepts are coupled with a passionate quest for paradise – the mythological place of origin, of creation itself. The touristic 'return' to paradise is a symbolic 'return' to the origins of mankind, in order to make us feel like being without sin (p. 82).

Obviously, Romanticism is not only linked to a movement against the dominance of reason and rationality of the Enlightenment but also to the quintessence of Protestantism. These characteristics are still very common in the Protestant countries of Europe, in particular among the elderly generations. Although he doesn't refer to Protestantism explicitly, Hofstede found many results that are consistent with these characteristics. The Protestant countries of Europe share a small 'power distance' ('the extent to which the less powerful members of institutions and organizations within a country expect and accept that power is distributed unequally') (1991, p. 28). In small-power-distance countries there is limited dependence of subordinates on bosses, and a preference for consultation, that is, *interdependence* between boss and subordinate. The emotional distance between them is relatively small (p. 27). Parents and children, students and teachers treat each other as equals.

The Protestant countries of Europe – and even more so the USA, Australia, Canada and New Zealand – also have a high score on *individualism*. This pertains to societies in which the ties between individuals are loose: everyone is expected to look after himself or herself and his or her immediate family. The opposite is *collectivism*. This pertains to societies in which people from birth onwards are integrated into strong, cohesive groups, which throughout people's lifetime continue to protect them in exchange for unquestioning loyalty (p. 51).

Some of the Protestant countries of Europe (all Scandinavian countries and the Netherlands) also share a low score on the 'masculinity index'. Masculinity pertains to societies in which social gender roles are clearly distinct (i.e. men are supposed to be assertive, tough, and focused on material success whereas women are supposed to be more modest, tender, and concerned with the quality of life); femininity pertains to societies in which social gender roles overlap (i.e. both men and women are supposed to be modest, tender, and concerned with the quality of life)

(Hofstede, 1991, pp. 82–83). In the Scandinavian countries and the Netherlands dominant values are (among others): caring for others and preservation, warm relationships between people, modesty, sympathy for the weak, stress on equality, solidarity, and quality of work life, resolution of conflicts by compromise and negotiation (p. 96). Similarly, in the research of Inglehart *et al.* (1998), the Protestant countries valued 'Third World Development' and 'Environment' much higher than other countries.

According to these authors, a new worldview is gradually replacing the outlook that has dominated industrializing societies since the Industrial Revolution. 'Postmaterialism' is growing at the expense of 'Materialism'.

> The transition from agrarian society to industrial society was facilitated by a Modernization shift, from a worldview shaped by a steady-state economy, which discouraged social mobility and emphasized tradition, inherited status, and communal obligations, backed up by absolute religious norms, to a worldview that encouraged economic achievement, individualism and innovation, accompanied by increasingly secular and flexible social norms.
>
> (Inglehart *et al.*, 1998, p. 9)

Industrialization and modernization required breaking certain cultural constraints on accumulation that are found in any steady-state economy. In West European history this was achieved by what Weber described as the rise of the Protestant Ethic, which was like a random mutation from a functional perspective. If it had occurred two centuries earlier it might have died out. In the environment of its time, it found a niche: technological developments were making rapid economic growth possible and the Calvinist worldview complemented these developments beautifully, forming a cultural–economic syndrome that led to the rise of capitalism and, eventually, to the industrial revolution. Once this had occurred, economic accumulation (for individuals) and economic growth (for societies) became top priorities for an increasing part of the world's population, and are still the central goals for the greater part of humanity. But eventually, diminishing returns from economic growth lead to a Postmodern shift.

Advanced industrial societies are now changing their basic value systems in a number of related ways. Increasing emphasis on individual economic achievement was one of the crucial changes that made modernization possible. This shift toward materialistic priorities entailed a de-emphasis on communal obligations and an acceptance of social mobility: increasingly, social status became something that an individual could achieve, rather than something into which one was born. Economic growth came to be equated with progress and was seen as the hallmark of a successful society.

In Postmodern society, this emphasis on economic achievement as the top priority is now giving way to an increasing emphasis on the quality of life. In a major part of the world, the disciplined, self-denying and achievement-oriented norms of industrial society are yielding to an increasingly broad latitude for individual choice of life styles and individual self-expression. This shift from 'Materialist' values, emphasizing economic and physical security, to 'Postmaterialist' values, emphasizing individual self-expression and quality of life concerns, is the most amply documented aspect of this change; but it is only one component of a much broader syndrome of cultural change (Inglehart *et al.*, 1998, pp. 9–10).

The Postmodern shift involves an intergenerational change in a wide variety of basic social norms. Moreover, the sharply differentiated gender roles that characterize virtually all pre-industrial societies, give way to increasingly similar gender roles in advanced industrial society (p. 12). Today, increasingly, support for the Left comes from middle class Postmaterialists, while a new Right draws support from less secure segments of the working class. A new Postmodern political cleavage pits culturally conservative, often xenophobic parties, disproportionately supported by Materialists, against change-oriented parties, often emphasizing environmental protection and emancipation of minority groups, and disproportionately supported by Postmaterialists (p. 13).

In terms of GNP per capita, the Protestant countries are the most prosperous countries of the world, with the exception of Japan as the only non-Protestant country among the top ten (p. 3). At the same time, the 'Historically Protestant' countries of the world are supporting Postmaterialist values much more than all other countries. Among the 'Historically Protestant' countries, the Scandinavian countries and the Netherlands are ahead of German and English-speaking countries in supporting these values (p. 20). This value system has clear repercussions for the appreciation of nature, culture and environment in relation to tourism, as will be discussed in much more detail later on.

## McDonaldization

In sharp contrast to romantic gazing at undisturbed nature and culture is a modern perspective developed by Ritzer (2000) in *The McDonaldization of Society*. This perspective, strongly influenced by Weber's theory of rationalization, is a modern grand narrative viewing the world as growing increasingly efficient, calculable, predictable and dominated by controlling non-human technologies.

McDonaldization refers to the global success of McDonald's fast-food chain, a process that is often referred to in Latin America as *cocacolaïzación* of society. According to Ritzer, McDonald's has succeeded because it offers consumers, workers and managers efficiency, calculability, predictability and control (2000, p. 12).

There are many clones of McDonald's, not only in the fast-food industry but in many other settings as well. Many other nations have been invaded by McDonaldized American businesses, and many nations have created indigenous versions of those enterprises. Most important, McDonaldization has become even more deeply ingrained not only in the culture of the United States but also in many other cultures around the world.

(Ritzer, 2000, p. xiii)

There are degrees of McDonaldization. Fast-food restaurants, for example, have been heavily McDonaldized, universities moderately McDonaldized, and mom-and-pop grocers only slightly McDonaldized (p. 19).

Both the McDonald's chain and the Disney theme parks can be seen as paradigms of the *McDonaldization of Society*. If McDonald's has been the paradigm of rationality for society as a whole, Disney has certainly been the model for the tourist industry (Ritzer and Liska, 1997, p. 97). Whereas society as a whole has been McDonaldized, the tourism industry in general, and, virtually every theme and amusement park in particular has been McDisneyized, at least to some extent (p. 98). Disney theme parks are efficient in many ways, especially in the way they process the large numbers of people that would easily overwhelm less rationalized theme parks. The set prices for a daily or weekly pass, as well as the abundant signs indicating how long a wait one can expect at a given attraction, illustrate calculability. The parks are also highly predictable. The staff works hard to be sure that the visitor experiences no surprises at all. And the Disney parks are a triumph of non-human technology over humans (p. 98).

According to Ritzer and Liska, Las Vegas hotels, and the city in general, are increasingly coming to exemplify the Disney model. In the beginning of the current century cruise ships, all-inclusive holiday resorts, theme parks and shopping malls are booming business. Cruise ships take on the appearance increasingly of floating theme parks. Beyond cruise ships, all-inclusives, theme parks and casinos, shopping malls have been McDisneyized, coming to look more and more like amusement parks (p. 98). Rigidly standardized tours are still popular in many Western (and Asian) countries. In addition to that, many package tours are more flexible. So much of the larger society has been McDonaldized that there is less need to McDonaldize the package tour itself. For example, tourists can generally be safely left on their own at most locales since those who want standardized meals will almost undoubtedly find them readily available at a local McDonald's, or an outlet of some other international chain of fast-food restaurants. As a general rule (p. 99), as society itself grows more and more McDonaldized, there is less and less need to standardize the package tour rigidly.

The McDonaldization thesis leads to the view that people increasingly travel to other locales in order to experience much of what they experience in their day-to-day lives. That is, they want their tourist experiences to be about as much McDonaldized as their day-to-day lives (p. 99).

Accustomed to a McDonaldized lifeworld, many people appear to want:

1.  Highly predictable vacations. One could argue that as our everyday life grows more and more predictable, we have less and less tolerance for, and ability to handle, unpredictable events. The last thing most of today's tourists want to experience is an unpalatable meal, a wild animal, or a rat-infested hotel room. In addition to avoiding the unfamiliar associated with a different culture, many tourists want the things they are familiar with on a day-to-day basis.

2.  Highly efficient vacations. The same point applies here: accustomed to efficiency in their everyday lives, many people tend to have little tolerance for inefficient vacations. They tend to want the most vacation for the money (hence the popularity of cruises and package tours), to see and do as much as possible in the time allotted, and so on.

3.  Highly calculable vacations. Many people want to know in advance how much a vacation is going to cost and they abhor cost overruns. They also want to have itineraries that define precisely where they will be at a given time and for how long.

4.  Highly controlled vacations. This can take various forms, from a preference for dealing with people whose behaviour is tightly controlled by scripts, as in the Disney parks, to the routines on cruises. Sites which house advanced technologies (modern aeroplanes, cruise ships, hotels, amusement parks) can be preferred both in their own right as well as for the control they exercise over both employees and other tourists (pp. 99–100).

Ritzer and Liska stress that our vacations are more and more like the rest of our lives, rather than escaping from it to other worlds, looking for a 'centre-out-there', or seeking authenticity. According to them, many tourists today are in search of inauthenticity (p. 107).

McDonaldization and McDisneyization are rationalized processes. However, 'rational systems inevitably spawn irrationalities that limit, eventually compromise, and perhaps even undermine their rationality' (Ritzer, 2000, p. 123). Ritzer refers to the 'irrationality of rationality' as a label for many of the negative aspects of McDonaldization, including actual inefficiency, illusions of various types, disenchantment (things lose their magic and mystery), dehumanization and homogenization (p. 124).

## The disorder of things

A more psychological line of thought leads to a different explanation of tourism. In the words of Wang (2000, p. 29), Logos versions of modernity tell the story of how reason and rationality have gained victory and ascendance over irrational or non-rational factors, and how irrational or non-rational factors have been successfully subdued, repressed, controlled, or constrained through the powers of both rational agency (such as modern surveillance and management) and rational mechanisms (such as formal organizations).

No society in the West, however, has ever been totally governed by Logos in its absolute form. The Logos version of modernity fails to recognize the irrational and playful elements of modernity. In terms of Rojek (1995): opposed to Modernity 1, 'The Roots of Order', is Modernity 2, 'The Disorder of Things'. Whereas Modernity 1 aims at a rational order of things and emphasizes the harmony and ascendancy of science, Modernity 2 stresses change, flux, de-differentiation and metamorphosis. It has a more poetic emphasis upon phenomenology and experience. Referring to Nietzsche, Rojek argues that modern life struggles to reconcile the conflicting impulses symbolized by Apollo and Dionysus. Apollo, the Greek god of music and poetry, is traditionally associated with structure, order and self-discipline, whereas Dionysus, the god of wine, is associated with sensuality, abandon and intoxication. Apollonian culture has achieved material abundance and superficial order. But is has done so at a ghastly cost to human life. Under Apollonian culture the individual is isolated from others by the specialized character of his or her activities and the legal and symbolic ties of his or her possessions. The fundamental Dionysian impulse for union, contact and affirmation is denied. However, precisely because of its fundamental nature it can never be ignored (Rojek, 1995, p. 80). Modernity 1's attempt to arrange the rational differentiation of society, e.g. between work and leisure, generated irresistible de-differentiating tendencies. Modernity 2 should be understood basically in terms of a process of de-differentiation (pp. 101–102). It emphasizes the messiness and untidiness of human relations (p. 106). The dialectic between Modernity 1 and Modernity 2 can be understood as producing a perpetual sense of corrosive restlessness in the human psyche (p. 109).

Wang's approach is similar to Rojek's. Civilization is highly ambivalent. It has made great achievements at the expense of Eros (Wang, 2000, p. 34). He discusses the dialectic between the Logos version of modernity and its opposite, an Eros version, referring to the carnivalesque, playful, romantic, or Dionysian features of modernity. Thus, opposed to the space of Logos as the key source of order and control, there is a 'poetic space', a 'space of desires', a 'space of pleasure', a 'space of play', in short, a 'space of Eros':

> Although Logos dominates the spaces of modernity, there is some evidence to demonstrate that modernity has also supplied Eros with a certain space. In reality, modernity has not only witnessed a process in which rationality has subdued and restrained irrational and non-rational factors (Logos-modernity); it has also involved a process in which certain irrational and

non-rational factors (Eros) have been *licensed and channelled to approved, safe, structurally separated zones, to be released and celebrated*, rather than repressed and constrained.

(Wang, 2000, p. 35, emphasis in original)

Leisure time in particular offers such 'legitimate' zones, where instincts, impulses, desires, drives of play and pleasure, feelings, emotions, imaginations and so on are no longer required to be subdued, constrained and controlled, but released, satisfied, or consumed. On one hand, Wang refers to the emergence of a private life of modern man that allows, in Giddens' terms (1991), 'privatization of passion', which offers additional scope for a free emotional life. On the other hand, there are the institutionalized 'spectator sports', which set up a safe and harmless channel for the release of violent impulses and emotions that are considered to be dangerous in mainstream institutional areas of civilized societies (Elias and Dunning, 1986). Moreover, there are 'free areas' or 'escape routes' where the rules of rational self-constraint are relaxed and activities that may not be consistent with the requirements of rationality are permitted. Lengkeek (1996) uses the term 'contra-structure' to denote these 'free areas' that are both opposed and complementary to everyday life's reality. Cohen and Taylor (1976) regard the holiday as the archetypical free area, the institutionalized setting for temporary excursions away from the domain of paramount reality (1992, p. 131). They classify three different free areas: first, activity enclaves, which include hobbies, games, gambling and sex; second, new landscapes, which consist of holidays and adventures; third, mindscape, which refers to drugs and therapy. All these free areas offer ways to escape the mundane, routine, boredom, and paramount reality. They offer the structurally separated (mostly) legitimate zones, where irrationality and emotion are no longer required to be subdued, but, on the contrary, they offer opportunities both to 'escape from' constraints and 'escape to' freedom and extraordinary experiences. As Elias and Dunning put it, 'the quest for excitement . . . in our leisure activities is complementary to the control and restraint of overt emotionality in our ordinary life. One cannot understand the one without the other' (1986, p. 66).

Wang divides Eros into 'poetic Eros' (cultivated emotional and imaginative pleasure, romanticism, or sublimation of instinctual pleasures in a Freudian sense) and 'carnivalesque Eros' (sensual pleasure, sensation seeking, or the Dionysian spirit in a Nietzschean sense). The poetic Eros version of modernity can peacefully coexist with Logos (reason and rational order), hence reinforces the order that Logos requires. It channels the energies of Eros into sublimation, into spiritual transcendence, and artistic creative activities: music poetry, painting and so on. In other words it mainly consists of cultivated, refined and sublimated 'high cultures' or elitist cultures. Under modernity, such 'high cultures' are the most legitimate zones in which the demands of Eros are satisfied (pp. 35–36). They are middle class cultures pre-eminently. Because the poetic Eros version of modernity gets along well with Logos, Wang compares it to Rojek's Modernity 1.

Linked to carnivalesque Eros, in contrast, are mainly the direct, less-sublimated, less cultivated, even crude and 'dirty' forms of gratification of Eros, particularly the sensual aspects of Eros (instinctual pleasure). Here Logos recedes and Eros surfaces as the main preoccupation. Rather than seeking gratification as sublimation, *carnivalesque Eros* demands its own satisfaction in a direct, crude, primitive, or less cultivated way. Pleasure is the only goal. People seek pleasure for pleasure's sake (p. 36). Wang compares the carnivalesque Eros version of modernity to Rojek's Modernity 2.

Eros versions of modernity, in particular 'space of desires' and 'space of pleasure', have won much ground in recent years in modern societies, as will be argued later. Current leisure and tourism cannot be understood without taking an Eros version of modernity into account.

Repression and control have turned out to be a source of considerable psychological tension.

> The rationality that is intrinsic to modern technology imposes itself upon both the activity and the consciousness of the individual as control, limitation and, by the same token, frustration. Irrational impulses of all sorts are progressively subjected to controls. . . . The individual is forced to 'manage' his emotional life, transferring to it the engineering ethos of modern technology.
>
> (Berger *et al.* in Wang, 2000, p. 29)

Freud can be given the credits for having identified and explained the syndrome of neurosis. This syndrome refers to emotional disturbances that are the results of inadequate solutions of mainly unconscious intrapsychic conflicts. All human beings have to find their way in the interplay between innate biological drives, instincts, impulses on one hand and social bans, values, norms, ideals that are internalized as a result of socialization on the other. In addition to that, modern man has to cope with repression and control of instinctual drives and impulses by rationality, which imposes a 'surplus-repression' (Wang, 2000, p. 34). Neurotic symptoms are characteristic of modernity. A syndrome, commonly referred to as stress (to be discussed later), is even more characteristic of our present times.

## Modern consumer culture

The roots of modern consumer culture trace back to both Romanticism (Campbell, 1983, 1987; Corrigan, 1997) and Protestantism, in particular the Puritan ethic (Campbell, 1983, 1987; Baudrillard, 1988; Corrigan, 1997). Both traces will be explained.

First, let us follow Corrigan (1997, pp. 11–12) in his explanation of Campbell's view on the emergence of the 'Self' during Romanticism. Romanticism began as a reaction against industrial society and all it stood for, including materialist and rationalist philosophies and the reason and science that were so important during the period of the Enlightenment. It preferred feeling to knowing, imagination to the intellect, and the inner world to the outer one. More important for present purposes, it replaced the old idea of the individual with a new one (Campbell, 1983, pp. 284–285). The pre-Romantic individual 'emphasized the commonality of mankind, the sense in which all men shared a common status leading to possession of common rights' (p. 285). The Romantics saw the individual as a distinct and autonomous being – the uniqueness rather than the generalizable side of the individual came to dominate views of what it was to be a person. If in pre-Romantic times the individual was seen as linked to society in formal ways and perhaps an individual only through these links, the Romantics saw an opposition, rather than a continuity, between the two: self and the nasty society outside came to be understood as opposing, rather than complementary concepts. The individual becomes understood as something divorced from society, and its job comes to be the development of its own uniqueness – this, indeed, becomes a duty. One major way in which he can do this is through the cultivation of more and more diverse experiences, and this generally meant going outside the constraints of society that tried to limit experiential possibilities. The Romantic was duty-bound to rebel against constraints, for only without constraints could individuals freely experience all the world had to offer. This, of course, included all sorts of pleasurable experiences. As Campbell remarks:

> What the romantics did was to redefine the doctrine of individualism and the associated idea of improvement or advancement. Instead of individuals improving themselves in this world through hard work, discipline and self-denial they substituted the idea of individuals 'expressing' or 'realizing' themselves through exposure to powerful feelings and by means of many and varied intense experiences.
>
> (Campbell, 1983, p. 287)

The idea was to seek out newer and more diverse forms of gratification, and this was clearly behaviour of an anti-traditional kind. It may be a little easier now to see links between this Romantic ethic of the experiencing individual and the practices of consumption. Central to these links is the idea of the self. Notions of self-expression and self-development seem to us now such obviously good things that it is perhaps hard to realize that they are relatively recent concepts (Corrigan, 1997, p. 12). Campbell considers the case of what he calls 'that "specialist of the self", the modern artist' (1983, p. 288). Artists were happy enough at the overthrow of traditional society, because it meant that they could escape from the ties of patronage and experiment on their own. Different from artists of an earlier era like Michelangelo, Rembrandt or Johann Sebastian Bach, romantic artists came up with what Campbell (p. 288) calls the 'expressive' theory of art: artists were not merely engaging in a craft producing work by order, but geniuses whose works expressed their superior sensibilities. The artistic genius did not really exist before the Romantics. If the consumer of pre-Romantic art was supposed to draw moral lessons from the work (that is, something not really tied to the person of the artist but to more general meaning), Campbell's romantic consumer was supposed to try to re-create the experiences and feelings of artists as expressed through the work.

> Hence, romantic doctrines provided a new set of motivations and justifications for consuming cultural products, ones which emphasized the value of the subjectively-apprehended experience of consumption itself. When this is coupled with the powerful insistence which the romantics placed upon the freedom of the artist to create without hindrance from any traditional, moral, or religious taboos and restrictions, one can see how a natural consequence of these new doctrines would be the freedom of the consumer to experience all and any form of artistically mediated experience. In effect, therefore, one of the consequences of the romantic teachings on art and the artist was to provide powerful cultural support for the principle of consumer sovereignty in relation to cultural products; a consequence, which in reality, few of them would probably have approved.
>
> (Campbell, 1983, p. 289)

But cultural products were not just expensive paintings appreciated by an elite audience. Novelists were also artists, and their works were perfectly accessible to the vast 'uncultured' hordes of the rising middle classes of the 18th and 19th centuries. Romanticism, then, could also provide a new way of experiencing the world for the masses. Campbell (1983, pp. 289–290) points out that the novel, because of its form and wide distribution, was one of the most important means by which Romantic values and ideas disseminated. It did not really matter whether the novels passed as high literature or as low literature such as the Gothic novels that were the most popular form in the late 18th and early 19th centuries: the Romantic attitude could be taken by both. He maintains that young middle-class women were the great consumers of novels, and so it was through this group that the Romantic ethic was most influentially carried. The pre-Romantic reader read for instruction or improvement, and writings had an uplifting moral purpose, while the Romantic reader wanted experiences and more experiences of the novelist-genius, and so novels could logically become quite sensationalist. People were now reading for amusement and entertainment rather than instruction or morals, and this was considered by many to be quite a shocking development (p. 290). Apart from being accused of spreading immorality and notions of romantic love (which was quite serious, as romantic love based on ideas of the individual was bound to undermine a marriage system based on transfer of property), the novel was accused of creating dissatisfaction in the reader. She was plunged into an imaginative world of apparently infinite possibility, a world which showed up the constraints of her own life and experiences and made her rather unhappy with her lot. As the 19th century wore on and literacy spread to the working classes, more and more groups of people picked up the habit of reading fiction and so more and more social classes became discontented with their station and experiences in life. People wanted more and more in order to fulfil themselves, and traditional constraints on behaviour began to seem intolerable. From paintings and novels we can work outwards to all sorts of other cultural products, and thus to consumption of such products on a great scale (Corrigan, 1997, p. 13).

The second root of modern consumer culture traces back to Protestantism, in particular the Puritan ethic, which seems contradictory to present consumer culture at first sight. According to Weber in his famous book *The Protestant Ethic and the Spirit of Capitalism* (1976), the Reformation brought about the conditions for economic activities to flourish. It was not Luther who paved the way for a profit-oriented economic system, in fact he disapproved of commerce as an occupation. From his perspective, commerce did not involve any real work. He also believed that each person should earn an income which would meet his basic needs, but to accumulate or horde wealth was sinful (Hill, 1996, p. 4). According to Weber, it was Calvin who introduced the theological doctrines that formed a significant new attitude towards work and, as such, were the foundations of capitalism. An important concept is the Calvinist idea of the 'calling': God had ordained for each of us a place in the world so that we could carry out his plan. A Godly man would perform his duty in His plan diligently and enthusiastically. A Godly man, moreover, would not allow affairs of this world to pull his mind away from God. Secular enjoyment and consumption was therefore a potential danger. The net effect of Calvinist theology on individual psychology was to break the link between production and consumption (Bradford de Long, 1989, p. 8). The Godly produced because diligent application to one's calling was a duty owed to God; they did not consume too much because a second duty owed to God was to avoid excessive enjoyment of the things of the world. As a result they accumulated. Weber quotes Benjamin Franklin who believes that a good man is diligent in his business and sober in his pleasure because such is his duty. In Weber's words:

The earning of more and more money, combined with the strict avoidance of all spontaneous enjoyment of life, is above all completely devoid of any eudae-monistic, not to say hedonistic, admixture. It is thought of so purely as an end in itself, that from the point of view of the happiness of, or utility to, the single individual, it appears entirely transcendental and absolutely irrational. Man is dominated by the making of money, by acquisition as the ultimate purpose of his life. Economic acquisition is no longer subordinated to man as the means for the satisfaction of his material needs. This reversal of what we should call the natural relationship, so irrational from a naïve point of view, is evidently as definitely a leading principle of capitalism as it is foreign to all peoples not under capitalistic influence. . .. The earning of money within the modern economic order is, so long as it is done legally, the result and the expression of virtue and proficiency in a calling; and this virtue and proficiency are, as it is now not difficult to see, the real Alpha and Omega of Franklin's ethic.

(Weber, 1976, pp. 53–54)

This, in Weber's view, is the true relationship between Protestantism and economic development. Radical Protestantism led to an ethos of diligence in one's business combined with the 'avoidance of all spontaneous enjoyment of life' that outlasted the original religious impulse. The presence of entrepreneurial classes that held to this ethos played an important role in the process of accumulation. And Darwinian mechanisms (the 'survival of the richest') in the marketplace ensured that those who held to this ethos would come to dominate the economy and set the tone for future generations (Bradford de Long, 1989, p. 8). It must be noted (p. 9) that the key to the growth of industrial capitalism is not the presence of a *Protestant* ethic but the presence of a *work* ethic. Any other ethic of hard work and accumulation would have served as well as the Protestant ethic from an economic point of view (and, indeed, has done so elsewhere according to Robert Bellah, cited in Bradford de Long, who has argued that Japanese variants of Buddhism played the same role in Japanese commercialization and industrialization as Calvinism did in European industrialization). Calvin taught that all men must work, even the rich, because to work was the will of God. It was the duty of men to serve as God's instruments here on earth, to reshape the world in the fashion of the Kingdom of God, and to become a part of the continuing process of His creation. Men were not to lust after wealth, possessions, or easy living, but were to reinvest the profits of their labour into financing future ventures (Hill, 1996, p. 4). The Protestant ethic spread throughout Europe and to America through the Protestant sects. In particular, the English Puritans, the French Huguenots, and the Swiss and Dutch Reformed Church subscribed to Calvinist theology that was especially conducive to productivity and capital growth. As time passed, attitudes and beliefs which supported hard work became secularized, and were woven into norms of Western culture (Rodgers, 1978). For

example, in America of the mid-19th century, the work ethic had become
secularized in a number of ways. The idea of work as a 'calling' had been
replaced by the concept of public usefulness. Economists warned of the
poverty and decay that would befall the country if people failed to work
hard, and moralists stressed the social duty of each person to be productive (Rodgers, 1978). Schools taught, along with the alphabet and the
spelling book, that idleness was a disgrace.

The English, Dutch, and American Puritans were the most rigid
among the Calvinists. The Puritans wanted to purify their Protestantism
(in England the Anglican Church) from the last remnants of Roman
Catholicism. In the early days of Puritanism (in the 16th century), they
were characterized by the exact opposite of the joy of living (Weber, 1976,
p. 41). Asceticism was the key word. Contrary to many popular ideas, the
end of this asceticism was to be able to lead an alert, intelligent life: the
most urgent task the destruction of spontaneous, impulsive enjoyment,
the most important means was to bring order into the conduct of its
adherents (p. 119). It attempted to subject man to the supremacy of a purposeful will, to bring his actions under constant self-control with a careful
consideration of their ethical consequences. Characteristic of Calvinistic
'this-worldly asceticism' is activity within the world, proving one's faith in
worldly activity, rather than passive contemplation (p. 121). For Puritans,
wealth as such was a great danger; its temptations never end, and its pursuit is not only senseless as compared with the dominating importance of
the Kingdom of God, but it is morally suspect. The real moral objection is to
relaxation in the security of possession, the enjoyment of wealth with the
consequence of idleness and the temptations of the flesh, above all of dis-
traction from the pursuit of a righteous life. In fact, it is only because possession involves this danger of relaxation that it is objectionable at all (p. 157).
Only activity serves to increase the glory of God, not leisure and enjoyment.
Waste of time is thus the first and, in principle, the deadliest of sins. The
span of human life is infinitely short and precious to make sure of one's
own election. Loss of time through sociability, idle talk, luxury, even more
sleep than is necessary for health, 6 to at most 8 hours, is worthy of absolute
moral condemnation (pp. 157–158).

Although Puritanism lost its rigid character after the 16th century, it
has deeply influenced the Protestant ethic of later centuries, not only
in various Protestant sects such as Calvinists, Methodists, Pietists,
Quakers and Baptists, but also, more importantly, in the modern culture
of Protestant European countries and the countries in the New World that
were influenced by migrants from these parts of Europe (see the section
'The Protestant ethic').

In *The Romantic Ethic and the Spirit of Modern Consumerism* (1987),
Campbell demonstrates how the problem of explaining the consumer revolution, and hence the emergence of modern consumer society, connects

with the fate of the Protestant ethic. 'Puritanism, even today, is recognized as a tradition of thought which, out of a basis in intense moral and religious concern, condemns all idleness, luxury and indulgence, espousing in contrast an ethic of asceticism and industry' (1987, p. 31). 'What is surprising is that the evidence strongly suggests that the consumer revolution was carried through by exactly those sections of English society with the strongest Puritan traditions, that is, the middle or trading classes. . . . How could this have come about?' (p. 31) How can the Puritan ethic in fact be intimately tied to the new pleasure-seeking activities of the consuming actor? (Corrigan, 1997, p. 15).

Let's follow Corrigan (1997) again. We commonly make a distinction between necessities and luxuries. From necessities we derive satisfaction, but from luxuries we derive pleasure. Necessities may provide what we need for existence and relieve discomfort, but luxuries are the way to pleasure rather than mere comfort. Campbell (1987, p. 60) remarks that these are in fact two contrasting models of human action: satisfying needs and pursuing pleasures are not at all the same thing. The first relates to a lack that needs to be filled so that some sort of imbalance can be righted, while the second aims to experience greater stimulation. Pleasure is tied to our capacity to evaluate stimuli, so that for example we may gain all sorts of pleasures from thinking about certain foods, but we can only gain satisfaction from actually eating the food. For pleasure, we do not actually have to eat it, although of course we may. So how does pleasure-seeking operate? Campbell contrasts traditional with modern forms of hedonism. In traditional societies, the search for pleasure is the search for sensations. This search applied only to the wealthy elite group whose general satisfactions could be guaranteed – they were not going to go hungry or lack shelter. The scarce commodity under these circumstances is not bread but pleasure dissociated from the guaranteed needs, pleasure as an end in itself. In general, traditional hedonism is characterized by the search for pleasures that are tied to quite specific practices, such as eating, drinking, sex and so on. A different, more modern, strategy is to look for pleasurable aspects in all experiences. Pleasure in traditional hedonism will be found in very particular experiences, pleasure in modern hedonism can be found in any or all experiences: experience of life itself seems to become the seat of pleasure. But how do we move from traditional to modern modes? The central change, argues Campbell (1987, p. 69), appears to be the shift from seeking pleasure in *sensations* to seeking pleasure in *emotions* – he sees the advantage here in the capacity of emotion to provide prolonged stimulation that can be coupled with a significant degree of 'autonomous control'. Of course one of our first reactions even to ourselves when we are 'tired and emotional' is to think that control is the last thing we seem to have. Are emotions and control not in contradiction? We tend to see emotions as taking control of us, rather than ourselves as taking control of emotions. Before we can talk of enjoying an emotion, maintains Campbell, it must become:

> Subject to willed control, adjustable in its intensity, and separated from its association with involuntary overt behaviour . . . it is precisely in the degree to which an individual comes to possess the ability to decide the nature and strength of his own feelings that the secret of modern hedonism lies.
>
> (Campbell, 1987, p. 70)

So we must be able to take a distance from our emotions in order to enjoy them. But how can this come about? Campbell sees the advent of Puritanism as a key event in this context. Although Puritans may have managed to suppress the evidence of unwanted emotion, it would be misleading to think that that was all they did – the capacity they had to suppress emotion could also be used to *express* emotion in a *controlled* way (p. 74). The Puritan ethic worked against the expression of 'natural' emotion, emotion of the kind that takes us over and controls us, and so it left the door open to the expression of what we might call 'artificial' emotion: we could now express emotions, emotions no longer expressed us. As Campbell puts it, Puritanism 'contributed greatly to the development of an individualistic ability to manipulate the meaning of objects and events, and hence toward the self-determination of emotional experience' (p. 74). We now had the capacity to take what meanings we liked from various symbols: we enjoy being frightened by horror films because we know that we have voluntarily chosen to suspend disbelief for a particular period of time. The horror is under control in the end, so we can be amused by it. So a big difference between traditional and modern hedonism lies in the fact that the former tried to control objects and events in the world in order to gain pleasure from them, while the latter finds pleasure in control over the meaning of things. The modern pleasure seeker, then, can find pleasure in almost anything. This would seem to be necessary in order for the world of consumer goods to appear as the hedonistic playground we take it to be today (Corrigan, 1997, pp. 15–16).

Although more pessimistic in his approach, Baudrillard (1988) arrives at a similar explanation of the relationship between Puritanism and modern consumer culture:

> There has not been a revolution in morals; puritan ideology is still in place. In the analysis of leisure, we will see how it permeates what appear to be hedonistic practices. We can affirm that puritan ethics, and what it implies about sublimation, transcendence, and repression (in a word, morality), *haunts* consumption and needs. It is what motivates it from within and that which gives needs and consumption its compulsive and boundless character. And puritan ideology is itself reactivated by the process of consumption; this is what makes consumption the powerful factor of integration and social control we know it to be. Whereas from the perspective of consumption/pleasure, this remains paradoxical and inexplicable. It can all be explained only if we acknowledge that needs and

consumption are in fact an *organized extension of productive forces*. This is not surprising since they both emerged from the productivist and puritan ethics which was the dominant morality of the industrial era.

(Baudrillard, 1988, p. 43)

The modern consumer society is characterized, according to Baudrillard, by the control of consumer demand by the system of production. Briefly summarizing the position of Galbraith in his books *The Affluent Society* and *The New Industrial State*, Baudrillard (p. 38) sees the fundamental problem of contemporary capitalism no longer in the contradiction between the 'maximization of profit' and the 'rationalization of production' (from the point of view of the producer), but rather a contradiction between a virtually unlimited productivity (at the level of the technostructure) and the need to dispose of the product. It becomes vital for the system at this stage to control not only the mechanism of production, but also consumer demand. Galbraith refers to the 'revised sequence', in opposition to the 'accepted sequence' whereby the consumer is presumed to have the initiative which will reflect back, through the market, to the manufacturers. Baudrillard agrees with Galbraith (and others) in acknowledging that the liberty and sovereignty of the consumer are nothing more than a mystification, but whereas Galbraith says 'needs are in reality the fruits of production' (Baudrillard, 1988, p. 41), Baudrillard states that *the system of needs is the product of the system of production* (p. 42, emphasis in original). Needs are not produced one at a time, in relation to their respective objects, but are rather produced as a 'force of consumption'. As a system, needs are also radically different from pleasure and satisfaction. They are produced *as elements of a system* and not *as a relation between an individual and an object* (p. 42, emphasis in original). Consumption, in Baudrillard's view, is a 'function of production' and not a function of pleasure, and therefore, like material production, is not an individual function but one that is *directly and totally* collective (p. 46). In his view consumption is a system which assures the regulation of signs and the integration of the group: it is simultaneously a morality (a system of ideological values) and a system of communication, a structure of exchange.

Here the views of Campbell and Baudrillard diverge. Whereas according to Campbell the modern hedonistic consumer finds pleasure in control over the meaning of things, Baudrillard prefers to talk about 'the denial of pleasure'. According to him consumption is defined as 'exclusive of pleasure'.

Pleasure would define consumption *for itself*, as autonomous and final. But consumption is never thus. Although we experience pleasure for ourselves, when we consume we never do it on our own (the isolated consumer is the carefully maintained illusion of the *ideological* discourse on consumption). Consumers are mutually implicated, despite themselves, in a general system of exchange and in the production of coded values. In this sense, consumption is a system of meaning, like language, or like the kinship system in primitive societies.

(Baudrillard, 1988, p. 46)

Marketing, purchasing, sales, the acquisition of differentiated commodities and objects/signs – all of these presently constitute our language, a code with which our entire society *communicates* and speaks of and to itself. Such is the present day structure of communication: a language (*langue*) in opposition to which individual needs and pleasures are but the *effects of speech* (*parole*).

(p. 48)

Baudrillard concludes that nowadays pleasure is constrained and institutionalized, not as a right of enjoyment, but as the citizen's *duty* (p. 48). In this respect he clearly agrees with his compatriot Bourdieu who wrote a few years earlier:

Thus, whereas the old morality of duty, based on the opposition between plea-sure and good, induces a generalized suspicion of the 'charming and attrac-tive', a fear of pleasure and a relation to the body made up of 'reserve', 'modesty' and 'restraint', and associates every satisfaction of the forbidden impulses with guilt, the new ethical avant-garde urges a morality of pleasure as a duty. This doctrine makes it a failure, a threat to self-esteem, not to 'have fun'.

(Bourdieu, 1984, p. 367)

According to Baudrillard, the consumer, the modern citizen, cannot evade the constraints of happiness and pleasure, which in the new ethics is equivalent to the traditional constraints of labour and production. Modern man must constantly be ready to actualize all of his potential, all of his capacity for consumption. If he forgets, he will be gently and instantly reminded that he has no right not to be happy. He is engaged in continuous activity. Otherwise he runs the risk of being satisfied with what he has and of becoming asocial (Baudrillard, 1988, p. 48).

In Campbell's view (1987), daydreaming and anticipation are pro-cesses central to modern consumerism. Individuals do not seek satisfac-tion from products, from their actual selection, purchase and actual use. Rather satisfaction stems from anticipation, from imaginative pleasure-seeking. However, since 'reality' rarely provides the perfect pleasure encountered in daydreams, each purchase leads to disillusionment and to the longing for ever-new products. What has been consumed will soon lose its appeal, because the modern consumer always desires to consume the new. 'It is not so much that we desire very particular things, although of course we might sometimes, it is rather that we want to want, we desire to desire, and we want new and different things in an endless pattern of discontent' (Campbell, 1983, p. 282). As soon as 1957 Erich Fromm wrote:

Man's happiness today consists in 'having fun'. Having fun lies in the satis-faction of consuming and 'taking in' commodities, sights, food, drinks, ciga-rettes, people, lectures, books, movies – all are consumed, swallowed. The world is one great breast; we are the sucklers, the eternally expectant ones, the hopeful ones – and the eternally disappointed ones.

(Fromm, 1957, p. 64)

In the words of Baudrillard in 1988:

*Everything* must be tried ('Try Jesus!' says an American slogan): since man as consumer is haunted by the fear of 'missing' something, any kind of pleasure. One never knows if such and such a contact, or experience (Christmas in the Canaries, eel in whisky, the Prado, LSD, love Japanese style) will not elicit a 'sensation'. It is no longer desire, nor even 'taste' nor a specific preference which are at issue, but a generalized curiosity driven by a diffuse obsession, a *fun morality*, whose imperative is enjoyment and the complete exploitation of all possibilities of being thrilled, experiencing pleasure, and being gratified.

(Baudrillard, 1988, pp. 48–49)

Modern consumer culture is perfectly reflected in contemporary holiday behaviour. People in modern societies have learned to desire holidays and have come to think of them as essential for their psychological well-being. Tourism offers surplus value, compared to material consumer goods. In the words of Wang:

Tourism has been popular not merely because there has been improvement in living standards, but also because it is one of the best spheres in which individuals can demonstrate their overcoming the limits of daily consumption. If material goods are relatively slow to innovate, then experiences, especially tourist experiences, are easy and quick to change. This situation makes tourism an exemplary domain to explore and satisfy the generalized consuming needs of modern consumers.

(Wang, 2002, p. 293)

## 2.2 Tourism and Modernity

This brief review of the lines of thought about modernity, and the explanations of the tourism phenomenon that are associated with these lines, clearly demonstrates that modernity is a controversial and ambivalent concept. Consequently, there is no univocal, unambiguous explanation of tourism. Much debate has arisen on the question of whether the West has undergone or is undergoing a transition from 'Fordism' to 'post-Fordism', from 'Materialist' values to 'Postmaterialist' values, or, in tourism terms, from 'tourism' to 'post-tourism'. Usually, Fordism is linked to modernity and post-Fordism to postmodernity. Fordism is named after Henry Ford, the inventor of the assembly line, which is representative of the modern mass-production system. It grew throughout the 20th century in the West, reaching its peak in the 1950s and 1960s, and showing signs of decline from the mid-1970s. Some major features of Fordism include the mass production of homogeneous products, the use of inflexible technologies, economies of scale and a mass market for the homogenized products of mass-production industries. Clearly the period in which Fordism triumphed was also the time in which mass tourism reached its peak (Wang, 2000, p. 102). Poon (1993) preferred to talk about 'old' tourism (before 1978) versus 'new' tourism (after 1978) rather than 'post-tourism. 'Old' tourism is associated with mass tourism, with standardized and rigidly packaged trips, whereas 'new' tourism is flexible, independent, segmented, environmentally-conscious (id). The debate is ongoing, but it is for sure that Fordism has not yet entirely disappeared; on the contrary, many of its elements are still alive and coexist with post-Fordism. Ritzer's McDonaldization of society is a clear example of the great influence of Fordism in contemporary years. Standardized packaged tours, cruises, all-inclusive resorts are booming faster than they ever did before.

Whether or not we stand at the opening of a new era, which is taking us beyond modernity itself, is not to be discussed here. According to Giddens, we are moving into a period in which the consequences of modernity are becoming more radicalized and universalized than before, rather than entering a period of post-modernity (1990, p. 3). Wang (2000, p. 16) prefers to treat so-called postmodernity as late modernity, because postmodern changes have not transcended rationalization, but, on the contrary, postmodernity is viewed as a new form of the same order (rationalization). Still, current years are different from recent decades in several respects. First, the clear and fixed dichotomies of the 1970s and 1980s, such as work versus leisure, everyday life versus holidays, home versus away, real versus fake, authentic versus inauthentic no longer apply as they once did. Second, as a consequence of the first respect, leisure in general and tourism in particular cannot be seen any more as 'escape' from everyday or 'normal' life, but are an integral part of it. Whether late modern or post-modern, this de-differentiation of traditional categories is a recent phenomenon. Third, the centrality of production in postwar years has given way to a consumer culture in the end of the 20th century. Fourth, what characterizes 'liquid modernity' according to Bauman (2000) is the abandonment of the search for a blueprint for human society to impose a newer, better solid form of social order. Instead, we have slowly but surely undermined and undone all forms of inflexibility and restraint, most dramatically perhaps with nation state borders and the freedom to travel – whether the cargo is trade goods, information or human travellers.

> It is precisely this world that we need to grasp, yet, like all liquids it does not hold its shape for long. Transformation and states of becoming are the social realities we have to deal with and Bauman has characterized our central roles as consumers in liquid modernity as rather like tourists.
>
> (Franklin, 2003b, p. 205)

These four aspects will be explained in some more detail now, the first two taken together.

## De-differentiation of traditional categories

The emergence of tourism as a modern mass phenomenon is traditionally explained in terms of 'escape' or 'push-motives'. At least three lines of thought lead to escape motives. One is the line of rationalization, which views tourism as a rational and functional escape, as a necessary complement to and a compensation for work, as a means of enhancing productivity and efficiency, and as an essential element of a reasonable standard of living (Hessels, 1973; Pimlott, 1976). A holiday allows workers to refill the batteries and re-energize to be able to do their jobs efficiently. In addition to that, Cohen (1979a) refers to tourism as a 'pressure-valve': when modern man cannot take the pressures of daily living any more, he goes on vacation.

Today, compensation motives are still very much alive. It is true that – on paper – we have more leisure time than ever before, but life is hectic, for every type of worker as well as for their employers. The work itself, the care for children and household, the maintenance of properties, the use of the media, our social network, congestion and traffic jams, and a differentiated consumption pattern, all add up to an agitated way of life. The felt need for frequent travelling is more pressing than ever. Surveys conducted in Western European countries demonstrate that 'getting away from it all', 'relaxation', 'having a break', '*Erholung*' are the principal motives for going on holiday (van Egmond, 1996). Again, destinations can be anywhere.

A second line is MacCannell's and Cohen's line of alienation. MacCannell (1976) found escape motives explicitly in the alienation of individuals from society. Only by breaking the bonds of their everyday existence can modern man or woman have authentic experiences. Meaning is sought in the life of others. Cohen (1979a), too, takes modern individuals' alienation from their society as a starting point. Whereas MacCannell thought of one single mode to cope with alienation, that is, the search for authenticity, Cohen specified five ways in which the individual could try to find a spiritual centre away from their everyday world (recreational, diversionary, experiential, experimental and existential modes, to be explained elsewhere).

Although the views of MacCannell and Cohen turned out to be very influential in tourism discourse, being cited frequently, the empirical support for these views is limited. One of (Erik) Cohen's modes of tourist experiences, the diversionary mode, refers to 'a mere escape from the boredom and meaninglessness of routine, everyday existence, into the forgetfulness of a vacation, which may heal the body and soothe the spirit' (1979a, p. 96). This mode is quite similar to the view formulated by (Stanley) Cohen and Taylor (1976, 1992) who regard the holiday as the archetypical free area, the institutionalized setting for contemporary excursions away from the domain of paramount reality. In this line of thought both leisure in general and tourism in particular offer ways of escape, not in order to recuperate and renew energy for daily work, but escape from the constraints of reason and rationality. They offer 'structur- ally separated (mostly) legitimate zones, where instincts, impulses, desires, drives of play and pleasure, feelings, emotions, imaginations, and so on are no longer required to be subdued, constrained and controlled, but released, satisfied, or consumed' (Wang, 2000, p.35), that is, they offer opportunities both to 'escape from' constraints and 'escape to' freedom and extraordinary experiences. In addition to that they offer therapeutic opportunities to those who are victimized by repression and control of irrational factors and impulses.

Although their theoretical perspectives might be different, this approach of leisure and tourism in terms of escape from rationalization, external control, alienation, boredom, routine and meaninglessness of work life or everyday life has been very common among researchers in the 1970s and 1980s. The early years of tourism thus evoked many critical, even pessimistic discourses about the origin and nature of tourism.

A possible explanation of this pessimistic approach is offered by the concept of *long waves in history*. This concept is based on the Kondratiev- cycles and developed by Gaus (2001). It offers a framework to explain the dynamics in the appreciation of tourism over the years. The Russian statis- tician Kondratiev gave the name 'long waves' in 1925 to the well-known phenomenon of cyclic trends in the economy. Gaus elaborated upon the Kondratiev cycles by postulating cycles of increasing and decreasing uncer- tainty and anxiety among citizens. Like the Kondratiev cycles these cycles of anxiety take 50 years, about 25 years of increasing (the descending phase) and 25 years of decreasing anxiety (the ascending phase) respec- tively. In recent years anxiety is presumed to have increased between 1971 and 1990 and from 1990 on we are becoming less uncertain and less anxious. With growing uncertainty and existential anxiety everyday life becomes increasingly displeasing. Escape routes from the conscious experi- ence of the present-day life will become popular. That is why the emer- gence of mass tourism in the 1970s was associated by many writers with escape, compensation or 'push' motives. Growing interest in nature has, according to Gaus, undoubtedly its roots in that it offers a universe free of people in which all those feelings which make the life of the anxious and uncertain human so troublesome are absent (2001, p. 155). The always emo- tional and arguably romantic return to nature therefore only occurs if human society in the long run has lost a lot of its attractiveness because of its more uncertain and anxious perception (p. 155). Moreover, the descending phase brought along pessimism about the future of our planet, including the impacts of tourism, whereas the ascending phase focuses rather on corporate social responsibility and sustainable development issues. In the ascending phase that is supposed to have started in the early 1990s, escape motives will lose ground, whereas exploratory ('pull') motives and adventure seeking, including seeking physical risks, will gain interest. Publications about tourism will lose their pessimistic view or even bring an ode to 'The Holiday' (Löfgren, 1999; Inglis, 2000). Playfulness is not appreciated by uncertain and anxious people. In the current ascending phase playfulness, carnivalesque Eros, *homo ludens* will get a greater share in people's daily life. Whether or not this concept is valid, it demarcates the transition between explanations of tourism in terms of escape motives to late modern or postmodern explanations.

The dichotomy between 'everyday life' and holiday no longer applies. Although compensation motives may still play an important role in holiday motivation and participation, it is not fruitful any more to regard leisure in general and holidays in particular as search for a 'centre-out-there' or escape from daily life conditions. 'Tourism is now so pervasive in postmodern society that, rather than conceiving tourism as a "departure" from the routines and practices of everyday life, tourism has become an established part of everyday life culture and consumption' (McCabe, 2002, p. 63).

Consequently, tourism not only represents a microcosm of everyday life and provides a frame through which everyday life is not abandoned, but enriched and heightened (p. 70), but the routines and practices of everyday life are more and more part of tourism as well. Everyday life's rationalization, external control, alienation, boredom, routine and meaninglessness permeate in contemporary holidays. Holidays seem more and more dominated by everyday rationalizations and routines (Bargeman, 2001, p. 24).

How can holidays become part of routines and practices of everyday life? Can even long-haul trips to exotic destinations that, for long, were supposed to be extreme contrasts to 'normal' life, become routinized?

To explain this several concepts will be used. These are: 'novelty seeking', as developed by Berlyne (1960) and Lee and Crompton (1992), 'restlessness', as developed by Rojek (1995), Giddens (1990) 'symbolic tokens, expert systems and trust', and Schutz's 'world within attainable reach'.

A variety of definitions of novelty have been proposed, but the prevailing view is to define it as the degree of contrast between present perception and past experience (Lee and Crompton, 1992, p. 733). Thus, in assessing whether a stimulus is novel, individuals compare it with other stimuli present at that time and with stimuli they have encountered in the past. In the present context, a tourist's perception of the extent to which novelty will be present at a vacation destination will be a function of the perceived novelty of objects (e.g. historical landmarks), the environment (the cultural atmosphere) and other people (residents or visitors). The degree of perceived novelty associated with objects, environment, or other people may be expressed in terms of experience. The antithesis of novelty is familiarity (p. 733). Berlyne (1960) reported a direct relationship between novelty and exploratory behaviour. Exploratory behaviour is an overt expression of curiosity that is aroused by an environment perceived to be novel. Berlyne postulated that every individual has a unique, normal, and adaptive optimal level of arousal he or she seeks to maintain, ranging from a high level of arousal that is characteristic of arousal seekers, to a low level that is characteristic for arousal avoiders.

This psychological approach of tourism seeking an optimal level of arousal is static and a-historical. The optimum in level of arousal, however, is changing. In our present 'modern consumer culture or global information culture' (Lash, 1999) we are used to more stimuli to reach an optimal level of arousal than ever before. 'The ever-changing stimuli of modern culture flood our senses' (Simmel, in Rojek, 1995, p. 109). According to Rojek (p. 109), the dialectic between Modernity 1 and Modernity 2 can be understood as producing a perpetual sense of corrosive restlessness in the human psyche. This is reflected in leisure behaviour in, for example, the endless pursuit of novelty. Some individuals might develop strategies to defend themselves against today's sweeping and overwhelming information flows. The most common defensive strategy is ignoring these flows and withdrawing oneself into a small controllable life world. Others might fall victim to stress or neurasthenia, physical disease or the tightening of the nerves, as a response to the constant assault of ever-changing stimuli. But many are getting used to 'a state of tension and expectancy' and 'flit from activity to activity in search of genuine escape and satisfaction' (Rojek, 1995, p. 109). Novelty seeking becomes routinized. What's challenging and thrilling today will be boring tomorrow. Yesterday's kick becomes today's routine. In the end this might lead to what Simmel (in Rojek, 1995) refers to as the 'blasé attitude', an incapacity to react to new sensations.

> Unable to commit ourselves to any of the ephemeral stimulations that we encounter, we are nonetheless incapable of living without them. Leisure is experienced as colourless, unvarying and incapable of providing genuine release. Our leisure activities simply become ways of killing time. Nevertheless, because our craving for escape has not been satisfied, we are driven on to helplessly search for excitement, escape and release.
>
> (Rojek, 1995, p. 109)

Restless novelty seeking is the quintessence of our modern consumer culture. 'Wanting new and different things in an endless pattern of discontent' (Campbell, 1983, p. 282) brings along a search for ever-new stimulations, sensations and activities. The fear of missing something has become a major motivator of consumer behaviour. In the words of Rojek:

> We crave the latest commodity or commodified experience but forget them almost as soon as we have consumed them. We are captivated by the style and boldness of the latest advertising campaign or fashion craze but we have trouble remembering anything about them six months later. Our leisure seems to be crunched up in the endless search for novelty and variety but leaves nothing memorable behind. Modern leisure experience, it might be said, is often marked by a disappointing sense of anti-climax – a feeling that despite all of the excitement that surrounds us there is nothing really exciting left to do any more.
>
> (Rojek, 1995, p. 109)

Consequently, the roller coasters in amusement parks have to grow longer and more exciting all the time, sex and violence in movies and on television must become more and more explicit and extreme, the most remote areas of the world are exploited touristically, the main subject of conversation during our holiday is what the next holiday will be like. New disciplines emerge in academia to study *imagineering*: how to create concepts that bring the thrill, adventure, surprise, novelty, boredom alleviation modern consumers demand.

During the 1990s long-haul exotic holidays became part of touristic consumption of many. Having started as a mass phenomenon only after the economic crisis of the early 1980s, it is a recent phenomenon. How can exotic long-haul trips become routinized? Let's first turn to two types of disembedding mechanisms mentioned by Giddens (1990). By disembedding he means the 'lifting out' of social relations from local contexts of interaction and their restructuring across indefinite spans of time-space (1990, p. 21). The two types of disembedding mechanisms Giddens distinguishes are the creation of 'symbolic tokens' and the establishment of 'expert systems'. By symbolic tokens he means media of interchange which can be 'passed around' without regard to the specific characteristics of individuals or groups that handle them at any particular juncture (p. 22). Money is an excellent example of such a medium of interchange, credit cards are even better examples when international tourism is concerned. Money/credit cards permit the exchange of things, wherever in the world, regardless of whether the goods involved share any substantive qualities in common with one another. The growth of the credit card made possible a massive increase in international consumer spending, without needing to purchase foreign currency. By expert systems Giddens means 'systems of technical accomplishment or professional expertise that organize large areas of the material and social environments in which we live today' (p. 27). The systems in which the knowledge of experts is integrated influence many aspects of what we do in a *continuous* way.

Driving a car, boarding a plane, booking an organized trip, paying with a credit card means relying on abstract expert systems. Both symbolic tokens and expert systems depend upon *trust*. Trust is therefore involved in a fundamental way with the institutions of modernity. Trust here is vested, not in individuals, but in abstract capacities (p. 26). All trust is in a certain sense blind trust. It rests upon faith in the correctness of principles of which one is ignorant, not upon faith in the 'moral uprightness' (good intentions) of others. It concerns the *proper* working of systems rather than their operation as such (p. 34).

Today's tourism and travel industry consists of various kinds of expert systems, from transnational hotel chains and transport systems to central reservation systems and tourist information systems. Thomas Cook's first inclusive group tour in 1841 heralded the new era of expert systems in the tourism and travel industry. These expert systems allow present-day consumers to book trips to the most remote areas of the globe without risks. Trust in aviation systems, tour operating systems, information systems and so on is justified because risks are minimized. Moreover, trust is supported by consumer protection systems that allow consumers to hold suppliers responsible for their services. According to Ritzer, many systems have been McDonaldized (Ritzer, 2000) or McDisneyized (Ritzer and Liska, 1997), in terms of efficiency, calculability, predictability and control through non-human technology. It is objectively safe now to book an organized trip to exotic countries. Consumers can trust that the tour operator has taken care of eliminating most of the physical, financial and psychological risks. It is also subjectively safe. In our globalized world the whole world has become our domain of consumption. We do not travel to discover the world, but because the world has been discovered. In the 1950s, Spain was a destination for pioneers. For any British or German holidaymaker the step to Spain in 1950 was a far bigger one – in terms of psychological impediments – than the step to Thailand, or even Vietnam, in present days. Whereas the first long-haul trip might have been a source of thrill and excitement, the fourth one was much more routinized. The first trip commonly goes to well-known destinations, where many predecessors have set foot. Consequently, there is a hierarchical order among destinations in terms of familiar high priority countries on top to unfamiliar ones at the base. This is a dynamic process, as is dramatically demonstrated on one hand by the rise of Vietnam and Namibia after war and the fall of tourism to former Yugoslavia on the other.

We are part of a collective learning process. We do not only learn from our own experience, but also from the experience of others and from mass communication. Holidays, even to exotic long-haul destinations, are now for many of us, in the terms of Schutz and Luckmann (1974), part of our 'stock of knowledge'. The sector of the world which is accessible to one's immediate experience is termed by them as *the world within actual reach.* It embraces not only actually perceived objects but also objects that can be perceived through attentive advertence (1974, p. 37). In addition to that they term a world which was never in one's reach, but which can be brought within it, 'the world within attainable reach' (p. 39). The whole world is gradually coming within our attainable reach. Indeterminate horizons are more and more experienced now as fundamentally determinable, as capable of explication and familiarization. This process has an important social dimension:

> The world that is in actual reach of my fellow-man is extensively but not completely different from the world that is in my actual reach. On the basis of my stock of knowledge it is . . . taken for granted by me that the entire sector of the world in another's actual reach can be brought into my actual reach through an exchange of locations.
>
> (Schutz and Luckmann, 1974, p. 40)

Mass communication contributes greatly to our collective learning process. Not only do mass media report about events in other parts of the world, they often recommend them explicitly. Tourism and travel are hot items. Generally speaking, the mass media display what options are on offer, whether they do so intentionally or not. In his informal social circles the consumer weighs these alternative options and determines whether they suit his personal preferences.

This process of familiarization of exotic destinations doesn't hold for organized trips only. Individual free unorganized tourists also travel to places that are well-documented in travel literature and on the Internet. For many the journey is led by the travel literature, often in the shape of a 'travel bible', which describes where one can find certain types of accommodation and restaurants and which attractions 'must' be visited. The consequence is that many free individual travellers meet each other in places described in these 'bibles'. Destinations for unorganized travellers show a similar hierarchical order, although not necessarily the same. Mass communication, personal experience and informal communication with friends and colleagues on one hand and expert systems on the other bring more and more previously unknown parts of the world within attainable reach. They even blur the distinction between attainable and actual reach. Even when we do not travel, many destinations will still be possible places to visit.

## Tourism as part of a modern consumer culture

Undoubtedly, a major characteristic of today's society is its consumer culture. In the vision of Baudrillard and Bourdieu pleasure is constrained and institutionalized, not as a right or enjoyment, but as the citizen's *duty*.

Whether or not Baudrillard is right in his analysis of the system of needs as the product of the system of production, pleasure as the citizen's duty, a fun morality, can be seen as the basis of modern consumer culture. This is the consumer culture at least in societies where the puritan ideology is still in place, that is, the Protestant countries of Europe, as well as North America. Modern consumer culture is perfectly reflected in contemporary holiday behaviour. People in modern societies have learned to desire holidays and have come to think of them as essential for their psychological well-being. A holiday is the perfect opportunity for spending time and money simultaneously in a hedonistic way. For this reason alone, going out becomes a 'must'. Holiday-taking in all forms, from long-haul trips to short breaks, has therefore risen sharply in the list of consumption priorities of the Western world. The decision-making process doesn't start any more with the question 'Are we going on holiday or not?' but rather 'Where are we going for the holiday(s)?' The symbolic aspect of touristic consumption can lead to social pressure. 'Not having a holiday' may become an indicator of deprivation.

Obviously, two opposite tendencies, enjoyment as the citizen's duty and the remnants of an ascetic Calvinistic life style paradoxically trace back to the same roots. This dimension, ranging from extreme hedonism on one pole to rigid asceticism on the other, is a useful instrument in describing tourist life-worlds, as will be demonstrated in Chapter 4.

## Tourism as a metaphor of the social world

Several contemporary authors don't see tourists as consumers who leave their place temporarily for holidays or 'vacations of everyday life', but rather see consumers as tourists. The tourist becomes a metaphor of the social world. According to Dann, in the book that has this very title (2002), 'the tourist, potentially at least, could reveal more about conditions in the generating society than ever (s)he did about the way of life in the receiving society – more about home than away' (2002, p. 6). How right he is, is demonstrated by Bauman (2002), who characterizes our central role as consumers in liquid modernity as rather like tourists (liquid modernity by contrast to solid is the abandonment of the search for a blueprint, to search out and impose a newer, better solid form of social order (Franklin, 20003, p. 206)). He refers to certain aspects of the tourist condition and/or experience – like being in a place temporarily and knowing it, not belonging to the place, not locked into local life 'for better or worse'. That condition is shared with the modality of ordinary life, with the way we are all 'inserted' in the company of others everywhere – in places where we live or work; not only during the summer holidays, but seven days a week, all year round, year by year. It is that characteristic of contemporary life to which Bauman primarily refers when he speaks of 'the tourist syndrome' (Franklin, 2003, p. 207). Much follows from that characteristic (p. 207). Perhaps the most important is the *looseness* of ties with the place (physical, geographic, social): there is no firm commitment, no fixed date of staying; it's all 'until further notice'. Presumption of temporariness is built into the way of being and behaving. This is very different from one very important expectation which was so typical of former 'solid modernity': the assumption that 'we will meet again'. If people know/believe that they are going to meet again and again, they strive to work out a certain modus co-vivendi, elaborate certain ways of living together, compose rules (norms) by which, as they assume, all of them will abide by (p. 207).

Another feature of the tourist syndrome is 'grazing behaviour'. Tourists seek pleasurable experiences – unlike the experiences they lived through before. According to Bauman, tourists have by definition, a 'pure relationship' to the place they visit – 'pure' meaning that it has no other purpose than the consumption of pleasurable sensations and that once the satisfaction wanes you move to another relationship, hopefully as 'pure' as the last one. The world of pure relationships is a huge collection of grazing grounds, and living in such a world is shaped after the pattern of wandering from one succulent and fragrant meadow to another (Bauman, 2002, p. 208).

A third feature is the frailty of relationships which tourists enter into wherever they go. This feature of the tourist syndrome is intimately connected to the previous ones: as they are a priori temporary and reduced to the consumption of (limited and fast shrinking) sensations, the effort to construct a hard and tough frame of mutual rights and obligations and mutually binding rules of conduct is completely redundant – a waste of time and energy. We don't trust the relationships to last, we have no idea how long we (tourists, workers, partners) will stay there. Living from one moment to another, living for the moment is a crucial trait of the tourist syndrome (id: 208–209).

## 2.3 Life-worlds and Distinctive Preferences

Early publications about tourism generally failed to take the heterogeneity, complexity and dynamics of the tourist phenomenon into account by reducing it to something simple and static and treating it as a unitary type. Many authors easily referred to 'THE tourist'. As a matter of fact, in the beginning of mass tourism tourists were more homogeneous and undifferentiated than they are now. The previous discussion of tourism and modernity clearly demonstrates that there is no simple explanation of tourism, neither can we talk about tourists as something homogeneous. The next section will endeavour to do justice to the complexity of the phenomenon.

Moreover, during the 1960s and 1970s, even 1980s, authors writing about tourism not only saw tourism as an escape from everyday life, but most of them also bemoaned the disappearance of the traveller and despised the shallow modern mass tourist. Boorstin (1961) and Turner and Ash (1975) were the most prominent among academic writers, Paul Theroux, Ted Simon, Nick Danziger among the travel writers. 'Travellers' versus 'Tourists' has been a recurring theme in literature since, tourists being denigrated by the use of nouns as 'flocks', 'insects', 'barbarians' or 'senseless mobs', whereas travellers abandon the tourism centre for the periphery (Dann, 1999, p. 165). Harrison (2003, p. 4) refers to the disdain many express for the 'hackneyed image of the camera-toting, garishly dressed, vociferous, culturally insensitive tourist, who is disconnectedly shunted, sheep-like, from destination to destination on a package tour'. Most of those who leave home for purposes of leisure prefer to be seen as 'travellers, guests, visitors, adventurers, possibly even explorers' (p. 4). Reporting middle class and/or elitist preoccupations with mass tourism, as opposed to travelling, most publications are evaluative rather than analytical in their approaches of tourism issues. The next section will demonstrate that tourists' life-worlds are more complex than the dichotomy between travellers and tourists suggests.

A special place in tourism literature is taken by Erik Cohen (1972, 1974, 1979a, b), by being one of the first authors who maintains that there is no single tourist as such but a variety of types of tourist behaviour (1972) or modes of tourist experience (1979a). His influential article 'A phenomenology of tourist experiences' (1979a) is concerned with the individual's 'spiritual' centre, whether religious or cultural, i.e. the centre which for the individual symbolizes ultimate meanings (1979a, p. 92). According to Cohen, many moderns are alienated from their society. His phenomenological typology of tourist experiences specifies the different meanings that the interest in and appreciation of the culture, social life and natural environment of others can have for the individual traveller (p. 94). To what degree represents a journey a 'quest for the centre'? Five modes span the spectrum between the experience of the tourist as the traveller in pursuit of 'mere' pleasure in the strange and the novel, to that of the modern pilgrim in quest of meaning at somebody else's centre. The 'recreational mode' corresponds to the line of thought about modernity called Rationalization. It represents a structural–functional approach of society. The tourist is 'pushed' by his own society to seek recreation and entertainment, not 'pulled' by any particular place beyond its boundaries. The 'diversionary mode' represents a mere escape from the boredom and meaninglessness of routine, everyday existence, into the forgetfulness of a vacation. This escape does not 'recreate' – i.e. it does not re-establish adherence to a meaningful centre, but only makes alienation endurable. In the 'experiential mode' tourists look for meaning in the life of others. This is the approach of MacCannell, described in the line of thought about modernity called Alienation.

> If Boorstin is among the most outspoken critics of recreational and a fortiori diversionary tourism, which in his view encompass all modern tourism, MacCannell attempts to endow tourism with a new dignity by claiming that it is a modern form of the essentially religious quest for authenticity.
>
> (Cohen, 1979a, p. 98)

The 'experimental mode' is characteristic of people who do not adhere any more to the spiritual centre of their own society, but engage in a quest for an alternative. Travel is not the only possible form of their quest for meaning; mysticism, drugs, etc., may serve as alternative paths to the same goal (pp. 99–100).

> While the traveller in the *experiential mode* derives enjoyment and reassurance from the fact that *others* live authentically . . . and content merely to observe the authentic life of others, the traveller in the *experimental mode* engages in that authentic life, but refuses fully to commit himself to it; rather, he samples and compares the different alternatives, hoping eventually to discover one which will suit his particular needs and desires. In a sense, the 'experimental' tourist is in 'search of himself', . . . he seeks to discover that form of life, which elicits a resonance in himself; he is often not really aware of what he seeks. His is an essentially religious quest, but diffuse and without a clearly set goal.
>
> (Cohen, 1979a, p. 100)

The 'existential mode' in its extreme form is characteristic of the traveller who is fully committed to an 'elective' spiritual centre, i.e. one external to the mainstream of his native society and culture (p. 100). For the person attached to such an 'elective' external centre, life away from it is, as it were, living in 'exile'; the only meaningful life is at the centre. The experience of life at the centre during his visits sustains the traveller in his daily life in 'exile', in the same sense in which the pilgrim derives new spiritual strength, is 're-created', by his pilgrimage (p. 101). Many people – and their number is increasing in a growingly mobile world – will not be able or willing to move permanently to their 'elective' centre, for a variety of practical reasons. They live consequently in two worlds: the world of their everyday life, which for them is devoid of deeper meaning, and the world of their 'elective' centre, to which they will depart on periodical pilgrimages to derive spiritual sustenance (p. 101). Cohen realizes that some people (he calls them 'humanists') have broad conceptions of 'their' culture, in that every culture is a form in which the human spirit is manifested. They don't have a single 'spiritual' centre and are not alienated from their culture of origin (p. 103). Moreover, there are people (Cohen refers to 'dualists' or more broadly 'pluralists') who adhere simultaneously to two or more heterogeneous 'spiritual' centres. They feel equally at home in two or more 'worlds' and are not alienated from their own (pp. 103–104).

Cohen's model will prove to be still very useful for understanding certain types of tourism, in particular, free individual unorganized tourism, commonly referred to as backpacker tourism. To explain all tourism and tourist experiences in contemporary society, however, Cohen's approach has strong limitations. Modern man's alienation from his society and, consequently, his search for a 'spiritual' centre 'out-there', in the external world, is Cohen's starting point (although some may be so completely alienated as not to look for any centre at all). Whether alienation and the search for a spiritual centre are nowadays the most important explanatory factors can be seriously questioned. The previous analysis of tourism and modernity tried to demonstrate that alienation is only one possible root of tourism and that, more importantly, tourism has become an established part of everyday life culture and consumption rather than a departure from the routines of everyday life in search of a centre elsewhere. For several contemporary authors tourism is even a metaphor of the social world, consumers in liquid modernity are like tourists (Bauman, 2002). According to Elands and Lengkeek (2000, p. 4), one of the charms of Cohen's phenomenological model is its simplicity. A scientific model is not a direct reflection of complex reality, but a reduction and simplification that makes scientific comprehension possible and manageable. For understanding present-day tourism, however, Cohen's model is too simplistic. Tourists' behaviour and experiences are now so complex and heterogeneous that one simple model leads to an unacceptable reduction of complex reality.

Rather than trying to develop a new, more complex model of tourist experiences, this study will try to describe the span of heterogeneous life-worlds of tourists and their consequent tastes or distinctive preferences, behaviour and experiences, according to the diagram presented in Appendix A.

First, let's turn to an explanation of tourists' life-worlds, using the explanation of the everyday life-world and the natural attitude by Schutz and Luckmann (1974). By the 'everyday life-world' they mean that province of reality which the wide-awake and normal adult simply takes for granted in the attitude of common sense. By this taken-for-grantedness, we designate everything which we experience as unquestionable and unproblematic until further notice (1974, pp. 3–4). In the natural attitude, we always find ourselves in a world which is for us taken for granted and self-evidently 'real'. This world appears to us in coherent arrangements of well-circumscribed objects having determinate properties (p. 4). Moreover, we simply take it for granted that other human beings also exist in our world endowed with a consciousness that is essentially the same as ours. Thus from the outset, our life-world is not our private world but, rather, is intersubjective; the fundamental structure of its reality is that it is shared by us. Furthermore, we take for granted that the significance of this world is fundamentally the same for our fellow beings as for us, since it is brought into a common frame of interpretation (p. 4). Consequently, we can enter into interrelationships and reciprocal actions with our fellow beings and can make ourselves understood to them (p. 5). Each step of our explication and understanding of the world is based at any given time on a stock of previous experiences, our own immediate experiences as well as such experiences as are transmitted to us from our social environment and the media. All of these communicated and immediate experiences are included in a certain unity having the form of our stock of knowledge, which serves us as the reference schema for the actual step of our explication of the world (p. 7).

In the natural attitude, we only become aware of the deficient tone of our stock of knowledge if a novel experience does not fit into what has up until now been taken for granted. If an actual new experience in a similar life-worldly situation can without contradiction be classified into a type formed out of previous experiences (and thus if it 'fits' into a relevant reference schema), then it, for its part, confirms the validity of the stock of experience (p. 10). Otherwise, the reality of the life-world demands the re-explication of our experience. Meaning is, according to Schutz and Luckmann, the result of our explication of past lived experiences which are grasped reflectively from an actual now and from an actually valid reference schema.

> Lived experiences first become meaningful, then, when they are explicated *post hoc* and become comprehensible to me as well-circumscribed experiences. Thus only those lived experiences are subjectively meaningful which are memorially brought forth in their actuality, which are examined as regards their constitution, and which are explicated in respect to their position in a reference schema that is at hand.
>
> (Schutz and Luckmann, 1974, p. 16)

Schutz and Luckmann stress that the orders of reality do not become constituted through the ontological structure of their Objects, but rather through the meaning of our experience. For that reason they speak of 'finite provinces of meaning', upon each of which one could confer the accent of reality. 'A finite province of meaning thus consists of meaning-compatible experiences. Otherwise put, all experiences that belong to a finite province of meaning point to a particular style of lived experience – viz., a cognitive style' (p. 23).

For our present purposes, it is important to realize that the everyday life-world is fundamentally intersubjective; it is a social world. Interpretation of meaning, understanding, is a fundamental principle of the natural attitude with regard to other people. Even more important is it to realize that there are many realities, each with its own particular cognitive style. So, what we are up to now is a specification of intersubjective everyday life-worlds or cognitive styles of tourists.

Whereas Schutz and Luckmann explain the principles of finite provinces of meaning and cognitive styles in general, Bourdieu (1984) goes a
step further in specifying how reference schemata come about and how
they lead to individual and group 'tastes' or distinctive preferences. His
concept of *habitus* is similar to the cognitive style of Schutz and Luckmann
Habitus refers to the habitual way of doing things and viewing the world
that prevails in certain groups. It is essentially a classifying tool, a reference schema, which helps us to relate to the external world. Bourdieu
(1984, p. 171) specifies the habitus ('a structured and structuring structure'!) into a system of schemes generating classifiable practices and works
and a system of schemes of perception and appreciation ('taste'). In other
words, the habitus consists of the capacity to produce classifiable practices
and works on one hand and the capacity to differentiate and appreciate
these practices and products (taste) on the other. In the words of Rojek:

> Habitus refers to an imprinted generative schema. The term 'generative'
> means a motivating or propelling force in social behaviour. The term 'schema'
> means a distinctive pattern or system of social conduct. For Bourdieu the
> socialization process imprints generative schemata onto the individual. We
> learn systems of speech, deportment, style and value from our families and
> local communities. Bourdieu argues that these systems thoroughly organize
> the individual. At the most basic level they teach us ways of blowing our
> nose, walking and gesticulating. However, they also structure our conscious
> and unconscious responses to, *inter alia*, questions of sex, race and morality.
>
> (Rojek, 1995, p. 67)

'Lifestyles' are, in Bourdieu's vision, 'systems of classified and classifying practices, i.e. distinctive signs ("tastes")' (1984, p. 171). Taste is 'the
generative formula of life-style, a unitary set of distinctive preferences'
(p. 173). These distinctive preferences are linked by Bourdieu to social
classes, as expressions of a particular class of conditions of existence. By
means of taste, classes distinguish themselves from other classes.
    In the process of socialization and education, lifestyles and tastes are
learned both consciously and unconsciously, both by active and passive
learning. The acquisition of cultural capital is a major part of this learning
process. Economic capital is immediately and directly convertible into
money and may be institutionalized in the form of property rights. Social
capital is made up of social obligations ('connections'). It is the aggregate
of the actual and potential resources which are linked to possession of a
durable network of more or less institutionalized relationships of mutual
acquaintance and recognition – or in other words, to membership in a
group (Bourdieu, 1986, p. 250). Cultural capital can exist in three forms
(p. 245): 'in the *embodied* state, i.e. in the form of long-lasting dispositions
of the mind and body; in the *objectified* state, in the form of cultural goods
(pictures, books, dictionaries, instruments, machines, etc.), . . .; and in the

*institutionalized* state', the objectification of cultural capital in the form of academic qualifications (p. 249). The embodied state is the most important one for our present purposes.

> The accumulation of cultural capital in the embodied state, i.e., in the form of what is called culture, cultivation, *Bildung*, presupposes a process of em-bodiment, incorporation, which, insofar as it implies a labour of inculcation and assimilation, costs time, time which must be invested personally by the investor.
>
> (Bourdieu, 1986, p. 246)

'The embodied capital, external wealth converted into an integral part of the person, into a habitus, cannot be transmitted instantaneously . . . by gift or bequest, purchase or exchange' (p. 247). On the contrary, the work of acquisition is work on oneself (self-improvement), an effort that presupposes a personal cost, an investment, above all of time, but also of that socially constituted form of libido, *libido sciendi* (the desire to learn and to know). In addition to that, cultural capital can be acquired, to a varying extent, depending on the period, the society and the social class, in the absence of any deliberate inculcation, and therefore quite unconsciously. It cannot be accumulated beyond the appropriating capacities of an individual agent; it declines and dies with its bearer (p. 247).

Accumulation of cultural capital, *libido sciendi*, the desire to learn and to know, in particular, is considered here as opposite to Simmel's *blasé attitude*, an incapacity to commit ourselves to any of the ephemeral stimulations that we encounter. So, in addition to the dimension hedonism versus asceticism, a second dimension, ranging from an extreme blasé attitude on one pole to an eager desire to learn and to know on the other, will be a useful instrument in describing tourist life-worlds and distinctive preferences, as is demonstrated in the next section.

Next to the capacity to accumulate cultural capital, the possession of economic capital and, to a lesser extent, social capital, plays, in Bourdieu's view, an extremely important role in structuring our lifestyles and the distinctive signs and tastes that are linked to that. The choices we make in life have an expressive function: the clothes we buy, the music we listen to, the groups of people we interact with, the holidays we choose, they all express what lifestyle we have or want to be associated with. Every choice entails a certain psychological risk: 'do people see me the way I want to be seen?' In structuring holiday preferences the role of economic and cultural capital is particularly important. In our egalitarian society tourism is one of the last battlefields for status and distinction (Obbema, in Bargeman, 2001, p. 35).

Consequently, two more dimensions will be used to describe tourist life-worlds and distinctive preferences: low versus high economic capital and low versus high cultural capital.

Few authors have tried to use Bourdieu's concepts in describing or analysing tourist preferences. Mowforth and Munt (2nd edition, 2003) made an interesting start by specifying 'Ecotourists' versus 'Ego-tourists'. The first category consists of the new bourgeoisie, in Bourdieu's terms (p. 121). They are located firmly within the service sector with jobs involving finance, marketing and purchasing, for example, and are high in terms of economic capital. They are also high in terms of their ability to accumulate cultural capital. They can afford expensive holidays that are exclusive in terms of price affordability and the numbers of tourists permitted: private game reserves with luxury accommodation and limited capacity, for example. They are class fractions, therefore, which can take holidays in environments which, by virtue of price, are exclusive (p. 121). 'Ecotourist' has a double meaning; it signals an interest and focus of this type of tourist on the 'environment' (*ecology*) and also indicates the ability to pay the high prices that such holidays command (*eco*nomic capital). Luxurious eating is another of this fraction's cultural characteristics (p. 121).

'Ego-tourists' represent Bourdieu's 'new petit bourgeoisie'. This social class is characterized by the increasing numbers working in employment involving 'presentation and representation', such as media and advertising, but it also encompasses a wide range of service jobs (such as guides working for small tour operators) and the growth in the number of people working for charities, for example (p. 122). These Ego-tourists are not so economically well endowed and must seek out cultural capital in order to establish their social class identity. 'In this way the burden of class differentiation weighs most heavily on this social class who must differentiate themselves from the working classes below and the high spending bourgeois middle classes above' (p. 122). Part of the reaction has been for the new petit bourgeoisie to deem themselves unclassifiable, 'excluded', 'dropped out' or perhaps, in popular tourism discourse, 'alternative'. This slide into individualism is an expression of a 'new ideology founded upon the pursuit of difference, diversity and distinction' (p. 123). Ego-tourists must search for a style of travel which is both reflective of an 'alternative' lifestyle and which is capable of maintaining and enhancing their cultural capital. Furthermore, it is a class fraction that attempts to compensate for insufficient economic capital, with an obsessional quest for the authentication of experiences (p. 123). Ultimately it is a competition for uniqueness with which Ego-tourists engage (p. 123).

Ecotourists and Ego-tourists, as described by Mowforth and Munt, are clear examples of specifications of life-worlds of groups of tourists and the distinctive preferences that are linked to these life-worlds. They are, however, only a few of all possible examples. Several more life-worlds will be specified in the next section, without the pretension of covering the full range of examples.

## 2.4 Concepts to Explain Individual Decision-making

The theoretical perspectives described above offer sociological and historical explanations of tourism in contemporary society. Several dimensions have been specified that refer to individual psychological processes. These dimensions are hedonism versus asceticism, blasé attitude versus desire to learn and to know, low versus high cultural capital, low versus high economic capital. Some additional psychological concepts are needed to explain individual decision-making processes and experiences. These are seeking novelty and change, seeking authenticity, seeking intrinsic psychological rewards, the tourist gaze, venturesomeness, the travel career ladder and the travel life cycle.

The concept of 'need for novelty and change' has been introduced by Berlyne (1960). Curiosity is a biological and psychological phenomenon. It can be defined as a drive (partly innate, biological, partly learned) to explore novelty, strangeness, or diversity. According to Berlyne, all organisms permanently strive to reach a condition of *optimal arousal*. It is about balancing between 'novelty' or 'strangeness' and 'familiarity'. Extremely novel stimuli may discourage exploration. Extreme unpredictability of stimuli is highly disagreeable because one is missing any perceived control of the situation. Should unpredictability of stimuli continue for some time, one would soon be demonstrating symptoms of stress, or rather, physical symptoms stemming from this lack of control. Extreme predictability of stimuli, that is, extremely little novelty, is just as unpleasant. If everything or virtually everything around us is known and predictable, we will be bored to death ('being bored to death' is a common expression in many languages), or, otherwise, we will demonstrate psychotic disorders, that is, disoriented behaviour combined with hallucinations. Consequently, the relationship between exploratory behaviour and novelty is an inverted U-shaped function, with the maximum level of curiosity and exploratory behaviour being exhibited in the presence of moderately novel stimuli. People strive to achieve an agreeable balance between the two extremes. Berlyne noted that 'we are indifferent to things that are either too remote from our experience or too familiar' (1960, p. 21). But, as noted before, we are learning continuously. We do not only learn from our own experience, but also from the experience of others and from mass communication. We are participating in a collective learning process. Holidays, even to exotic long-haul destinations, are now for many of us, in the terms of Schutz and Luckmann (1974), part of our 'stock of knowledge'. The whole world is gradually coming within our attainable reach. Indeterminate horizons are more and more experienced now as fundamentally determinable, as capable of explication and familiarization without fear.

MacCannell's (1973, 1976) well-known concept of 'search for authenticity', as well as Cohen's (1979a) revision of it have led to numerous comments and discourses. With the concept of authenticity being widely used,
its ambiguity and limitations have been increasingly exposed. Critics have
questioned its usefulness and validity because many tourist motivations
or experiences cannot be explained solely in terms of the conventional
concept of authenticity (Wang, 2000, p. 46). Most of the common tourist
activities have little or nothing to do with authenticity in MacCannell's
sense of the term. According to Wang (2000), authenticity will be used in
three different meanings, in order to justify and enhance its explanatory
power. First of all, authenticity in tourism can be differentiated into two
separate issues – the authenticity of tourist *experiences* (existential authenticity) and that of toured objects. The first is activity-related, the latter
object-related. Object-related authenticity consists of objective authenticity and constructive authenticity. Objective authenticity is linked to the
museum usage of the term. It refers to the authenticity of the *original* that
is also the toured object. Consequently, the authenticity of tourist experience depends on the toured object being perceived as authentic. In this
way of thinking, an *absolute* and *objective* criterion is used to measure
authenticity (2000, p. 48). Thus, even though tourists themselves may think
that they have had an authentic experience, it can still be judged objectively as *in*authentic, given that many toured objects are in fact false and
contrived, or form part of what MacCannell (1973) calls 'staged authenticity'. The opposite, called 'contrived authenticity' by Cohen (1979b), is also
possible, though less frequent: tourists perceive originals as staged. *Constructive* authenticity is the result of social construction. Authenticity is
not seen as an objectively measurable quality. According to Lengkeek
(1996, p. 186), authenticity is a value judgement; it depends on a person's
perception of reality. Authenticity and illusions are not contradictions,
but rather results of subjective perception (p. 199). Things appear authentic not because they are so but because they are constructed as such in
terms of social viewpoints, beliefs, perspectives, or powers (Wang, 2000,
p. 49). Authenticity is thus relative, negotiable, even ideological. According to Wang (2000, p. 53), a few common viewpoints on authenticity in
tourism can be identified. First, there is no absolute and static original or
origin upon which the absolute authenticity of originals relies. Second,
origins and traditions are themselves invented and constructed in terms
of living context and the needs of the present. Third, (in)authenticity is a
result of how persons see things and of their perspectives and interpretations. Fourth, with respect to the different cultures or peoples that are to
be toured, authenticity is a label attached to toured cultures in terms of
the stereotyped images and expectations held by members of a tourist-
sending society. Fifth, even though something in the beginning may be
inauthentic or artificial, it can subsequently become 'emergent authenticity'

as time goes by. Even Disneyland can become authentic. Cohen (1995, p. 16) notes that, although Disneyland was created for commercial purposes, over time it became an American cultural landmark. Despite its 'contrived' origins, it acquired a measure of 'authenticity'. In effect, according to Wang, for constructivists, tourists are indeed in search of authenticity; however, what they seek is not objective authenticity (i.e. authenticity as originals) but a *symbolic* authenticity which is the result of social construction. Symbolic authenticity has little to do with reality. It is more often than not a projection of certain stereotypical images held and circulated within tourist-sending societies, particularly within the mass media and the promotional tourism materials of Western societies (p. 54). Eco and Baudrillard (in Moore, 2002, p. 54) go as far to comment that the present world (and American life in particular) has generated the loss of the distinction between the original (or the 'true') and 'simulacra' (the simulated 'real').

Cohen (1995) adds an important notion to the attractiveness of 'contrived' authenticity. On one hand, there is a growing scarcity and diminishing attractiveness of 'natural' attractions, which make them more and more sought after. 'Unmarked' natural attractions are those sites and sights which have not yet undergone any intervention – physical or symbolic – to make them more appealing, accessible, or even more easily noticed by tourists. On the other hand, a new type of 'contrived' attraction has emerged, from 'historic theme parks' and 'living museums' to staged ethnic villages. These 'contrived' natural, ethnic and historical reconstructions have become increasingly popular with the travelling public (1995, p. 20). They are a substitute for 'natural' attractions which are becoming ever scarcer, but they are also a 'show'; they therefore appeal to the tourist's predisposition for playfulness, his or her readiness ludically (playfully) to accept 'contrived' attractions as if they were real. This predisposition becomes culturally sanctioned by the post-modern ethos (p. 20).

> If the culturally sanctioned mode of travel of the modern tourist has been that of the serious quest for authenticity, the mode of the post-modern tourist is that of playful search for enjoyment. In the former, there is a cognitive preoccupation with the penetration of staged fronts into real backs (MacCannell 1973), in the latter there is an aesthetic enjoyment of surfaces, whatever their cognitive status may be.
>
> (Cohen, 1995, p. 21)

In common-sense terms, 'existential authenticity' denotes a special existential state of Being in which individuals are true to themselves, one which acts as a counterbalance to the loss of 'true self' in public roles and public spheres in modern Western society (Wang, 2000, p. 56). Wang cites Selwyn who refers to authenticity as the 'alienation-smashing feeling' (p. 57). In terms of tourist roles, in contrast to everyday roles: tourism is thus regarded as a simpler, freer, more spontaneous, more authentic, or less serious, less utilitarian, and romantic lifestyle which enables tourists to keep a distance from, or transcend, their daily lives (Wang, 2000, p. 59). In this sense tourists are less concerned about the authenticity of toured objects, but rather are they seeking their authentic selves with the aid of tourist activities and toured objects. The rising popularity of nature-based tourism, rural tourism and ethnic tourism is commonly explained in these 'nostalgic' terms.

According to Mannell and Iso-Ahola (1987, p. 315) any leisure activity (e.g. tourism behaviour) has two motivational forces. On the one hand, leisure activities are sought because they provide change or novelty to daily routine; engagement in leisure activities allows one to leave the everyday environment behind. This is consistent with escape motives mentioned before. The other motivational force is the individual tendency 'to seek psychological (intrinsic) rewards' from participation in leisure activities. The intrinsic rewards that the individual pursues through leisure participation can be divided into personal and interpersonal. The personal rewards consist mainly of self-determination (one's ability to exercise freedom in choosing a leisure activity), sense of competence or mastery, challenge, learning, exploration and relaxation. Wang's 'experiencing one's authentic self' can be seen as an intrinsic personal reward of touring objects. Csikszentmihalyi's 'flow' (1975) is another type of intrinsic personal reward. Flow is the phenomenological experience resulting from man at play, the experience as 'one of complete involvement of the actor with his activity' (1975, p. 36). A sense of flow results from a balance between the individual's level of competency and the level of the challenge.

Seeking interpersonal rewards is an optimizing and dialectical process. Crowding is felt when the privacy-controlling mechanisms fail, producing more social interaction than is desired (Iso-Ahola, 1980, p. 300). Less social interaction than desired results in social isolation. The optimal level of social interaction coincides with the top of an inverted U-shaped curve.

In 1990 Urry introduced *The Tourist Gaze*. A second edition of the book was published in 2002. Based on the medical gaze described by Foucault, Urry formulated a tourist gaze that is as socially organized and systematized as is the gaze of the medic (2002, p. 1). In tourism we gaze at what we encounter, we visually consume places. The tourist gaze presupposes a system of social activities and signs which locate the particular tourist practices, not in terms of some intrinsic characteristics, but through the contrasts implied with non-tourist social practices, particularly those based within the home and paid work (2002). There is no single tourist gaze as such. It varies by society, by social group and by historical period (p. 1). In 1990, Urry made a distinction between a 'romantic' tourist gaze and a 'collective'. 'Undisturbed natural beauty' constitutes the typical object of the 'romantic' gaze. The 'collective' gaze necessitates the presence of large numbers of other people, as is the case in mass tourism resorts and other public places like major cities. Characteristic of the collective gaze is that it is thoroughly based on popular pleasures, on an anti-elitism with little separation of art from social life; it typically involves not contemplation but high levels of audience participation; and there's much emphasis on pastiche, or what others might call kitsch (p. 78). The romantic gaze is much more obviously auratic, concerned with the more elitist – and solitary – appreciation of magnificent scenery, an appreciation which requires considerable cultural capital (p. 78). It implies solitude, privacy and a personal, semi-spiritual relationship with the object of the gaze. Tourists expect to look at the object privately or at least only with 'significant others'. Large numbers of strangers visiting intrude upon and spoil that lonely contemplation. The collective tourist gaze involves conviviality. Other people also viewing the site are necessary to give liveliness or a sense of carnival or movement. Large numbers of people that are present can indicate that this is *the* place to be (p. 150). However, beyond these two forms of the gaze, various writers have recently shown that there are other gazes, other ways in which places get visually consumed, both while people are stationary and while they are moving. These vary in terms of the socialities involved, the length of time taken and the character of visual appreciation (p. 150). In the second edition of *The Tourist Gaze*, Urry consequently extended the number of tourist gazes. First, there is the *spectatorial* gaze, that involves the collective glancing at and collecting of different signs that have been very briefly seen in passing, at a glance such as from a tourist bus window (Urry, 2002, p. 50). Then there is the notion of the *reverential* gaze used to describe how, for example, Muslims spiritually consume the sacred site of the Taj Mahal (Edensor, 1998, pp. 127–128). An *anthropological* gaze describes how individual visitors scan a variety of sights/sites and are able to locate them interpretatively within an historical array of meanings and symbols. Somewhat related is the *environmental* gaze. This involves a scholarly or NGO-authorised discourse of scanning various tourist practices for their footprint upon the 'environment'. And finally, there is the *mediatised* gaze. This is a collective gaze where particular sites famous for their 'mediated' nature are viewed. Those gazing on the scene relive elements or aspects of the media event (Urry, 2002, p. 151).

Urry's *Tourist Gaze* emphasizes that tourism is an essentially visual phenomenon and a visual practice. Moreover, it is organized in visual terms as a set of signs and mediated by a set of visual technologies. With several co-authors (Crawshaw and Urry, 1997; Macnaghten and Urry, 1998), Urry singled out the visual sense as the dominant sense in tourism. Whereas in traditional societies, great emphasis was given to multi-sensed experience, in modern societies, they argue, the visual has become dominant and sidelined other senses. Franklin (2003a, p. 86) points out that visualism is still very much a part of the tourist experience – 'how could it not be' – but the essentially passive nature of visual consumption in tourism, Urry's Tourist Gaze of 1990 and for that matter, most of the 20th century, is now in decline, and more fully embodied modes of tourism are increasingly sought after. Tourism is characterized by activity. Although the disembodied subjectivity of the gazing tourist is still an important part of tourism nowadays, tourists are increasingly doing things with their own bodies, with embodied objectives such as fitness, health, thrill, spirituality, risk, etc. (p. 213).

Personality traits obviously play an important role in both preferences, behaviours and experiences of tourists. Unfortunately, research that is able to specify this relationship is limited. Plog's distribution of psychographic segments has been the most influential. In 1971 Plog introduced the concept of allocentrism/psychocentrism. In 1995 this concept was re-labelled as 'venturesomeness'. Allocentrics/venturers have a high degree of self-confidence that leads to their willingness to be venturesome. They tend to be relatively achievement oriented and have a positive view about life and the experiences it offers (Plog, 1998, p. 255). They also spend more of their income especially on travel. And, finally, they make decisions easily – about what to buy, where to go, and how to get there (p. 255). Psychocentrics/dependables, on the other hand, are followers, characterized by indecisiveness, a low level feeling of dread or anxiety that tends to pervade much of their lives because of this indecisiveness, and a desire to make very safe and comfortable choices. They travel less and they tend to select destinations that are very well known and over-developed. Once having 'discovered' a destination that they like, they are likely to return to it year after year, rather than seeking out new places. According to Plog the psychocentric/allocentric or dependable/ venturer dimension distributes relatively normally across the population, with limited proportions of 'pure' venturers (4 per cent) and dependables (2.5 per cent), whereas the majority of the (American) population fits in the middle of the curve as *centrics* (about 60 per cent of the total (p. 255)).

In 1988 Pearce introduced the notion of a 'travel career ladder' (TCL). The model is based upon Maslow's (1970) hierarchy of needs and conceptualizations of psychological maturation towards a goal of self-actualization, which may be interpreted as a state of psychological maturity or 'good health'. Like Maslow, Pearce's model specified five different hierarchical steps. These steps are: i) Relaxation; ii) Stimulation; iii) Relationship; iv) Self-Esteem and Development; and v) Fulfilment. The model postulates a career goal in tourism behaviour, and as tourists become more experienced they increasingly seek satisfaction of higher needs. The crux of this theoretical framework is that it is developmental and dynamic. In an appraisal study of the TCL, Ryan (1998) questions the evidence that people are progressing on a 'ladder' of experience. One problem in both Pearce's study and many of those that adopt his ladder concept is that individuals are not being questioned over time. It simply cannot be sustained that length of years is really a suitable proxy for experience, for individuals learn at different rates. Second, there is a question at the heart of Maslow's hierarchical concept. He argues that people ascend towards self actualization as lower needs become fulfilled. Yet, many do not become 'self-actualized' (p. 950). Moreover, while the model implies an upward movement on the ladder over time, it cannot be said to be a predictive theory (p. 952). When we leave Pearce's ladder concept as an elegant and appealing formulation based on a humanistic interpretation of behaviour (p. 953), a 'travel career' concept still can be very useful. Pearce himself mentioned: 'Like a career at work, people may start at different levels, they are likely to change levels during their life-cycle and they can be prevented from moving by money, health or other people. They may also retire from their travel career' (Pearce, 1988, p. 121). According to Oppermann (1995, p. 538), the basic points are that travel patterns change as the individual moves through her/his life-span and/or family career, that tourism destination choice and patterns vary according to previous experience including the time of childhood, and that external and personal barriers influence annual tourism decisions.

Oppermann (1995) introduced a similar concept, named the 'travel life cycle'. Although the life cycle theory is a widely used concept, its application in tourism studies is restricted to destination areas as introduced by Butler (1980). In a pilot study in Germany, it has been suggested that there is an increasing travel frequency (i.e. more trips), particularly with respect to secondary and tertiary trips and a tendency to travel longer distances, in this way exploring new horizons. 'A cross-sectional analysis of travel patterns indicated that destination choice, travel purpose, and month of travel varies according to age. A cohort analysis disclosed that successive generations have different travel patterns. . . . Through their travelling the young gain different travel experiences, which makes it unlikely that they will select the same destinations as previous generations in later stages of their life span' (Oppermann, 1995, p. 549). Destination choice seems to vary along two axes: with the stage of the life course of the individual and with successive generations.

In sum, our everyday life-world is fundamentally intersubjective, it is a social world. However, rather than one common everyday life-world, we have many realities, many distinct intersubjective life-worlds. In the end, there are as many realities as individuals in society, but groups of individuals share common reference schemata, meaningful experiences, cognitive styles, or, in the terms of Bourdieu, share common habitus and, consequently, common lifestyles and distinctive preferences.

Now we can turn to the intersubjective realities of 'Western' tourists in the South and try to specify distinctive preferences of tourists.

# Towards Understanding Western Tourists: Empirical Studies

**3**

## 3.1 Introduction

The empirical data presented in this chapter are derived from both primary and secondary sources. Primary data have been compiled by the author, assisted by students of Tourism Management. Secondary data have been collected from tourism journals, students' theses and selected books.

A visit from the West to the South commonly takes the form of 'travelling' or 'round trip', i.e. a trip to multitude of sites and objects, as opposed to stationary visits to a specific place. The trip is either organized or unorganized (although there are more and more hybrids). Organized round trips imply interventions by tour operators and (in the case of indirect selling) travel agencies in the country of origin. Tourists book the trip or tour in their home country. It includes flight, accommodation and transport in the destination areas, as well as guiding. The tour is 'consumed' in a group. Most participants will not know each other, prior to the start of the tour. A tour leader or tour manager accompanies the group during the whole trip, local guides might be called in 'on the spot'.

Unorganized trips don't make use of tour operator interventions in the country of origin. Unorganized tourists or individual travellers arrange the trip themselves, i.e. they book flights, accommodation and local transport without the intervention of a tour operator. In the countries visited they might buy excursions from local tour operators. Quite a few unorganized individual travellers can be labelled 'backpackers'. Examples of hybrids are organized trips with a lot of 'free' time in which participants can do whatever they want and 'modular' trips in which the tourist puts together an individual, tailor-made tour derived from the programmes of several tour operators.

The primary data concern organized round trips, as this type of tourism is still an unexplored domain. Because individual travellers, backpackers in particular, have become the focus of increased academic interest in recent years, the secondary data concern unorganized trips.

## Methodology

Many social researchers – economists and psychologists more than others – have sought respectability in the rigour of the scientific method. Tribe refers to economics when he states that :

> The effects of developing orthodox economics on scientific and mathematics methodologies have been that first economic theory has increasingly become separate from the phenomenal world that it seeks to describe, and second that phenomenal world is seen in a particular way.
>
> (Tribe, 1997, pp. 646–647)

*Mutatis mutandis* this holds true for psychology as well, in particular the behaviouristic tradition in psychology. Something similar happened in tourism studies. Whereas the 1970s generated broad visions on human motivation and experiences, in particular by MacCannell (1973, 1976) and Cohen (1979a), publications in the 1980s and 1990s showed a bias towards methodologies that placed the emphasis on the establishment of *significant* findings and causal connections. It is the kind of research that is frequently practised by economists and market researchers and also on occasion favoured by psychologists, sociologists and human geographers (Dann *et al.*, 1988, pp. 4–5). 'In its most exaggerated neopositivistic form, scant attention is paid to questions of theory or meaning. Instead there is an obsession with transforming reality into variables and a cultivation of statistical techniques for their own sake' (p. 5). The research that was published in tourism journals during the 1980s and – to a lesser extent – in the 1990s was characterized by quantification that described a burgeoning phenomenon of temporary migration and revenues generated (Riley and Love, 2000, p. 166). Quantitative research methods, as meant here, have indeed become separate from the tourist phenomenon and do not greatly contribute to the understanding of tourists' motivations, preferences and experiences. Acknowledging the usefulness of quantitative research for specific purposes, the studies in this chapter employ a qualitative or 'emic' approach. Qualitative research is, according to Denzin and Lincoln:

> Multimethod in focus, involving an interpretive, naturalistic approach to its subject matter. This means that qualitative researchers study things in their

natural settings, attempting to make sense of, or interpret, phenomena in terms of the meanings people bring to them.

(Denzin and Lincoln, 1994, p. 2)

Walle (1997b) describes an 'emic' approach, as opposed to an 'etic', referring to phonemics versus phonetics. Whereas an 'etic' approach advocates scientific methodology, formality, rigour, and favours mathematical tools, an emic approach advocates qualitative methodology, insight and understanding and qualitative data. Among the multitude of qualitative research methodologies, in-depth interviews, group discussions and both participant and non-participant observation are the most useful for present purposes. Using multiple methodologies may be viewed as bricolage, that is, 'a pieced-together, close-knit set of practices that provide solutions to a problem in a concrete situation' (Denzin and Lincoln, 1994, p. 2).

In recent years, predominantly in the current century, qualitative research has regained popularity. A lot of research reports are now being published that use a qualitative methodology and an emic approach. Tourism journals with the mission of addressing industry issues publish few qualitative articles, while the *Annals of Tourism Research*, adopting a social science orientation, has since its inception published qualitative articles consistently (Riley and Love, 2000, p. 176), the proportion of which has increased strongly since 2000. Consequently, this chapter will make a lot of references to the *Annals of Tourism Research*.

To collect primary data, 14 fourth-year students and two graduates of the Tourism Management programme of NHTV Breda University of Applied Sciences in the Netherlands were engaged to conduct research among organized tourists in the South. Fifteen countries were covered: Chile, Costa Rica, Ecuador, Guatemala, Hong Kong, Indonesia, Laos, Malaysia, Mexico, Nepal, Peru, South Africa, Tanzania, Thailand (2×), Turkey. These countries are either well-developed or emerging destinations for organized European tourists. They are well spread over the South geographically and represent the most important destinations for organized trips.

All researchers employed a qualitative and emic methodology. More specifically, they made use of in-depth interviews and both participant and non-participant observation. The interviews were tape-recorded, and worked up by the researchers into written interview records. The interviews with Scandinavians were carried out in English, almost all other interviews were conducted in the native language of the interviewee. The non-English interviews have been translated into English either by the researchers or by the author.

All students and graduates attended a thorough training programme in these research methods between September 2003 and January 2004. In addition to that, they were trained to understand the theoretical perspectives. Fieldwork was carried out between January and May 2004.

At the end of 2004 the researchers had produced 333 interview records. Of these records, some 272 were derived from tourists and 61 from tour managers, tour guides, local travel agents and other professionals, who were able to supply useful information and visions, in addition to the tourists' views. In about 50 per cent of the interviews with tourists, couples were involved, mostly married couples, but also regular travel partners, gay couples and friends. In a few interviews, groups of six or eight persons were involved. The total number of interviewees amounts to 475.

Quite a few nationalities were included, but in some countries (Ecuador, Mexico, South Africa) there was a strong bias towards Dutch respondents. The distribution of nationalities was: from the Netherlands 115 interviews, United Kingdom 42, Germany 35, Scandinavia (Denmark, Norway, Sweden) 20, Canada 14, Australia 10, USA 9, Belgium 8, and others (China, France, Switzerland, Turkey) 19.

A practical problem was anticipated by the researchers. As opposed to backpackers (see next section), organized tourists are commonly bound to a tight schedule, which makes it difficult to approach them. The researchers either addressed tourists during their 'free' days or participated in (part of) the tour, which enabled them to have interviews during the trip. Still, some interviews were broken off, because interviewees had to go to dinner, someone was waiting for them, or the bus was leaving. Generally speaking, tourists were quite willing to talk about their holidays and experiences. Taken together, the tourists interviewed cover both the mainstream and adventurous segments of the organized travel market adequately.

Apart from a bias towards Dutch respondents a bias towards age is worth considering. Most respondents were interviewed in January, February and March 2004, i.e. during the winter season in Europe and the summer season in the South. Some elderly respondents, in Asia in particular, referred to the winter conditions in their home country and/or the nice weather conditions in their destination country. Whereas organized tours attract, on average, more older consumers than individual unorganized trips, the average age may be relatively high in January/February/March.

Except for some respondents interviewed in Turkey, all respondents were middle-class citizens with comparatively high incomes and high educational levels.

The secondary data have been collected from tourism journals, the *Annals of Tourism Research* in particular, students' theses and selected books. These data concern backpackers, volunteers and romance tourists.

All of the selected studies used a qualitative and emic approach to obtain insight into motivations, value systems, preferences, experiences and actual behaviour of Western tourists. They are all based on in-depth semi-structured interviews and (participant) observation, in some cases completed by discussion sessions.

## 3.2   Organized Tourists

### The nature of organized tours

Organized tours cover a broad range of trips, from the conventional or mainstream, to the adventurous. Mainstream package tours go to tourism highlights or tourist icons (often 'must-see' sights) and are consequently part of a more or less fixed tourism circuit. For example, conventional package tours to South Africa arrive in Johannesburg, from where the group is going by coach to the Kruger Park. From this Park the trip continues along the cities on the east and south coast, down to Capetown. During this trip visits are paid to places of historical interest, native shows, crocodile farms, ostrich farms, cheetah reserves, museums and other sights. The night is spent in 'decent' (three/four star) accommodation. It is the 'white' South Africa that is offered to conventional tourists. In mainstream package tours no visit is paid to any black community. From Capetown the group will take a flight back to Johannesburg to leave for Europe. Outside this tourism circuit organized tourism is minimal. Tours to China, to give one more example, are restricted to either Beijing (including 'The Great Wall') – Shanghai – Xi'an (including the location of the 'terracotta warriors') or the Pearl River Delta (Hong Kong, sometimes Macao, Canton), increasingly offering Tibet (Lhasa) as an extension. There are only minor differences between tour operators.

Adventurous tours offer trips that pretend to go more into depth. 'Off the beaten track', 'getting in touch with exotic life' and 'exotic nature', 'great adventure people' are key words in travel brochures. The products are presumed to appeal to 'travellers' rather than 'tourists'. Extreme versions offer overland transport by trucks and wilderness camping for the night. According to the travel programmes, adventurous tours actually take travellers past the same tourist sights. In Peru, Machu Picchu must be visited, on Java, the Borobudur, in Cambodia, the Angkor Vat temples, in Yucatán, Mexico or Guatemala, the famous Maya sites, in South Africa, Kenya or Tanzania, the 'big five' (elephant, rhinoceros, lion, buffalo, leopard) parks, etc. Consequently, conventional and adventurous tourists will often meet. Adventurous tour operators cannot allow themselves to produce unpredictable and uncontrollable events. So, every single element of the trip is carefully planned, including visits to local communities. No company will randomly visit villages and communities. Rather, they select families and projects that meet certain standards of hygiene, safety, hospitality and awareness of visitor interests. In most adventurous programmes, however, visits to local families, in terms of having a meal or even spending the night in the family accommodation, will be restricted to once or twice only. Adventurous tours tend to have a smaller group size than conventional trips. They also tend to have a longer duration. Whereas most conventional trips take 2 or 3 weeks, adventurous tours take 2 to 6 weeks.

Accurate estimations of the volumes of types of organized tourism are not available. Neither WTO, nor WTTC, Mintel or any other umbrella organization or publishing company supply data on types of organized trips. The programmes offered by European and North American tour operators, though, suggest that conventional tourism – or mainstream tourism – outpaces adventurous tourism in terms of a much larger volume. Participants in adventurous trips tend to be slightly younger, on average, than participants in conventional tours.

## Motivation of organized tourists

Beyond any doubt, holidays are part of modern life in the traditionally Protestant countries of Europe, at least part of the life of the interviewees. The respondents have learned to want holidays and have come to think of them as essential for their psychological well-being. The decision-making process starts with the question 'Where are we going for the holidays?' or 'What kind of holidays do we want?' Even long-haul travelling is a normal part of life. Most respondents are well-travelled. They display a common travel career pattern. Europeans start travelling in Europe, mostly unorganized. Having visited (or even 'done') quite a few countries, they might develop an interest in long-haul destinations. The most obvious long-haul destination for Europeans is North America, the United States in particular. Going to the South is for well-travelled consumers. Only in exceptional cases does one start travelling to the South from the very beginning.

Elderly married couples often refer to their family situation. When their children were young, they had domestic holidays or went to neighbouring countries. Now that the children have left home, the parents are 'catching up' and enjoy their newly gained freedom.

Many respondents make long-haul trips every year. Commonly, they make one long-haul trip per year and several short-haul trips inside Europe, often city breaks. Some elderly Germans proudly mention how many countries they have 'collected' ('I have visited 64 countries by now' or 'I still have to do several Central-African countries'). Others 'want to see all the countries of the world' or say 'I will regret on my dying day not having seen everything' (Dutchman, age 35, Thailand).

What are the reasons people mention for travelling to developing countries? The most important reasons have nothing to do with the South or the specific destinations which the people are visiting. Respondents refer to hectic and stressful daily lives that prompt them to have a break. They need a holiday to relax. Some 'treat themselves', because they have worked hard and now 'deserve a holiday'.

'We needed a holiday to escape the pressure of the job'
'I like my job, but it's very busy, a lot of stress, so I needed a break'
'I need to get away from the rat race . . . get some vitality back'
'We love to be away from home and have no worries about the children'
'I did not know what to expect, but we really needed a holiday, so we booked our trip'
'Because I really needed some time to relax, we thought let's treat ourselves'

'Having a break' means going away from home for a fixed period of time and returning home on a fixed date to go back to 'normal' life. Although some respondents might be critical about their home country, life at home is taken for granted. Quite a few British mention crime and racial problems in the cities as a big issue at home, but they would not want to live in a different place. Only one respondent (English man, age 32, living in Bradford, interviewed in Thailand) referred to 'getting away from the westernization of things'. In Thailand, for that matter, the researchers came across several German, Dutch and British persons who settled there permanently, preferring it to their home country. Evidently, push motives or compensation motives are still very much alive, even among long-haul travellers. In addition to 'having a break' other push motives were mentioned, such as 'having time for each other' or, rather, 'having some quality time together', referring to hectic and tightly scheduled lives at home that are at the expense of intimate personal relationships of couples, parents and children or friends. Some push motives are personal and are not easily communicated, such as problems back home and looking for 'peace of mind' elsewhere.

> Some people, you know, after spending some time with them, you ask him or her why they are actually here, and then you find out it is actually not only because of the game. People have family problems, have a broken heart, had a divorce, somebody died. . . . so many times there is another reason behind it.
> (Tour guides in Tanzania, conducting game safaris for adventurous tour operators)

Having a break from daily life to relax is not sufficient to explain long-haul travel to the South. A beach holiday in a Mediterranean destination might serve the same purpose, as might camping in the countryside and many other activities inside Europe. It is the difference that matters. Reasons people mention to go to the South are seeing different cultures, lifestyles, landscapes and learning more about the world. It is about the visual consumption of places that are different from the familiar, but to a certain extent only, as will be discussed shortly. Rather than seeing specific things, respondents want to see and do as much as possible. Time should not be wasted. The programmes organized by European tour operators consequently include as many interesting ingredients as possible, leading to tight travel schedules. Frequently respondents refer negatively to beach holidays in terms of 'I don't like to laze my time away on a beach', 'I don't like to do nothing' or 'I am proud of not going on a simple beach holiday'.

> We couldn't come here to sit on the beach and do nothing. That would be such a waste of time and money . . . I would not be able to forgive myself if I would go to a place like Thailand and just lie on the beach.
>
> (Scottish woman, age 64)

'Doing nothing' and relaxing on a beach when the trip is over is something quite different. Having had a busy trip and having seen a lot, many respondents feel entitled to spend some days on a beach and do nothing. At the end of the trip they 'deserve' a couple of days on a beach. Some are extreme in this respect:

> Sometimes this trip is hard because you always have to do things. After a stressful period at home I am quite tired and I really need to relax. But I just think about the days that I am going to spend on the beach afterwards. I know that I need to motivate myself to go and see something, . . . but I'm also really looking forward to my days on the beach.
>
> (Swiss woman, age 50, Thailand)

To meet this demand, most tour operators offer the opportunity for a beach extension in destinations such as Thailand and Malaysia.

### Choice of a destination

The holiday destination is chosen arbitrarily. One wants to make a long-haul trip to see a lot and do a lot and then weighing the various alternatives begins. Recommendations in one's social circles, from friends in particular, play a decisive role in selecting a continent or a country. Destinations constitute a hierarchical order. The most popular destinations are at the top, the least popular at the base. Individual travel careers commonly develop in the top-down direction. Figure 3.1 shows the hierarchy of long-haul destinations for organized round trips in the South in the early 21st century. The hierarchy applies to Germans, British, Dutch and, probably, other European nationalities as well.

Although Thailand is a major beach destination (the research was carried out before the December 2004 tsunami), it is among the top destinations for round trips too. Whereas the beach resorts are located in the western part of the country, round trips cover the whole country, with an accent on the exotic cultures in the northern hills. The following quotes illustrate the special attraction of Thailand:

> Friends of ours . . . told us all the time that we had to go to Bangkok and the south of Thailand; they said it was super, that the people were so nice and that the atmosphere was so relaxed and friendly, that there was no stress at all. Especially the part about no stress sounded so good to us (smiling).
>
> (German couple in their forties)

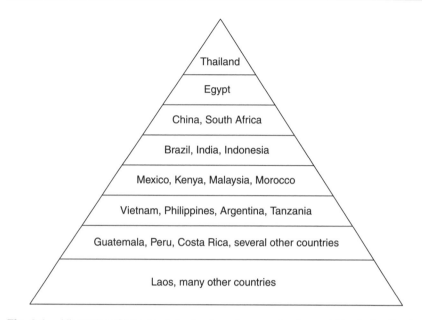

**Fig. 3.1.** Hierarchy of long-haul destinations for organized round trips in the South.

> I think the Thai are the most friendly people in the world, well . . . together with the people of Indonesia, we have been there as well. Maybe it has to do with Buddhism, all the people are friendly and they are always willing to help you out.
>
> (German man, age 54)

> It is nice to meet people who are respectful, who want to honour the people that are older . . . at home that is so hard to find.
>
> (English woman, age 57)

Friendly people, in addition to a nice climate, good accessibility and well-developed tourist facilities explain the present popularity of Thailand. The friendliness of the Thai is perhaps most appealing to Germans, as several German interviewees complain about the cold and cheerless atmosphere in German public space. Whereas most destinations are visited only once, Thailand is able to generate repeat visits and even destination loyalty. As mentioned before, quite a few Europeans live in Thailand permanently, reminding of Cohen's (1979a) existential mode.

This hierarchical order is dynamic, i.e. destinations may rise and fall. South Africa, for example, has risen sharply in the hierarchy after the abolition of apartheid in 1994. Competition between destinations takes place on the horizontal level rather than the vertical one. This competition is worldwide. Thailand is not a competitor to its neighbouring countries but rather an opportunity. The popularity of Vietnam, Cambodia and Laos is rising due to the fact that many people have come to appreciate Thailand and now want to see more of South-east Asia. Some examples of alternatives that were balanced against each other by respondents are:

> Middle East vs South-east Asia, South America vs Southeast Asia, South Africa vs China, Thailand vs Turkey, Cuba vs South Africa, Tanzania vs Australia, Indonesia vs Kenya, Indonesia vs Mexico, Peru vs Nepal, Laos vs Namibia

Destinations are easily exchanged, particularly on the horizontal level. When Indonesia isn't attractive any more because of political unrest or visa requirements, people might turn to Malaysia, which is perceived as the most similar alternative. The destinations that respondents have actually chosen may be the second or third option, if the first one was fully booked or cancelled. During their trip many discuss the destination to go to next time, probably next year. Where one has been in the past and where one is planning to go next time is a commonly discussed theme of interest in the travel group.

In Chile (3), Ecuador (2), Guatemala (2), Nepal and South Africa, the researchers interviewed participants in organized trips who happened to be visiting their children who worked or volunteered there, studied Spanish or did a work placement. Visiting their children by way of an organized trip turned out to be easier and cheaper than arranging a visit independently.

The organized tourists interviewed in (West and South) Turkey were extremely accidental tourists. Most of them did not plan to go to Turkey nor did they have any special interest in Turkey. They were seduced by extremely cheap offers they came across in advertisements and articles, or the trip was organized by their skittle club. They travelled outside Europe for the first time. It did not prevent them from being enthusiastic about the trip.

Whereas the average educational level of the interviewees in general appears to be relatively high, this is not the case with people interviewed in Turkey. Going to Turkey doesn't seem to be the start of long-haul travelling.

Characteristic of the common travel career pattern of Europeans is that destinations are visited only once. Having seen one country, people turn to another, at the same horizontal level or down the hierarchy, because 'the world is big', 'there are so many countries to see' or 'it's a waste to go twice'. Some tourists, however, develop interests in a specific destination or even lose their heart. They have 'a Love Affair with Elsewhere' in the words of Lengkeek (2002, p. 189) and develop a committed relationship by going there as frequently as possible, marrying a native person, adopting a native child, starting local projects, giving donations.

Sometimes one actually migrates to the beloved country. It might happen to any country, but it happens in particular to Thailand and Sub-Saharan Africa, as quite a few Europeans are captured by the colours and smells and the completely different way of life of Black Africa.

Whereas tourists usually visit a destination only once, their loyalty to the tour operator once they have proved to be good and reliable is strikingly great. Many book programmes from the same tour operator every year. Sometimes the choice for a destination is even dependent on the tour operator's supply.

## Why organized?

Most respondents have done some individual travelling in Europe. Why do these tourists prefer organized trips to long-haul destinations? Several reasons are mentioned. First, most people want to see a lot and do a lot during their trips. A good many respondents even refer to 'seeing as much as possible'. As the destinations are unknown, people easily rely on tour operators who 'know' the country, supply a tour manager and, even more important, guides who know the local ins and outs. Most respondents are convinced that they wouldn't have been able to arrange visits to so many interesting sights by themselves. Moreover, they arrive in places they wouldn't have been able to discover themselves.

Second, it is easier and less time-consuming to buy a package instead of arranging things by yourself. Having busy lives, many don't have the time and/or the energy to prepare and organize a trip. In addition to that, they can enjoy the trip without having to worry about where to go, where to eat, where to sleep.

Third, many don't feel at ease in unknown countries. People feel much more vulnerable in developing countries than in Europe or North America. Travelling in the familiar company of – mostly – compatriots makes the trip less threatening than travelling around individually. Safety issues play an important role, as many destinations in the South are perceived as unsafe, because of high crime rates or political unrest. Travelling in a group, within the tourism circuit, is presumed to be much safer than individual travel. The tour operator and guide will make sure that you do not end up in 'no go' areas accidentally.

Fourth, a package tour that includes a travel manager and local guides makes a destination accessible for people who haven't prepared themselves, don't speak the local languages and still want to learn about the country. Many interviewees regret that they don't speak the local language and are therefore unable to communicate with local people. Through the guide they can connect at least a little bit.

Fifth, provided that one chooses the 'right' programme and, consequently, the 'right' group, one will meet like-minded fellow-travellers. Shared interests might add to the enjoyment of the trip.

Sixth, people, women in particular, who don't have a travel partner and are not willing to travel alone can easily join an adventurous trip, rather than a conventional trip. Quite a few participants in adventurous tours have booked individually. In many of these tours, women outnumber men.

Some elderly respondents used to travel independently, but as they are ageing, they prefer to book organized trips now. Not surprisingly, both young and elderly respondents perceive organized group travel as something for the elderly who are no longer able to travel independently. Some elderly make long-haul organized trips as long as they are in good physical condition. They anticipate 'returning' to European destinations when their condition becomes more frail.

## Expectations

Being 'pulled' to a specific destination is exceptional among the respondents. Seeing the ikons of tourism, such as Machu Picchu in Peru, the big five in Tanzania or Hill Tribes in Northern Thailand are mentioned as specific reasons. For most respondents, however, seeing different things/seeing something new is the driving force rather than interest in specific features of a destination. 'There are so many different people, different places, ways of life, cultures; . . . I just want to see what it is like, just a comparison', 'There are so many differences . . . and I like to see it', 'It is a privilege to see so many countries', 'I just want to have been there', 'As long as we see something new and are not bored', 'Get to know other cultures and broaden your view', etc. are very common statements. As far as interest in 'seeing something new' is concerned, there is no relationship between types of organized trips. Participants staying in luxurious accommodation such as four- and five-star hotels mention this interest as frequently as participants in adventurous trips. Similarly, some respondents refer to cruises as a nice way to see a lot of different cultures, demonstrating that, in their view, it is possible to see a lot of cultures in a brief glimpse.

'Getting in touch with local culture or local people' is often mentioned as an important ingredient of the trip, in adventurous trips more than in mainstream. In spite of this, actual interaction is extremely limited. Chapter 4 will address the discrepancy between this desire and actual behaviour.

Travel groups consist of participants from the same country (only adventurous trips incidentally have a mixture of nationalities). Participants expect the tour manager, who guides the trip from beginning to end, to speak their own language. When a local guide is called in, this person either speaks the language of the participants or English. 'We have very good staff who speak German fluently, that is really important. You understand things much better if it's told in your own language' (German woman, age 40). So, most people travel in a language bubble. Still, many respondents prefer not to see other tourists during their trips. Meeting compatriots in particular will spoil the effect of being away from home and having left daily life for some time. In a similar vein, apart from the 'must see' attractions, places should not be 'too touristy'.

Most respondents do not have specific expectations about destinations. Expectations commonly relate to: the tour operator will have arranged everything well, the group members will be like-minded, we will see a lot, people over there will be friendly, the local culture will be interesting, nature will be beautiful, and, above all, the trip will be mentally relaxing, because daily stress and routine are left at home. Dutch interviewees prefer non-luxury accommodation such as two-star hotels or local guesthouses. French, Belgian, American and German respondents tend to prefer more luxurious accommodation.

A specific reason for visiting countries that are low in the hierarchy, such as Laos, is related to advancing modernization. Several respondents are 'going there before it is too late', which means going there before these countries are Westernized and globalized and have lost their specific culture.

To prepare the trip people don't read a lot. All tour managers and guides agree that their clients do not prepare themselves by collecting information about the country they are going to visit, although most of them have a *Lonely Planet*, *Rough Guide* or other travel guide. These guides are used as books of reference during the trip rather than information sources prior to departure. Some statements of tourists refer to having an open mind with regard to the country visited: 'You should travel with an open mind. Let the country come the way it is', 'I don't visit the slide show offered by the tour operator prior to departure, I want to be surprised' or 'Preparing a lot would result in expectations. When your expectations are too high, you might get disappointed'. For others reading and learning is not important: 'We just look for comfort and have nothing on our mind', 'I don't read, otherwise it is not a real holiday', 'We don't want to learn from our trips, we just want to have a nice time and observe things', 'I don't need to meet new people or learn new things, I do that every day at work. I don't want to think too much here (smiling)', 'I am beyond learning, I am here to be here' or 'I'm actually just happy to pack'.

Whenever interviewees refer to interest in specific features of a destination it is about highlights and landmarks they know from the mass media, television in particular. See with your own eyes what you have heard about or have seen on TV. Tour guides and drivers in Northern Tanzanian national parks commonly mention something like: 'I think many people come to Tanzania to see the parks, because you see so much about them on TV. So people know about it.' Having seen professional films about Nazca lines in Peru, the big five in the Serengeti, funerals in Bali, some tourists are disappointed when confronted with reality. In the words of the same tour guides: 'Some people forget that it is not a zoo, and that it is the animals in their natural habitat, so they live how they want. That is disappointing for some people, because of this it is sometimes not possible to see all the big five'.

## Authenticity

For many interviewees seeing the 'real' Guatemala, Vietnam, South Africa, seeing 'original' villages', not seeing things for tourists, is important. For interviewees in newly emerging 'unspoilt' destinations such as Laos, seeing 'authenticity' is more important than for respondents visiting destinations at the top of the hierarchy. Although tourists' perceptions of 'realness' or 'originality' might be strongly biased, as will be discussed shortly, getting in touch with the 'real' country and meeting local people are mentioned by many. Seeing 'authentic family life', as it is promoted in travel brochures, is among the priorities for many rather than seeing ruins, museums or buildings. Adventurous tour operators in particular promote authenticity in terms of 'meet real local families', 'taste local culture', 'visit unspoilt places', 'meet indigenous people', 'back to basics' as selling points in their packages. 'Unspoilt' often has the connotation of 'not contaminated by other tourists'.

## Adventure

Some tour operators promote their trips as 'adventurous', as opposed to 'conventional' or 'mainstream' packages. Adventure is not a univocal concept. In literature one can find a range of definitions from 'adventure involves pursuing risk as an end in itself' (Walle, 1997, p. 269) and 'a search for competence with a valuation of risk and danger' (Ewert and Hollenhorst, 1989, p. 127) to 'adventure is quite obviously linked with exploration' (Weber, 2001, p. 363). 'Adventure' in terms of pursuing risks is not relevant here, as every single element of the trip is carefully planned. In the words of a travel manager of an adventurous tour operator (Guatemala): 'There is nothing adventurous about it; every aspect is taken well care of. Our participants do not appreciate spontaneous change of plans.' A 'search for competence with a valuation of risk and danger' isn't relevant either. The link with exploration is evident. Adventurous tour operators claim that their trips are more exploratory than conventional trips, but, as said before, adventurous tours visit the same highlights as conventional tours. In some cases, such as overland tours through Africa, transport (trucks) and accommodation (tents) are more primitive, allowing participants to go 'deeper' into the region. For individual respondents, adventure appears to be something strictly personal. For some, adventure is 'not knowing what to expect', 'going off-road', 'going unorganized', 'travelling all by yourself'. For others, participating in an organized trip isn't adventurous at all.

## Behaviour

Conventional trips have a common pattern. Participants book the trip in groups of two or four persons, often couples. Having arrived at the airport in the destination, they are collected by the tour manager. Most group members will meet for the first time. Group size is between 20 and 30, sometimes more than 30. Some groups are smaller, if they are not fully booked. Group dynamics start as soon as people meet. Some groups easily grow into strongly cohesive groups, others are incoherent from the very beginning. Incidentally tension arises between participants, possibly to a level that is at the expense of a positive holiday experience. Tour managers often refer to 'in-group–out-group processes' in that groups perceive themselves in no time as the 'coolest' group. When travel groups meet, they say, people tend to see their own group as much more positive and attractive than other groups and try to outdo other groups in terms of having had more interesting experiences.

By means of prearranged transportation (usually coach) the group is brought to the accommodation. The tour consists of travelling by coach or minibus, lunch in fastfood restaurants or 'reliable' local restaurants and arriving in another hotel in the late afternoon. Breakfast and dinner in the hotel are part of the deal. Normally they are European (or American) style. Luxury hotels boast a bar, shops and a swimming pool. During the tour, the tour manager will give both practical tips and information about the destination. Depending on the programme and the country a local guide might be called in (compulsory in some countries). Whereas the tour manager is a compatriot of the participants – at least speaks their language – the local guide is native of the destination country, often indigenous to the region visited. Generally speaking, it is through the local guide that interaction between tourists and residents is possible. Most conventional round trips do not visit local communities or only allow participants a brief glimpse through the windows of the coach. When visits are paid to communities, it is to carefully selected local families and businesses.

If visits to local communities are limited, what do tourists actually do when travelling around? First of all, they visit tourism highlights, often 'must see' sights. In Mexico and Guatemala these are Maya sites, in Peru, Cusco and Machu Picchu, in Ecuador, Otavalo (Indian market), in Tanzania, the big five, in Nepal, Kathmandu (capital), Bakhtapur (famous medieval city), Pokhara (trekking centre) and Chitwan National Park (elephant ride), etc. Second, though depending on the type of trip, they visit nature areas, mostly national parks (e.g. volcanoes, rain forests, wildlife) and cultural landscapes (e.g. rice terraces, plantations). Third, trips commonly start and end in capitals. Most programmes include a stay for one or more days in these cities, paying visits to the highlights (e.g. museums, palaces, monuments, shopping centres) and/ or making a city tour. Fourth, when the country is toured, places of secondary interest are visited, such as ostrich farms, crocodile farms, elephant nurseries, local museums, local factories (e.g. jeans, textile, pottery, basketry) and art centres (e.g. wood carving, sculpture). Fifth, indigenous culture is observed either by means of watching 'native shows' and going to visitor centres or by paying a visit to selected and adapted ('staged') villages and households. Local markets that are frequented by residents are popular spots for a stop, allowing tourists to smell the *couleur locale* informally and have some interaction with local people ('the market is a real place, it is not set up for tourists, but for the locals and you can really see them doing their shopping').

Depending on the programme (adventurous trips more than conventional ones), some afternoons or days are 'free', i.e. there is no fixed programme, participants can do whatever they want. Most tours offer optional excursions on free days. According to the tour managers interviewed, most participants will choose the excursions rather than spending the day by themselves. Still, they appreciate having the opportunity to choose.

Adventurous tours have much in common with conventional or mainstream tours. The group size tends to be (much) smaller (the trips are more expensive for that reason). The size is less than 20, but often, if the tour is not fully booked, less than ten. Consequently, interaction between group members is more intensive and much more a critical success factor than in conventional trips. According to tour managers, 'groups can make or break a holiday'. When participants click with each other, this may contribute to a great experience; when they don't, this might spoil the trip. When groups travel on trucks, prepare their meals along the road and sleep in the wilderness, as is the case in overland tours, group interaction is a critical success factor to an even greater extent.

Adventurous tour operators claim to go much more 'into depth' than mainstream operators. Overland tours that make use of campsites in the wilderness or sleeping in local guesthouses allow their participants to have a 'deeper', more intense, experience indeed. Most adventurous tours, however, do not differ materially from conventional tours. Accommodation may be more modest, e.g. two-star hotels versus four-star hotels, transportation may be a little less luxurious, but the route is virtually the same. Visits to experience the 'local culture' are also visits to carefully selected local families and businesses. According to an adventurous tour manager (Mexico), 'there is no difference, except that adventurous tourists have a backpack and conventional tourists have a Samsonite'. Still, it is important for quite a few participants in adventurous trips to see themselves as travellers rather than tourists.

Organized tourists do not spend much money in the destination visited. The travel costs are paid to the tour operator in the country of origin.

Some 50 per cent of the travel costs actually arrive in the destination country (Smith and Jenner, 1992). During the trip participants make use of prepaid facilities. Souvenirs, some snacks and drinks, some meals (depending on the programme), some shopping, as well as tips and donations are among the main reasons for tourists to open their purse. Boxes 1 to 4 in Appendix B give an overview of tourist expenditures per type of organized trip. The economic impacts that these expenditures generate in the area that is visited will be discussed in Chapter 5.

## Experiences

Although tourist experiences are strictly personal, some common trends can be identified. The vast majority of interviewees really enjoy the tour. Seeing a lot and doing a lot, or even seeing and doing as much as possible, is tiring, exhausting for some, but also satisfactory. Some retired people mention that they don't mind being exhausted, because they can relax when they are back home. Others have a beach extension to relax. Most respondents refer to mental relaxation, having been away from daily routine, having seen interesting things, having had interesting experiences, never mind the busy programme. Moreover, time is perceived differently. Especially during the first days of the trip, time is not going as fast as it is in the daily routine back home. Waking up early in the morning to be able to do a lot also contributes to 'long days'. For some, having to rise early is not in line with their 'holiday feeling', but most take that for granted. Complaints concern the quality of the facilities (toilets in particular), local people who are not clean and throw away their waste, places being too commercial and too 'touristy', sites not meeting expectations.

> It has to be at least as comfortable as it is at home, otherwise there is no need of going on holidays! The hotel has to be clean absolutely. I think that Indonesian people are not very clean. . . . I thought it would be the same as in France.
>
> (Elderly French woman, Indonesia)

> No toilet, but just a hole in the ground, no toilet paper; I will not be able go to the toilet for days.
>
> (Dutch woman, age 24, overland tour Tanzania)

> We thought that we would see more Indians in Santiago, but we don't see them, that is probably because a lot of them died in the war.
>
> (American couple in their early sixties, Santiago de Chile)

> Actually we are a bit disappointed about Chile, it is not as developed as we thought.
>
> (German couple in their fifties, Santiago de Chile)

We had a totally different perception of Santiago de Chile. We thought it would have an inner city with lots of historical buildings, but we find it too European.

(Another German couple)

Complaints also concern visiting 'too many temples'. In Thailand particularly, several respondents state that 'After having seen a couple of temples, I have seen them all' and 'I like to see a lot, but after some time I'm fed up with temples'.

## Interaction with local people

In spite of the frequently mentioned desire to meet local people, interaction between tourists and residents is extremely limited. Most tours, conventional tours in particular, avoid local villages and communities. As a consequence, meetings between tourists and locals are only accidental. A casual chat with a waiter, street vendor, shoeshine boy or market vendor often constitutes the only direct interaction. Still, remarkably, many interviewees remember these casual meetings as the highlights of the trip. Some tours, adventurous more than conventional, include visits to local communities. The group pays a visit to one or more indigenous families to have lunch, dinner or even spend the night. These carefully selected families have children around, have 'indigenous' furniture and kitchen equipment and, in general, represent 'traditional life', but have been trained to serve tourists. When more and more groups are passing by, hosting tourists becomes a matter of routine. Still, once more, participants perceive this type of interaction as the highlight of their trip. Even when they are happy to eat in a decent restaurant or sleep in a comfortable bed afterwards, many describe this interaction as something memorable. Tour operators who want to include villages in the tour have to select these villages carefully as well. In the words of a Tanzanian tour guide, referring to Masai villages: 'It is difficult to just go to a village next to the road, so we have to go to an organized village. We try to keep it as natural as possible, and that is what the clients like best'. Interaction is difficult, because 'we have limited time and there is a language barrier. So, maybe we do not really go into the culture very deep, but the people get a sense of how they live'. All villages visited are more or less staged for tourists, otherwise visiting a village would be too risky for the tour operator and much too disturbing for local communities. When visiting a (staged) village, many tourists appear to be hesitant or afraid of direct interaction.

I would say between 20 and 30 per cent actually wants to mingle with the local culture, so that is not that many. The other people rather just learn about it from a distance.

(Tanzanian tour guide)

> Actually the tourists do not get involved. It is like they don't feel comfortable to interact with local people.
>
> (Tanzanian driver)

> What I often notice is that people, when we take them to a cultural village, are embarrassed to be there. . . . They step back and don't ask anything. . . . They want to see the locals, but when you take them there, it is more like they don't feel comfortable there.
>
> (Tanzanian tour operator)

Quite a few respondents are straightforward in stating that they don't want contact with local people, they just like to 'observe' local life. They feel safer and more comfortable then. Several tour managers and tour guides refer to the helplessness of participants who strayed from the group and felt 'lost' in a village.

A special type of interaction many interviewees refer to is harassment by local vendors, masseuses, shoeshine boys, informal guides, prostitutes, etc. These people are especially drawn to highly developed tourism areas. On the one hand, contacts with these representatives of local informal economy may constitute the highlights of the tour, on the other hand, being approached continuously by people who want your money one way or another is annoying. It is clearly at the expense of satisfactory interaction from tourists' point of view. A tour guide in Zanzibar aptly remarked:

> You know, usually it is a very difficult situation, because people in the tourism areas have an interest and that interest is tourists. So, when they see a tourist, it is 'my friend, my friend'. You as a tourist do not like that. You feel like your privacy is being invaded. Therefore, that automatically puts a barrier between you and the local people, because as soon as you want to start communicating to somebody, somebody wants to sell you something. In the end, you don't start communicating any more.

Local perspectives have not been studied in most countries. Only in Tanzania and Zanzibar, as well as in a study in Namibia (de Groot, 2004), have indigenous tour guides and community representatives supplied some interesting visions on European tourists. European tourists happened to be perceived much more favourably than European residents in Africa. According to a tour guide in Arusha, tourists are friendly and polite, they are touched by what they see and are interested to learn about a country, whereas residents see Africa as a good place to become rich. 'The whites that live here won't really say anything to us on the streets, but when a white person sees a white person they say "hi" '. A driver said: 'I met genuine people. Because I'm African, sometimes people don't really trust you. It is that way. . . . Some of the European and South African crew won't talk to me, but most tourists have respect for the Africans.' The Namibian results were consistent. International tourists (mostly European) were perceived more positive, more polite, than Afrikaner. In the eyes of the villagers, tourists are very curious, they ask many questions (2004, p. 65), but they are friendly, whereas Afrikaner are rude and ignore black people. The African interviewees do not understand why tourists ask so many questions, nor do they understand why Europeans want to be alone or among themselves as if they are scared of black people. An old woman said:

> Tourists are very sensitive, they want to be treated right. When they arrive . . .
> they do not want to see other people, they want to be left in peace. Tourists
> come to relax and enjoy their rest. They do not like it when you jump upon
> them with goods. Let them get off the car calmly, and show them your ware
> quietly, let them ask you questions! You have to encourage them carefully
> and invite them. If we are nice to them they will lose the fear in their hearts.
>                                                              (de Groot, 2004, p. 75)

But, 'only a few tourists like to mingle with the black population, most of them are scared' and 'tourists are afraid to touch black people, maybe they think we give off colour' (p. 75). According to De Groot, the poor black Namibians want tourists to be friendly, because after all tourism is one of the very few options to alleviate their poverty (p. 76). An elderly Canadian woman expressed her surprise that black Africans are very friendly and want to come into contact with tourists: 'I would think they would be very resentful but they don't seem to act that way'.

Ironically, whereas many European tourists are looking for 'paradise' in developing countries, several African respondents describe Europe as 'paradise' (p. 84).

### Observing local culture

In the travel programmes, as described in the section 'Behaviour', 'local culture' is mainly represented by markets, museums, small factories, art centres, 'native shows', visitor centres and selected and adapted ('staged') villages and households. Apart from markets, 'local culture' is either created for tourists or adapted for tourism purposes. Commonly, 'real life', i.e. non-tourism life, is not visited explicitly. Exceptions are to be found among 'adventurous' programmes in countries that are low in the destination hierarchy, such as Laos. Local culture, in terms of local life, is only observed in marketplaces, public places in cities and through the windows of the coach or minibus. There is an evident discrepancy between this conclusion and the frequently mentioned tourists' desire to see 'original villages', 'unspoilt life', 'authentic culture', etc. Whereas some tourists are completely happy with 'tourist things', others must find strategies to cope with this discrepancy. Several strategies were found. First, many respondents enjoy incidental contacts with local vendors, children in particular, as contact with 'real life'. As such these contacts represent the highlights of the tour. A second strategy is to perceive selected villages and families as 'authentic'. Although most tourists are aware that these villages and households are adapted for tourists, they are still perceived as 'real', i.e. 'people really live like that'. Third, for some, observing authentic culture is a very socially desirable value rather than desirable practice. Saying that you are not interested in local life is not done, not going there is much more acceptable. Common practice is that tour guides give a lot of information about the region or villages the group is passing by, while group members have a sense of place in terms of being there physically. Another general strategy is to compare one's own experiences to those of other tourists. Adventurous tourists in particular, who want to be travellers rather than tourists, easily refer to tourists as people who only visit 'tourist things', whereas travellers go much more into 'depth', even when there are no substantial differences between the programmes. In a similar way, backpackers are contrasted to tourists (see section 3.2). 'Organized travellers' react against mainstream tourists, but also against 'those depressing backpackers who don't know how to behave' (Dutch couple, in their fifties, Laos). According to these respondents, 'backpackers are a plague' that must be 'avoided' during the trip. 'They claim to have such nice contacts with local people, but they really haven't'.

Preoccupation with other tourists is something common among the respondents. When 'originality' and 'authenticity' are very socially desirable, many tourists don't appreciate – or are even 'allergic to' – other tourists. This is more urgent in countries that are low in the destination hierarchy, such as Laos and Guatemala, than in Thailand or Turkey. According to a travel manager of an adventurous tour operator (Guatemala), 'meeting other organized groups kills their experience of discovery and the feeling of being unique'. In Mexico interviewees complained about running into other groups several times a week. Conversely, 'not having seen any tourists makes this experience very special' (Dutchman in his forties, Laos). Even tourists who stay in Hilton Hua Hin (Thailand) and play golf might complain that 'there are more tourists than Thai people, I think it is too touristy' (German, age 54) and 'On my holidays, I don't want to come across many tourists' (Swedish man, age 50, sitting on a crowded Thai beach).

In a similar vein, the desire to see 'original villages', 'unspoilt life', 'authentic culture', etc. brings along a preoccupation with change and commercialization of local culture among several interviewees. Again, this is more urgent among respondents in Laos than in Thailand. Tourists are conservative when change of local culture is concerned.

> What you actually want as a tourist is that these villages stay the way they are so that you as a Westerner can see all the old traditions. . . . I realize, of course, that countries change, we have to accept that. But from a tourist point of view tears come to my eyes when I see all those traditions disappear.
>
> (Dutch couple, age 48 and 69, Laos)

I just see a sleepy version of Thailand, sleepier, more chilled out, a more relaxed version. But I have this certain feeling that in a number of years it will chase the tourist dollars as much as Vietnam. Economically it will be good, but I think from a cultural point of view it will be a great shame.

(English woman, age 34, Laos)

It has become more and more commercial, which is a shame. Especially in the tourism areas. I think the real Thailand can still be found in the non-tourism areas.

(English man, age 57, Thailand)

American fastfood chains are perceived as the ultimate symbols of commercialization and standardization of facilities.

I hate the fact that we have a Burger King and a McDonald's on Samui now, I'm afraid the Thai culture will be vanished in a couple of years.

(Welshman, age 49, Thailand)

I don't like the fact that the Thai adapt their country so much to the tourists; their culture should remain Thai and not Western. I hate seeing a McDonald's next to a Wat, for example.

(English woman, age 43, Thailand)

'Authentic local life' is often romanticized. A great many respondents perceive the residents of the countries visited as 'poor but happy'. Their lives are 'simple', often poor, but they are friendly and relaxed. Additional associations are: 'innocent' and 'unspoilt' people, who are 'proud of their culture', with 'strong family ties' and 'strong community ties', who 'don't quarrel' and 'live peacefully together', who are 'poor, but so rich at the same time' or 'materially poor, but spiritually rich', whose life is 'closer to its origin', they have 'more connection with life', etc. Inevitably, this generates reflections among many tourists on their own lives. These reflections tend to be critical of their own society and life back home, but at the end of the day everybody is happy to return to his or her own place. An obvious comparison concerns 'relaxed' life in the countries visited, as opposed to hectic and stressful lives in European and American societies. Whether it is in Africa, Asia or Latin America, local life is perceived as 'relaxed'. 'People enjoy life more than we do'. Reflections also often relate to poverty in comparison to material wealth in 'Western' countries. In materially prosperous countries in Europe and North America we know how to make money but not how to live and enjoy life.

We Western people have to learn how to live. We are too busy making money that we forget to live. The people who live in these underdeveloped countries do not have much wealth, but they know how to live. You are richer with happiness than you are with lots of money.

(Canadian / Dutch couple in their fifties, Chile)

It is hard for a lot of us to understand, I think. They are poor, well, at least they don't have a lot of money, and still they seem happier than most of the people living in Europe.

(German man, age 36, Thailand)

The people have a simple life here, more simple than in Europe, but they are happy with it, they don't know any better. The people in Europe are very materialistic, too materialistic I think.

(Norwegian woman, age 30, Thailand)

And they are very, very, very, very innocent people, especially the monks. . . . These people could survive for years and years and are not depending on some kind of cash corrupted world. . . . And there are so many people in the United States that are desperate for this sense of simplicity and spirituality.

(American man, age 64, Laos)

Another comparison between observed life and life back home concerns perceived family ties. People in the countries visited are presumed to have strong ties and care for each other, whereas in individualistic European and American countries we seem to have lost family life and every man has to face the world on his own.

Well, what really affected us was to see how people here are having a real close family life. We do not really see that anymore in our country.

(Group interview with Australians, Peru)

They stick together, they take care of each other. More than we do. They take care of the older people, they take care of the young, brothers and sisters take care of each other.

(Norwegian woman, age 52, Peru)

In many places where I have been people really live together, and then I really mean live together. . . . Everyone knows what the other is thinking. If the entire world would be like that, there would be far fewer troubles.

(Elderly English man, Indonesia)

'Respect' is another keyword. People in the countries visited seem to respect each other, and respect their guests consequently. The elderly in particular are highly respected, as opposed to the elderly in 'Western' countries. For many older ones among the tourists this is a special reason to feel welcome during their trip. Respect for women is less self-evident. Buddhist countries in South-east Asia are perceived as less male-chauvinist than most other countries. One female English respondent referred to Buddhist countries, such as Thailand and Laos, as 'feminine', as opposed to Latin American 'macho' countries. In Buddhist countries women feel at ease, they can move freely without being harassed. It is definitely a major selling point for South-east Asia. Conversely, several women admitted that they were reluctant to go to Muslim countries such as Pakistan or Iran that are supposed to be unfriendly to women.

Romanticizing 'authentic local culture' is strongly supported by most tour operators, not only by referring in their brochures to 'unspoilt villages and people' and 'exotic culture', but also by selecting appropriate villages and sites and avoiding possibly shocking real life. Appropriate sites are, according to one of the tour managers, 'postcard-like' sites. According to several tour managers, real life does not appeal to tourists at all. Real villages are dirty and smelly, waste and garbage are everywhere. Poverty is often distressing. Tourists do not like real local food that doesn't meet their hygiene and quality standards. A ride in a local bus is perceived as 'cool', but travelling by local transport isn't appreciated at all. A night with a local family, as is part of some adventurous packages, might be an interesting experience, as long as the next night will be in a comfortable bed. The above-mentioned tour manager consequently refers to the *illusion* of authenticity.

## Coping with poverty

Observing poverty is a serious issue for many respondents. A great many people are deeply touched when they observe poverty, poor children in particular. Reactions range from embarrassment and helplessness to guilt and shame.

> We feel sorry for those people. Why should people have to live like that?
>
> (English couple in their sixties, South Africa)

> I felt terrible when I saw all those poor people over there.
>
> (German man, age 54, referring to Mexico and South Africa)

> It is hard to see, I don't know how to handle it. It bothers me, but you are not really sure what to do.
>
> (American woman, age?, Peru)

> Sometimes I was so ashamed. When we were in the bus we saw children outside walking to school without shoes. This made me feel very bad.
>
> (Dutch girl, age 15, travelling with her parents in South Africa)

Most tour operators advise their clients not to give money or sweets. Observing poverty, however, prompts many respondents to 'do something'. A wide range of strategies to cope with embarrassment and guilt is found. The most common strategy of tour operators is avoiding poor local life. When visits are paid to local communities, e.g. to townships in South Africa, grinding poverty is not shown to tourists. Rather, tour operators select households that are – in the words of a tour manager – 'cute and exotic'. When tourists, nevertheless, are confronted with poverty, they demonstrate various strategies. One, still, is giving money. But for most tourists giving money is not done, because 'you might spoil people'. Giving sweets to children is more common. Tourists enjoy their 'happy faces'. Every now and then, tourists give pens to children or schools. A more subtle way of giving things (sometimes promoted by tour managers) is 'leaving something behind' in a plastic bag (T-shirts, towels, shoes, etc.). Several respondents have sent some goods (e.g. cloths, books, school equipment, computers) after having returned home from a previous trip. Others have adopted a foster child (mentioned eight times), sponsor children, donate scholarships (mentioned five times), supply donations to schools or orphanages or start development projects. In particular, tourists who have 'fallen in love' with a destination country develop a committed relationship in one of these ways. This relationship allows them to come back frequently. Some interviewees (all female) want to stay and help or consider going back to the country as a volunteer ('to do something'). Several respondents want to help, but don't know how.

> Very touching, it gives me a feeling of helplessness. It is difficult to do something about it, especially on your own. . . . I would like to co-operate with a project in Nepal for several weeks. I want to do something more concrete.
> (Dutch woman, age 55, Nepal)

> It is frustrating when you see poor people, but unfortunately you can not do anything about it. . . . You want to help, but don't know how.
> (Canadian couple in Chile, referring to Nepal)

The most general strategy is buying things. Europeans often admit that it is difficult to find a balance between bargaining and paying a fair price. Most agree that it is better to buy useless things or have your shoes polished than give money. It is a common feeling that they contribute to economic development best by being there as tourists and spending money.

> It is the easiest way to have these people have their share in our welfare. Your money is going directly to the people. Today we had some soup, we bought water and postcards . . . that's the best way of development aid.
> (Dutch couple in their fifties, Laos)

One respondent recommends tour operators to support development projects and include an amount of money in the cost of the travel package. Some of the respondents are sceptical about 'doing something', because whatever you do will be 'just a drop in the ocean' and 'having compassion will spoil your holiday'.

The desire to 'do something', when confronted with poverty, is very general among respondents from the Protestant European countries. It is a desire to take action individually. This is in contrast to French and Belgian respondents who plead government intervention to reduce poverty.

Confrontation with poverty not only generates feelings of embarrassment or guilt but also some kind of reconsideration of life at home. On one hand, the romantic perception of relaxed and happy life makes interviewees critical towards their home society with its materialistic and individualistic values, but, on the other hand, observing poverty is generally conducive to a greater appreciation of life back home. It makes people happier with the conditions of life in the West. A few respondents said they had resolved to change their lifestyles after previous trips, in order to live less consumptive and materialistic lives, but after a short time they were drawn again into the vortex of hectic life.

Critical reflections on Western values and lifestyle induce some interviewees to question the blessings of modernization.

> Do we offer them more happiness by giving them more wealth? In our wealthy country 60 per cent of the population is stressed.
>
> (Dutch couple in their fifties, Laos)

### Learning

'Learning about other cultures' is among the central interests of the organized tourists interviewed. Some respondents are straightforward in stating that they just want to relax and enjoy themselves. They want to turn off their minds. Learning, in their view, resembles work and interferes with a 'holiday-feeling'. The vast majority, however, wants to learn something. Without intellectual stimulation, the virtues of a trip are seen to be limited. Although the qualitative research methods used in the present study do not supply accurate information about the participants' level of education, it is evident that this level tends to be comparatively high. Most respondents are assumed to have quite a lot of cultural capital in terms of Bourdieu's embodied and institutionalized state. From the top of the destination hierarchy to the bottom, the level of education seems to increase. Nevertheless, though some interviewees have read a lot about the country they are visiting, most did not engage in any preparation, except for buying or borrowing a travel guide. Actually, there is a great discrepancy between the desire to learn and understand, as expressed by the majority of respondents, and the perceptions of tour managers. The tour managers are rather negative about the participants' desire to learn. They all agree that the need to learn has strong limitations. The information that is supplied by tour manager and guide is sufficient for most participants. For some it is more than enough. Participants don't ask many questions. During lunch, tour guides are not approached for additional information. Some tour managers complain about participants who are sleeping during their presentations. One tour manager (Indonesia) explicitly states that 'some tourists aren't ripe yet to travel to countries like this one'. Another tour manager (Ecuador) noticed that tourists don't want to hear negative information. Their romantic expectations shouldn't be frustrated. When they are confronted with less positive experiences, this will affect their 'holiday feeling'. According to this tour manager, having seen grinding poverty, severely handicapped people, dirty places, people will feel guilty when they go on enjoying themselves. Quite a few interviewees admit that it is difficult to handle so much information. They either listen selectively and pick out the interesting things or were not fully committed to the explanations of tour manager and guide. They do not remember much of the information supplied to them. Likewise, they cannot give many details about previous trips. Reading their *Lonely Planet* or other travel guide during the trip or during the return flight often has the function of putting things into perspective.

Much learning is adapting information to one's existing reference schemata. A common way to do that is by comparing new information with the situation at home (e.g. see the section 'Coping with poverty') or by associating features of destinations with one another: 'Ecuador reminds me of Greece' (Dutch woman visiting her son in Ecuador), 'Ecuador has much in common with Mexico and Guatemala' (several Dutch respondents).

## Differences between nationalities

The limited number of American respondents (nine interviews, 14 interviewees) does not allow any comparison between Americans and Europeans. The opinions of tour guides, hotel managers and other staff who have been interviewed are, nonetheless, quite consistent in their perception of differences. According to Costa Rican and Mexican tour guides, the differences between Americans and Europeans are greater than the differences among Europeans. Americans are more demanding. They easily complain and want their money back, when they don't get the desired service. Americans are more direct, they say what they want to say. Europeans aren't that direct. Moreover, Europeans are better prepared while travelling, they know much more about the country. They know what to expect and have made enquiries in advance.

According to tour guides in Costa Rica, Ecuador, Mexico and Peru, Americans are not really interested in indigenous communities, although they all say they want to see 'the real life'. Visitors to community projects are mostly European.

Americans in Tanzanian National Parks are 'very organized people'. They like to arrange everything before they come. They don't want anything unexpected to happen. More than Europeans they want value for money. For many this means: see and do as much as possible, don't waste time. A tour guide in Zanzibar said:

> Americans are used to a remote control, more than Europeans. . . . We are forced to provide itineraries that resemble the remote control button. Value for money. If I sit down and start explaining the Muslim religion, they are going to say why am I wasting my time on this? I want to see some spices, taste some food, relax on the beach and go and see the dolphins. I want to go see

the historical Stone Town, don't forget the few gifts I want to buy. Unfortunately, that's reality.

A popular pastime among European tourists is reacting against other nationalities, especially Americans and Japanese – being much more 'typical tourists' than Europeans in their view.

> These Japanese are awful. They think they are kings, they think they are the only ones in the world.
>
> (German woman in her fifties, Peru)

> Those Israelis, they always stick together and don't adapt at all.
>
> (Dutch man, age 35, Thailand)

> Especially the Japanese have a bad influence on the Thai culture and prices.
>
> (English man, age 36, Thailand)

## 3.3 Backpackers

### Introduction

> During my many journeys as a backpacker I met numerous other backpackers. In the famous Thai backpacker paradise Kho Pha-Ngan I ran into young people who made a one-and-a-half-month trip and spent four weeks of it on the beach to dance and use drugs. In Guatemala I met backpackers who had gone there to learn Spanish, participate in volunteer projects and travel around. Backpackers I saw in Australia were selling telephone subscriptions in Sydney all year round to buy beer. Others made hiking trips of several days or weeks in the outback of the Oz. In Bangladesh I came across Western youngsters who lived with local people, were able to speak the local language, and were all skin and bone like the locals. Some backpackers in Indonesia hang around for two weeks in Kuta, Bali, to visit the big attractions of the island by tourist coach. Others travelled through this country by local public transport and reported passionately about the joviality of local people in the interior of Flores.
>
> (van Egmond, 2004, p. 3, translation by the author)

Backpackers are not a homogeneous category of tourists or travellers. Consequently, there's a lack of agreement on the definition of backpackers. Whatever definition is used, however, backpackers are undoubtedly a recent phenomenon. Though nomadism, according to Adler (1985), has been widely spread among young men from the lower classes in the pre-modern West, this nomadism was in quest of employment and survival rather than travelling for enjoyment and personal experiences. The emergence of contemporary backpacking as a large-scale tourism phenomenon is related to some distinctive traits of modern Western societies and the position of youth within them (Cohen, 2004, p. 44). As such it originates in the 1960s and 1970s.

The study of backpacking began when Cohen (1972) differentiated between non-institutionalized tourists and their institutionalized counter-parts (Uriely *et al.*, 2002, p. 520). According to Cohen, the latter comply with the conventional features of mass tourism, particularly mass tourists' preference for being confined to the Western 'environmental bubble', while the former are referred to as drifters (1972) or nomads (1973). A variety of names have been used in literature to describe drifter- or nomad-style travellers, but in recent years, studies tend to address them as backpackers (e.g. Pearce, 1990; Loker-Murphy and Pearce, 1995; Hampton, 1998; Spreitzhofer, 1998; Elsrud, 2001; Murphy, 2001; Uriely *et al.*, 2002; Sörensen, 2003; Noy, 2004; Richards and Wilson, 2004; van Egmond, 2004). Pearce (1990) is presumed to have coined the term 'backpackers'.

From the very beginning drifters/nomads/backpackers have been young (predominantly male) members of Europe's middle classes. During the 1950s hitchhiking became popular among young Europeans, particularly tertiary students who had time but not usually the funds for foreign travel (Westerhausen, 2002, p. 21). These hitchhikers were fol-lowed a decade later by the travelling hippie or drifter. While most youth were content to restrict their journeys to Europe, others began to travel to more remote locations. Soon North and East Africa as well as the Middle East entered the itinerary of many young Europeans, while others fol-lowed an emerging route through South and South-east Asia to Australia (p. 22). Young Westerners in the United States and Canada followed this trend pioneered by their European peers not only by criss-crossing their own countries and Europe but also by expanding their scope to the less-developed countries in Central and South America (Cohen, 1973, p. 92). During the late 1960s, thousands of young Westerners travelled to Asia following the Hippie Trail, the overland route from Europe via Iran and Afghanistan to India and Nepal. Their quest frequently had spiritual overtones, and their at least temporary renunciation of material comforts provided strong echoes of those religious traditions that valued poverty as spiritually uplifting (Westerhausen, 2002, p. 22). Cohen's observation (1973) of voluntary poverty among those who followed the trail is remi-niscent of pilgrims of earlier centuries. MacCannell's (1973, 1976) and Cohen's (1979a) reference to pilgrimage in search of a 'spiritual centre out-there', an essentially religious quest for authenticity in the life of others, is quite relevant here. Being able to take for granted the material security so desired by their parents, many young Westerners in the 1960s set their sights on more emotionally satisfying pursuits. Repelled by the material-ism of postwar Western society, quite a few started to look for more 'meaningful' and 'authentic' experiences than could be found in the stifling security the status quo seemed to provide (Westerhausen, 2002, p. 22). This resulted in all kinds of romantic countercultures in Western countries, from an anti-authoritarian ethos and a 'student revolution' (1968) to

'flower power' movements, support for Eastern spiritual gurus and experimentation with psychedelic drugs. These romantic countercultures went
hand in hand with drifter-style travel in the 1960s and 1970s. This mode of
travel was characterized by its anti-authoritarian ethos, minimal expenditure, desire to meet (often bewildered) locals, exclusive use of cheap transport or hitchhiking, and search for spiritual, sexual, cultural and narcotic
experiences (p. 23). Travelling according to this mode represented a lifestyle that managed to combine the appeal of 'flower power', the mystical
East, as well as a sense of adventure, spontaneity and individualism
young travellers felt were lacking at home. Their travel outside Europe
and North America was further motivated by the desire to meet others of
kindred spirits in an environment that permitted a counterculture lifestyle
away from the restrictions of their own societies. Western drifters
appeared on the scene all over Asia and parts of North Africa and quite
openly indulged in drug use and sexual experimentation. The drifter-style
travel during the 1960s was primarily motivated by the quest for adventure, authenticity, spontaneity and a chance to define themselves as individuals. In the early 1970s ever-larger sections of the baby-boomer
generation adopted modes of drifter-style travel, promoted by word of
mouth and alternative guidebooks. 'What had previously been a non-
institutionalized form of itinerancy now rapidly acquired the character of
an established youth culture. These developments led to significant
changes not only in the numbers of participants but also in the very nature
of the lifestyle'.

Initially (1973), Cohen distinguished four drifter types: both full-time
drifters and part-time drifters, who could be either outward or inward
oriented. Outward oriented full-time drifters were 'Adventurers', the original individual drifters. They were the pioneers among the travellers and
may have been an ideal to which many young travellers were attracted,
but only very few succeeded (Cohen, 2004, p. 45). Inward oriented
full-time drifters were the 'Itinerant Hippies', the travelling drop-outs,
moving between different drug scenes or drifting aimlessly from one
'hippie community' to another. Outward oriented part-time drifters were
the 'Mass Drifters', the predecessors of the majority of current backpackers. They were usually students who spent their extended holidays or had
a limited time-out to see the world, meet people and 'have experiences'.
Like most of the current backpackers they tended to stick to the drifter
tourist establishment of cheap lodgings and eating places. Finally, inward
oriented part-time drifters were 'Fellow Travellers', who imitated the
hippies and visited the hippie communities for short periods of time.
These part-timers returned to 'normal' life after the trip.

According to Westerhausen (2002, p. 155), this typology is no longer
accurate. The distinction between full-time and part-time travellers is
more problematic nowadays than three decades ago. Moreover, most

travellers now lead relatively conventional lives prior to their departure from the West, and they initially tend to postpone, rather than refuse, the assumption of social responsibilities. They don't represent a counter-culture any more, but are part of a backpacker subculture.

So, whereas drifter and nomad tourism in the 1960s and 1970s was supposed to be primarily motivated by alienation of young people from postwar materialistic Western lifestyle, backpacker tourism in the 1990s and 2000s is triggered in a different fashion, as the empirical data and consequent discussion will show.

Cohen's typology demonstrates that from the very beginning, drifters were not a homogeneous category of travellers. Nor are today's backpackers. Most definitions refer to what Uriely *et al.* (2002) call form-related attributes of tourism, as opposed to type-related. Forms refer to visible institutional arrangements and practices by which tourists organize their journey: length of trip, flexibility of the itinerary, visited destinations and attractions, means of transportation and accommodation, contact with locals, and so forth (2002, p. 521). A frequently used, predominantly form-related, definition is offered by Loker-Murphy and Pearce (1995) and Murphy (2001). According to this definition backpackers are young and budget-minded tourists who exhibit a preference for inexpensive accommodation, an emphasis on meeting other people (locals and outsiders), an independently organized and flexible itinerary, longer rather than brief vacations, and an emphasis on informal and participatory recreation activities.

Types refer to less tangible psychological attributes, such as tourists' attitudes towards the fundamental values of their own society, their motivations for travel, and the meanings they assign to their experiences (Uriely *et al.*, 2002, p. 521). According to these authors, form- and type-related attributes are used indistinguishably in drifter and backpacker literature, where a clear differentiation between backpacking as a form characterized by various practices and backpacking as a type identified by tourists' attitudes and motivations should be made. That's what the next section aims at.

## Empirical studies

In recent decades the youth tourism market has been a major growth segment within international tourism (Mintel Group, 2003). According to World Tourism Organization estimates, the proportion of all international tourism trips undertaken by young travellers grew from 14.6 per cent in 1980 to 20 per cent in 2001, and is presumed to have reached 25 per cent by 2005. In absolute numbers of arrivals this means 42 million in 1980, almost 140 million in 2001, and about 180 million in 2005. How many of these can be identified as backpackers is uncertain, because, on the one hand, there is no generally accepted definition of backpackers, and on the other hand, most destination statistics do not make a clear distinction between ages or types among inbound tourists. Young tourists that meet the broad definition given by Loker-Murphy and Pearce (1995) and Murphy (2001) will make up a considerable proportion of the 140 million youth arrivals. The majority of these young tourists will travel in their own continent. A rough estimation of young travellers heading for Asia, Latin America or Africa will arrive at 5 to 10 million.

Among the pioneer studies on backpacker-related issues are Cohen (1972, 1973) and Vogt (1976). Whereas Cohen referred to 'drifters' and 'nomads', Vogt preferred the term 'wanderers'. These authors contributed most to the early conceptualization of unorganized individual travelling by young Westerners. Cohen identified drifting as 'both a symptom and an expression of broader alienative forces current among contemporary youth' (1973, p. 94). Vogt observed a similar set of motivating characteristics, particularly with respect to their class-based origins (Ateljevic and Doorne, 2004, p. 63). Between the 1970s and the explosive growth of studies in recent years, Riley's study (1988) was the most prominent. According to her, the youthful traveller of the 1980s was neither accurately described as a drifter, nomad or hippie, nor as an exponent of a 'counter-culture'. Riley's long-term travellers were not aimless drifters, but college-educated low-budget travellers with flexible timetables and itineraries, who were at a juncture in life and expected to rejoin the work force in the society they left (1988, p. 326). Through this approach Riley built the bridge between early conceptualizations of drifter- and nomad-like travellers and contemporary conceptualizations of backpackers.

The discussion of empirical results is hampered by the variety of definitions of backpacking used in literature. Nine recent studies will be used here to describe contemporary backpacking practices. These studies are: Spreitzhofer, 1998; Elsrud, 2001; Murphy, 2001; Uriely *et al.*, 2002; Westerhausen, 2002; Sörensen, 2003; Noy, 2004; van Egmond, 2004; Welk, 2004.

Most of them employ form-related definitions like the one offered by Murphy (2001, p. 50), but use slightly different criteria related to age and minimum length of the trip and aim at different target groups. Table 3.1 gives an overview of the differences. In most of the studies the minimum length of the trip was two months or more, to exclude conventional tourists on annual leave but also youth tourists such as college students celebrating their annual holiday. Except for Australia, the destinations were in developing countries.

### Research methods
As Table 3.1 shows, most researches have been conducted in Asia, Southeast Asia in particular, and Australia. Africa and the Americas have been

**Table 3.1.**   Recent backpacker studies.

| Authors | Minimum length | Age | Research destination | Nationalities | No. of respondents |
|---|---|---|---|---|---|
| Elsrud (2001) | 1 year | 18–71 | Thailand | Northern Europe, USA | 35 |
| Murphy (2001) | No minimum | av. 23.8 | Australia | Many | 59 |
| Noy (2004) | 3 months | 22–25 | S. America, Asia | Israel | 40 |
| Sörensen (2003) | No minimum | 18–33 | Many | Many | 134 |
| Spreitzhofer (1998) | 2 months | n.s. | South-east Asia | n.s. | 81 |
| Uriely et al. (2002) | 3 months | 21–26 | Many | Israel | 38 |
| van Egmond (2004) | No minimum | 20–32 | Peru, Bolivia | Western Europe | 22 |
| Welk (2004) | 6 months | n.s. | Australia, Malaysia | n.s. | n.s. |
| Westerhausen (2002) | 3 months | <30 | Asia | 'Western' countries | 63 |

Note: n.s. means 'not specified'.

covered less, as have been the home continents of the backpackers. The researchers tend to be (former) backpackers themselves, who know the backpacker (sub)culture well and never lost their interest in this specific life-world. The double role as both a fellow-backpacker and researcher isn't seen as problematic by most of them. On the contrary, it produced research benefits, since the realization that they were being studied often triggered interesting reflections and deliberations from the informants (e.g. Sörensen, 2003, p. 851). Respondents were selected in hostels and other accommodation facilities, in restaurants, bars and the like, and during transport or excursions, often by means of 'snowball sampling'. Backpackers were easily identified. As a rule potential informants were well prepared to co-operate, because they were much interested in the subject and didn't have time constraints. In preparing the interviews most researchers first established a good relationship with the respondents and were deliberately straightforward about the goals and methodology of the ongoing research. Most respondents really appreciated being interviewed. Often they thanked the researcher for the interview (e.g. van Egmond, 2004, p. 8).

The number of respondents was not fixed. The methodology used required finding new respondents until a level of saturation was reached: when new respondents do not supply additional information and insight, one could stop.

## Generating and destination countries

Backpackers are from highly developed Western countries, i.e. primarily from Northern, Western and Central Europe (United Kingdom, Germany, the Netherlands, Scandinavia, Switzerland, Austria, Belgium) and, to a lesser extent, Canada, USA, Australia, New Zealand. With the exceptions of Austria and Belgium, these are the traditionally Protestant countries. Israel, as a non-Christian country, represents a very special case. Other developed countries like France, Spain, Italy, Japan also generate backpackers, but these are underrepresented in the international market.

Although more and more backpackers or travellers are over 30 years old, the vast majority of them are young. In the ISTC/ATLAS Survey of 2002, 12.8 per cent of youth travellers were under 20 and 5.2 per cent were over 30. Among long-term travellers the average age is a little higher than among short-term travellers. The age of starters tends to be ever younger. In the ISTC/ATLAS Survey, more than 70 per cent of the sample of young travellers had a trip length of less than 60 days, while in most of the studies mentioned the minimum length was 2 months.

Backpackers have an average high level of education. Most of them are students or former students, i.e. undergraduates, graduates, temporary quitters, drop-outs, or students-to-be. They all have, at least potentially, a high level of cultural capital in terms of Bourdieu's embodied state (i.e. cultivation and education), and many have a high cultural capital in the institutionalized state (i.e. academic qualifications). Their economic capital is limited, although they can afford to travel for months on a low-budget basis. Most of them, however, anticipate future conditions of high economic capital, having the academic qualifications to have or find well-paid jobs. Social capital is different per individual, but the ability to interact with fellow-backpackers and – even more so – local people is highly valued, as will be discussed later in this section.

As far as the gender distribution is concerned, Australian data suggest an even male/female split, while data from the developing world suggest a 60/40 male preponderance ratio, perhaps slightly higher in certain regions (Sörensen, 2003, p. 852).

Backpackers travel more frequently within their own world region than to other regions, consistent with the travel market as a whole. As travel experience grows, respondents travel increasingly further afield. Australia is the destination many European backpackers aim at for their first long-haul trip. In the hierarchy of long-haul destinations, Australia is at the top, with an increase of backpacker arrivals from 272,320 in 1995 to 447,000 in 2002 (Slaughter, 2004, p. 171). Figure 3.2 gives a rough indication of this hierarchy.

Thailand is the top destination in the developing world. Other Asian countries such as China, Vietnam and Cambodia are rising rapidly in the hierarchy, thus demonstrating that it is not static.

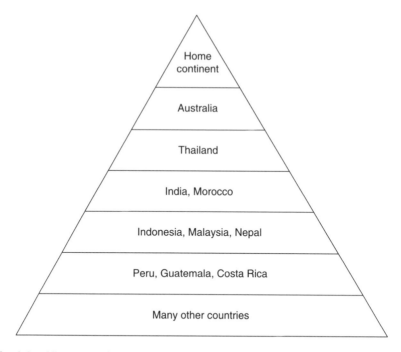

**Fig. 3.2.**   Hierarchy of backpacker destinations.

The great majority of respondents who are interviewed in developing countries will answer that they travel alone or with one person. In day-to-day practice, however, most of them spend their time in the company of other backpackers, in informal ad hoc groups formed along the backpacker track. These groups are fluid in character. Friendships arise rapidly and travel groups are formed and dissolved almost instantly.

According to the frequently-used definition of Loker-Murphy and Pearce (1995), backpackers are budget-minded tourists who exhibit a preference for inexpensive accommodation, transport and commodities and longer rather than brief vacations. Getting the best deal contributes to 'road status' among backpackers (see next section). Their relatively low daily expenditure is one of the possible explanations of the traditionally low popularity of backpackers in quite a few Third World countries. Gradually more and more destinations become aware, however, that total backpacker expenditure adds up to a substantial amount of money, which generates more economic dynamics in the destination area than expenditures by mainstream organized tourists. Boxes 1 to 9 in Appendix B give an overview of tourist expenditures per type of trip and throw light on the net economic results for the destination area. These results will be discussed in Chapter 5.

## Motivation of backpackers

The motivation to travel has only received limited attention. Westerhausen (2002, p. 28) found a significant qualitative difference in terms of motivation for long-term travel between those setting out for the first time (novices) and repeat travellers.

Four sets of motives tended to recur frequently among first-time travellers (pp. 29–30):

A) *The Long-Held Dream*. Rather than a deviation from their life plan, the decision to set off represents the fulfilment of a lifelong dream for these travellers.

B) *Journey into Adult Life*. Long-term travelling is viewed by these respondents, being primarily of college age, as a *rite de passage* consisting of self-testing, the broadening of one's horizons, prior to the assumption of adult responsibilities.

C) *The Final Fling*. The primary motivation for undertaking their journey is for this group the postponement of adult responsibilities. The journey affords a final opportunity to 'just once' experience an unencumbered lifestyle before settling down.

D) *The Escape*. For this final group of first-time travellers, the decision to leave often occurs quite spontaneously. Personal problems, the end of a relationship or disillusionment with unsatisfactory careers create a situation in which travel provides a 'time-out'.

The tourism mythology propagated in the media, literature and in the informal social circuit of many students frequently serves to reinforce these motives.

For repeat travellers (about a third of Westerhausen's respondents), the departure on subsequent journeys represents a return 'home' to a world with which they had not only become comfortable but to which nostalgia had added additional shine. They do not perceive the journey as just an episode in their lives after which they will move on to other things, but as a deliberate choice of lifestyle for the time being. 'Already familiar with what awaits them, they expect to reintegrate quickly within the subcultural lifestyle, are confident of easily adjusting back to life abroad, and hope that their new experiences resemble treasured memories of their earlier journeys' (Westerhausen, 2002, pp. 30–31).

Israeli backpackers are a special case. During the 1980s, young Israelis began to travel, first to Latin America, and later to South and East Asia as well. These backpackers are mostly young secular Jews of middle and upper middle class origin who have attended academically oriented high schools and completed their long army service (Uriely *et al.*, 2002, p. 528). This trend has assumed such a magnitude as to be considered part of the 'normal' route Israelis complete after their army service. Uriely *et al.* cite sources estimating that about 10 per cent of discharged soldiers from each Israel army cohort spend more than 5 months travelling in developing countries. According to Noy (2004, p. 82), these discharged soldiers express a desire for a radically different social environment to the one experienced in the army. In practice, their social conduct throughout the trip is reminiscent of a 'military mode', including travelling in small cohesive groups, seeking risky physical challenges, but confined to Israeli 'enclaves' as far as accommodation and restaurants are concerned.

## Backpacker culture

Over half of the respondents in the ISTC/ATLAS Survey (2002) identified themselves as 'travellers' as opposed to 'backpackers' or 'tourists'. Almost a third opted for 'backpackers'. By contrast fewer than 20 per cent considered themselves to be tourists. Unfortunately, the survey report doesn't specify what the respondents mean by these terms but the results are indicative of a culture and style of travel that appear to reject the label 'tourist'. More precisely: most backpackers readily accept that travelling contains elements of tourism. They nevertheless prefer to present themselves as 'better tourists', who arrange things themselves, whereas conventional tourists are led or herded (Sörensen, 2003; van Egmond, 2004). Anti-tourist sentiments are much more prominent among medium- and long-term travellers than among short-term travellers. Negative attitudes towards conventional tourists, or even 'mass tourists', are the glue of the backpacker community. In the words of Welk (2004, p. 83), what ties backpackers together as a community is the strongly defended differentiation against the community that lives closest to them. The distinction cannot be made in territorial terms, because as a global community they lack a 'neighbour' to differentiate themselves from. 'For backpackers, the closest (i.e. most similar) community is that of mainstream tourists, which is why backpacker ideology primarily stands in opposition to mainstream tourism' (p. 83). Wilson and Richards (2004, p. 139) refer to 'tourist angst' or, rather, 'backpacker angst' that represents 'a gnawing suspicion that after all . . . you are still a tourist like every other tourist'.

Ironically, it is difficult – if not impossible – to objectively distinguish backpackers from other tourists, but backpackers generally prefer to see themselves as different. Most backpackers make use of travel facilities offered by the tourism and travel industry, visit tourist attractions and famous sites, and purchase organized excursions, safaris, treks, etc. Still, despite the scene's own increasing resemblance to conventional tourism in recent years, anti-tourist attitudes are an important ingredient in the construction of backpacker identities (Welk, 2004, p. 90). Consequently, Cohen's 'parallel universes' where backpackers and conventional tourists 'flow along . . . segregated institutional channels' (1973, p. 95) are still relevant to present times. These segregated channels can be symbolic rather than physical. Tourists and backpackers alike might well be travelling to the *same* places, visiting the *same* sights, eating the *same* food, and visiting the *same* national parks, although they might stay in *different* accommodation, visit *different* restaurants and bars, mingle with *different* people (Welk, 2004, p. 86). Even when they run into each other at the same spot, backpackers generally will perceive tourists as 'them' as opposed to 'us' (tourists are much more indifferent to backpackers). In particular they are unified in their dislike of commercialized package tours. That's why, according to Sörensen, being both an individual perception and a socially constructed identity, 'backpacker' is more a social construct than a definition (2003, p. 852). The dissociation from mainstream tourism is constructed on a symbolic level with symbolic boundaries largely maintained through the adoption of an ideological, decidedly anti-tourist set of values (Welk, 2004, p. 90). Returning to the distinction Uriely *et al.* (2002) made between form- and type-related attributes of tourism, it can be stated that backpacking as a form of tourism may not differ much from the mainstream, but the backpacker as a type of tourist does constitute a distinct identity. Backpacking, long-term travelling in particular, is a way of life (Westerhausen, 2002).

Characteristic of backpacker culture (Sörensen, 2003), subculture (Westerhausen, 2002), or community (Welk, 2004) is an informal system of norms, values, social hierarchies and codes of conduct that are transmitted from experienced backpackers to newcomers, even without fixed and permanent social institutions that may facilitate this process. These norms, values, etc., however, are continuously negotiated, challenged, manipulated, and changed through social interaction. The opportunity for this is enhanced by the combination of, on the one hand, the continuous replacement of backpackers within the community, and on the other, a near absence of institutions that can hold and transfer meaning over time (Sörensen, 2003, p. 855). Sörensen refers to recent conceptions of culture in which the individual is ascribed an active role, as someone who *produces culture* rather than just representing it (p. 855). Backpacker culture is neither located nor bounded, i.e. it is neither limited to a fixed place nor to fixed groups. It can 'take place' anywhere. Backpacker culture illustrates that 'cultures travel as well as people' (Rojek and Urry, 1997, p. 11). Westerhausen (2002, p. xiv) refers to a mobile subculture that has replaced the more individual world of hitchhikers and drifters. Individuals do not become members of the subculture in any formal sense but instead come to share the subculture's ideology, activities and way of life (Macbeth, cited in Westerhausen, 2002, p. 5).

An important element of backpacker (sub)culture is 'road status'. This refers to an informal status hierarchy among backpackers in terms of travel experience. Interaction with local people, having 'authentic' experiences,

travelling off the beaten track, getting the best deal, low spending patterns, long-term travel, risk taking, independence, but also diseases and
deprivations contribute to road status. To establish a clear status hierarchy
all kinds of verbal and non-verbal communication are used. By relating to
specific narratives, particularly risk narratives expressing adventurous
identities, travellers can position themselves within the backpackers' hierarchy (Elsrud, 2001, p. 613). Within limits, it is expected and even
accepted that one lies about risks taken, prices paid, or interaction with
locals to enhance one's status, but too overt preoccupation with enhancing
one's status is improper (Sörensen, 2003, p. 857). Guidebooks such as the
*Lonely Planet* are much scorned and seen as a symbol of the lesser traveller.
'Real' travellers have left the *Lonely Planet* behind. As a consequence, 'bible bashing' is another parameter in the exchange of road status (p. 860).
Among non-verbal expressions equipment and clothes play an important
role. To dress properly means to dress down rather than up. Worn, ripped
clothes tell a story of 'rough' living and 'adventure' (Elsrud, 2001, p. 611).
Elsrud researched backpackers that were long-term travellers (> 1 year).
Among these backpackers those having endured the hardship of journey-
ing in India felt it made them more experienced than those travellers who
stuck to the 'average' route. This is the experience that leads to higher
road status among long-term travellers. For some the reason for going to
India may even be to suffer, rather than enjoy (2001, p. 608). Elsrud also
refers to an antagonistic relationship associated with the taking of anti-
malaria drugs and travel experience. The experienced travellers avoid
anti-malaria pills, the inexperienced do not (p. 610). Moreover, eating hab-
its can be used as statements about the unique 'self': 'streetsmart' travellers
eat in the cheapest food-stalls, whereas others look for the relative safety
of restaurants (p. 610).

Interaction with local people, indigenous people in particular, contributes highly to road status. There is a clear hierarchy in interaction, in
which observing local life is basic and 'living with locals' is the most
favoured type of interaction. Most travellers' experience of local society,
however, is that of interested observers rather than active participants
interacting with locals on their own level, although travellers are able to
access a far wider spectrum of the local society than conventional tourists,
and exhibit a greater readiness to talk with anyone willing to talk to them
(Westerhausen, 2002, pp. 88–90). 'Living with locals', having authentic
experiences and travelling off the beaten track represent highly valued
experiences among backpackers, among long-term travellers in particular. Although some of them are actually able to live with indigenous
people for some time, the vast majority does not, in spite of the social
desirability of doing so. The contacts are basically restricted to an
English-speaking minority employed in the low-budget tourism business
(Spreitzhofer, 1998, p. 982). For most backpackers there is a discrepancy

between their intentions and their practice. In Cohen's words (2004, p. 48): 'the actual practice of most backpackers is at considerable variance with the predominant image of the young traveller who roams far off places all alone.' One way to narrow this discrepancy between the model and actual behaviour is the 'creation' of experiences in backpacker narratives. Elsrud (2001) shows how risk and adventure on the trip are constructed by the backpackers. The focus of her research was consequently on the way in which they perceive and narrate their experiences, rather than whether they have 'real' adventures and face 'real' risks.

Social interaction is an integral part of the backpacking experience. For most this interaction is mainly limited to fellow-backpackers and, as mentioned, some English-speaking staff in the low-budget tourism business. This particularly applies to short-term travellers. Social interaction among backpackers often has a ritual character. The initial conversation focuses on where people have been and/or are going to and where they are from (Murphy, 2001, p. 55). Well-travelled long-term backpackers might even complain about the ritual and stereotypical character of the initial conversation. According to Murphy, this initial discussion is often used as a 'feeling out' period to decide whether they would like to continue the discussion/interaction with the other person. If they 'connect', the discussion moves on to more detailed tourism experiences and personal information. Backpackers from Mediterranean or Asian (mainly Japan) countries who are not representing the well-travelled countries of Northern parts of Europe and are less able to speak English tend to restrict interactions to their co-nationals. Backpackers from Israel find themselves in, or seek, the company of other Israelis, and spend a good deal of their time in Israeli 'enclaves', although they repeatedly express a desire to distance themselves from fellow Israelis and from state-related organizations (Noy, 2004, pp. 81–82).

Westerhausen (2002) is the only one who explicitly discusses women's experiences of life on the road. More than 90 per cent of the respondents answered 'yes' to the question 'Is travelling different for a woman?' The reasons mentioned referred to 'sexual harassment' (51.6 per cent), 'women are more restricted than male travellers in what they can do' (25.8 per cent), 'locals are not accustomed to or even disdainful of single women travelling alone' (25.8 per cent), 'sexist attitudes in Islamic countries' (22.5 per cent), 'travelling is more dangerous generally' (19.4 per cent), 'perceived threat of rape' (12.9 per cent), 'women are not regarded as equals in local culture' (12.9 per cent), 'women need to link up with guys or other women for protection' (12.9 per cent), etc. (p. 103). Often women travelling alone will join male travellers for company and greater safety in potentially hostile environments and call on male help when in trouble, mirroring traditional gender roles while on the road. Alternatively, a number of women will band together and overcome potentially troublesome sections of the trail as a group before returning to an individual travel mode (p. 104). Some countries are largely avoided by female backpackers (Pakistan, Iran), whereas others – Thailand in particular – are quite popular (p. 102).


## Psychological effects of backpacking

The psychological effects of backpacking have been researched by only a few. Obviously, it is much more complicated to study effects after backpackers have returned home than 'on the road'. Two studies have been able to study after-effects, Westerhausen (2002) and Noy (2004).

In Westerhausen's research among Western long-term travellers, 95.2 per cent answered 'yes' to the question 'Has travelling changed you?' (2002, p. 120). The most important reasons mentioned were: 'more broad-minded, wider horizons, more tolerant': 40.4 per cent, 'different priorities, change of direction in life': 26.2 per cent, more sociable, less introverted: 14.3 per cent, more respect for other cultures, less prejudiced: 11.9 per cent. Noy's research among Israeli backpackers showed consistent results. They consistently describe deep and profound personal changes that are always markedly positive (2004, p. 86). Noy (p. 90) points to differences in gender perspective. 'Male interviewees portrayed a clearer connection between the personal changes they had undergone, and specific, seemingly risky, activities (e.g. climbing volcanoes) in which they had participated. Female interviewees also described significant delineated experiences, but expressed criticism of the masculine features of the discourse pertaining to strenuous outdoor activities. Thus, they accounted for the changes by referring to the experience of the trip as a whole.' Noy presumes that among Israeli youth, masculine dimensions of adventure and risk are more salient than among 'Western' youth, due to both the general pervasiveness of militaristic, chauvinist discourse within Israeli society and a lengthy service in the army (p. 91). But also among European backpackers 'risk and adventure narrative of travel' is still at least partly gendered, according to Elsrud (2001, p. 614), embracing its masculine supporters while excluding female intruders. That's why it was mainly women who adopted an ironic tone when discussing risk and adventure (p. 614).

According to Westerhausen, the degree of change depends on the individual's perspective prior to departure (2002, p. 119). The smallest degree of change is reported by those who had been following an alternative lifestyle in the West and thus were able to internalize the subcultural ideology with minimal departure from their prior convictions. Conversely, the most dramatic changes to their previously held values and attitudes were noticed by those who had subscribed unquestioningly to Western values and mainstream ideology before leaving home (p. 121).

Personal change is expressed in terms of 'You get more tolerant to other kinds of people and other kinds of thinking', 'I am quite a bit quieter now than I used to be', 'I have become a lot more calm inside . . . I used to be running around', 'I know that I have become a lot more laid back. A lot more patient. Hopefully a lot more tolerant', 'I learned a hell of a lot. I have far more self-confidence now and relate a lot better to people' (Westerhausen, 2002, pp. 122–123), etc. Being able to travel individually, to manage well without family, friends and Western facilities is an important source of growing self-confidence, for female respondents in particular. Van Egmond (2004, p. 62) refers to the respondents' changing view of Western materialism. On the one hand they were aware of the advantage being from an affluent country but quite a few came to the conclusion that a less materialistic life might be preferred. A common reaction among respondents was that people in Third World countries might be happier than people in the First World. Considerations like these reflect the search for existential authenticity Wang (2000, p. 56) has elaborated upon. Many backpackers are in search of their 'real self', freed from roles and obligations in daily life, more spontaneous, less serious, less hectic, less materialistic, less utilitarian, in sum: more authentic. Personal change and Western values compared to local values are favourite subjects of backpacker conversation to an extent that some of them react aversively in terms of 'I am who I am', 'I tend not to think about myself so obsessively' (van Egmond, 2004, p. 46).

### Reversed culture shock
Westerhausen pays a lot of attention to returning home and 'reversed culture shock'. 'Often the transition back to "ordinary life" is difficult due to the profound sense of alienation from a society whose values are now foreign, and because of the absence of others back home who share the returning traveller's new ideological orientation' (2002, p. 122). Obviously, this transition is more difficult for long-term than for short-term travellers. Quite a few respondents among Westerhausen's long-term travellers said they found it difficult to fit back into life in the West. The main reasons were: 'was unable to relate to non-travellers'; 'was unhappy and wanted to return to life on the road as soon as possible'; 'felt alienated'; 'could only relate to other travellers'; 'could no longer make a permanent commitment to any aspect of life in the West'; 'changed outlook while away'; 'no longer in touch with life in the West' etc. (p. 139). Almost half of them were no longer committed to their previous home. This could take the form of 'no permanent home'; 'home is on the road'; 'not sure where home is'; or 'looking for home in another country'. Some even found a new home in the Third World and permanently settled abroad or were alternating between their base in the West and the subculture (2002, p. 129), reminding of Cohen's (1979a) 'existential mode'. Culture

shock, coined in 1960 by Oberg, refers to the confusion or even desperation that strikes us when the information rate of an unfamiliar environment is far beyond our powers of control (van Egmond, 2005, p. 92). Culture shock is anticipated by many backpackers when they arrive in a developing country. While often traumatic, it is usually of relatively short duration and decreasing severity. Adapting to the norms of this new world is aided by quickly meeting others who are in the same situation. Those unable to adapt quickly are able to return to the – as yet – unbroken familiarity of home (Westerhausen, 2002, p. 135). Travellers without prior experience coming home, however, are by no means prepared for the realities facing them upon their return (p. 136). Being strangers in their own society can be extremely disconcerting. This confusion or even desperation is commonly referred to as 'reversed culture shock'. It is tempting to draw a comparison to war veterans who have had profound experiences during war and aren't able to relate to people at home who haven't had these experiences. No wonder then, that the alienation from their own society travellers feel after having returned home is the main reason for repeated long-term travelling.

## 3.4   Other Types of West–South Tourists

Several types of tourists cannot be categorized as 'organized tourists' or 'backpackers'. Because of their relevance for a West–South tourism analysis, they will be discussed in this section separately. First, there is a substantial group of individual unorganized tourists that cannot be labelled 'backpackers'. They will be referred to as 'independently travelling luxury tourists'. Second, 'volunteers' are a relatively new category of tourists. They book organized trips that are different from mainstream holiday trips in several respects. Third, 'romance tourism' is distinguished from mainstream holiday tourism by its specific purpose. Fourth, 'adventurers' constitute a small but intriguing group of tourists, getting a lot of media exposure.

### Independently travelling luxury tourists
A considerable number of tourists who travel from the West to the South to make a round trip in one or more countries cannot be categorized as 'organized tourists' or 'backpackers'. They do not buy an organized package, nor do they meet frequently used definitions of backpackers in terms of young budget-minded tourists who prefer inexpensive accommodation. On average, they are much older than backpackers. They arrange everything themselves, including comparatively luxurious accommodation, such as three-, four- or five-star hotels. They have flexible itineraries.

Following Mager (2005), this section will refer to 'independently travelling luxury tourists'.

Unfortunately, studies aiming at analysing this type of tourism are almost entirely missing. Among the 333 interviews mentioned in section 3.1, some 5 per cent concerned independently travelling tourists, not all of them staying in luxurious accommodation. It turned out to be difficult to find differences between organized and independent travellers among the interviewees, in terms of motivation to travel, places visited, behaviour on the spot, travel experience, etc. Still, they exhibited a clear desire to distinguish themselves from organized tourists. The reasons for travelling independently are related to perceived freedom to go wherever and whenever you want, to be able to make your own decisions and 'expect the unexpected'. 'It's the feeling. We don't want to follow everybody to all the highlights' (Dutch couple in their thirties). Several independent travellers prefer unorganized trips in order to be better able to have contact with local people in the villages they visit. There is, however, no indication whatsoever that they actually do interact more with local people than organized tourists.

A valuable study has been done by Harrison (2003). She conducted in-depth interviews with 33 Canadian travellers, ranging in age from 30 to 75. Unfortunately, not all interviewees travelled independently and, moreover, her research was not restricted to tourism to the South. Harrison's conclusions and views will be discussed in Chapter 5.

### Volunteer tourism

The generic term 'volunteer tourism' applies to those tourists who, for various reasons, volunteer in an organized way to undertake holidays that might involve aiding or alleviating the material poverty of some groups in society, the restoration of certain environments or research into aspects of society or environment (Wearing, 2001, p. 1). Volunteer tourist operations are those offered by organizations such as Youth Challenge International, World Wide Fund for Nature and Earthwatch, to name a few, but also – more and more – by not-for-profit foundations and commercial tour operators. Although tourism to Israeli kibbutzim started quite a few decades ago, volunteer tourism has only gained quantitative significance in recent years.

Volunteer tourists will almost always pay in some way to participate in these 'working holidays'. Prices are comparable to those of organized adventurous trips. So, the question arises: what additional value to 'normal' holidays do volunteers seek?

The sources used are several. Wearing (2001) examined Australian students who participated in an ecotourism development project in Costa Rica, organized by Youth Challenge International. The average age was 21–22 years. Part of the programme is round trips through Costa Rica. Both

(2004) studied Dutch volunteers who participated in housing and social projects in Guatemala. The programme is organized by a Dutch tour operator, in cooperation with several Guatemalan organizations. The trip takes 3 weeks, half of which is spent on working, the other half on travelling through Guatemala. All respondents were women, ranging in age from 18 to 57. Among the 333 interviews mentioned in section 3.1, eight were with volunteers (Costa Rica, Ecuador, Guatemala, Laos, Nepal ×2, Peru ×2). Six respondents were Dutch, one was Danish and one Swedish. Their trips were mediated by various organizations. The youngest volunteer was 23, the oldest 54.

All studies made use of in-depth interviews. Wearing (2001) and Both (2004) interviewed volunteers prior to departure and after returning home, the other interviews were hold in the destination countries.

The motivations of the interviewees range from naive idealism to an excuse to travel. Among the idealistic considerations are: 'I want to give people a better life', 'I want to help people', 'I want to make children happy'. Excuses to travel relate to critical attitudes towards tourism. Several respondents want to travel, but don't want to 'just walk around like tourists'. A Dutch interviewee (age 18) said: 'I really feel bad when I just walk around and watch local people'. Another (age 36) referred to her conscience, that doesn't allow her to watch poverty and do nothing. The prevalent motivation has to do with 'I really want to do something', 'I want to do something valuable/worthwhile/constructive/helpful, rather than just going there and enjoy myself'. An Australian girl compared her previous holidays as 'a tourist' to her present volunteer trip: 'A tourist is someone who just comes and goes without giving anything. But in Costa Rica you can really do something that benefits the community'.

In addition to that, many respondents want to 'get to know local people', 'see a totally different culture', 'learn about children, how they live', 'converse with locals', etc. A Dutch woman (age 23) said: 'I really want to help people, but learning about cultures makes it even more interesting'.

Organized volunteer holidays offer the protection and safety of a group. It is a safe way to visit exotic countries: 'I'm too timid to go alone', 'I have never been that far from home before'.

Volunteer destinations are chosen arbitrarily. Any developing country will do, as long as it is safe, clean and not 'too touristy'. The choice depends on the countries and projects on offer on the Internet and through personal contacts. Prior to departure most volunteers do not know what to expect, resulting in general statements such as 'I think that the community will appreciate our presence', 'I expect it to be the most beautiful place', 'I expect to have a good feeling by doing something good'. Some specific expectations relate to social aspects. On the one hand, some respondents look forward to affiliating with like-minded people in the travel group, on the other hand, some are anticipating bonds of friendship with 'local people'.

One Dutch woman (age 36) is explicitly in search of solidarity among humans, something that is missing in her daily life.

Wearing (2002) stresses the opportunity volunteer tourism offers for an individual to engage in an altruistic attempt to explore 'oneself'. By living in and learning about other cultures, in an environment of mutual benefit and cooperation, a person is able to engage in a transformation and development of the self. They set volunteer tourism against mass tourism. Mass tourism serves as an escape from the stresses of everyday life or as a reward for hard work, rather than altering people's everyday lives in terms of the way they think, feel or act (2002, p. 242). Volunteer tourism is an alternative to mass tourism (Wearing, 2001, p. 30).

> Under volunteer tourism, no longer is culture consumed, photographed and taken home as memento of the tourist's brush with difference. Nor is it just about affluent 'cultural tourists' visiting 'exotic' destinations in poor countries and, in doing so, often quite inadvertently, causing considerable damage to the ecology, cultural lifestyle and economics of the host communities.
>
> (Wearing, 2002, p. 250)

It rather offers opportunities to develop one's self-awareness, a heightened awareness of one's beliefs and abilities, enhanced by cross-cultural comparisons through interaction with host communities.

Generally speaking, the volunteers were very positive about the experiences they had. Sheer idealism declined. Several respondents expressed some scepticism about the value of their activities in terms of contribution to poverty alleviation and happiness of their hosts. One woman, who participated in construction of houses for community members, felt she was hampering rather than helping local construction workers. But almost all had a great time.

Living for some time with a native family was experienced as 'impressive' and 'unique', the highlight of the trip. According to Both (2004, p. 56), all volunteers mentioned that adapting to the local culture is very important, but in fact they did not really adapt. They kept on speaking Dutch to construction workers and family members, because none of them was able to speak Spanish. Moreover, they worked according to their Dutch efficiency criteria and became impatient when things went slowly or inefficiently.

> Sometimes, when I was just sitting around and doing nothing, I wondered: what am I doing here?
>
> (Dutch woman, age 28)

> I feel lazy and a bit bad when I'm not working hard during working hours. After work it doesn't matter.
>
> (Swedish girl)

Volunteers don't want to be seen by locals as 'walking wallets'. They want to be accepted as individual human beings who are looking for genuine interaction and connection with local people. Some are disappointed in being addressed as tourists and asked for goods or money, but realize that local people do not understand why these volunteers pay so much money to come and help them.

Observing poverty is a major issue. One young respondent mentioned a severe culture shock, when she was confronted with poverty for the first time. Most participants are sincerely touched by observing children without shoes or wearing torn and dirty clothes. Their common response is buying food and furniture for the families. Many refer to 'good feelings in doing something good'. In Both's view, these families were ambivalent; on the one hand they appreciated this support, but, on the other hand they felt uncomfortable, sometimes embarrassed. According to her (2004, p. 56), the participants did not notice that.

Notwithstanding the pity interviewees feel when they observe poverty, they perceive community members as cheerful, happy and relaxed.

> They are happy with a coke, that's great, I think we can really learn from them.
> (Dutch woman, age 35)

> They are poor, but they have a lot of fun, they are not unhappy, anyway. Sometimes I wonder who are the happiest ones, we or they.
> (Dutch woman, age 57)

Family life is frequently mentioned as something really interesting and impressive. Originating from individualistic countries, Australian and European volunteers are touched by the perceived strong family ties and care for each other. For many, this compares unfavourably to the loose family life in their home countries.

Part of the volunteer programme is a tour of the host country. Some respondents refer to a 'reward' for having worked in the project. The tour leads along the tourism highlights. The volunteers consequently have to step into a different role as conventional tourists. This is a source of ambivalence and critical reflections on the tourist phenomenon. For some respondents the round trip is 'too touristy'. They would have preferred a tour that fits close to the volunteer role and doesn't force them to be 'tourists'. Others make fun of themselves and realize that they 'are not any better than tourists'. In general, tourists represent a species volunteers want to distance themselves from.

> They [tourists] don't have that sense of value for the place, they're just there passing through . . . You get upset that these people don't have the same sense of that really deep-felt appreciation for where you are.
> (Australian male student)

> Living among local people is much more satisfying than being a tourist. . . . When you watch such a tourist invasion of our village through the eyes of community members, you realize how ridiculous tourists are. You are going to see things from the other side.
> (Dutch woman, age 36)

The psychological effects of volunteering have only been assessed immediately after the participants' return back home. Long-term effects have not been studied. Wearing (2001, p. 126) uses four – obviously interrelated – categories to describe the personal development that volunteer tourists experience: (i) personal awareness and learning; (ii) interpersonal awareness and learning; (iii) confidence; and (iv) self-contentment. The first category relates to a wider awareness of self from an affective perspective, as well as beliefs, values, abilities and limitations (p. 127).

> I think my tolerance level and my acceptance levels aren't as black and white any more. . . . It doesn't matter that other people have a totally different system to the way we do things, just enjoy the difference.
>
> (Australian female student)

> You've got to get down to yourself and it's not all these other consumer things which we tend to take for granted. Then when you step back into that poor society, your sense-of-self, or your identity shrinks a fair bit. . . . It shrinks you down until you're just you.
>
> (Australian male student)

> It was much inspiring, the way we interacted with the family and grandfather and the construction workers. It was incredibly inspiring. We got lots of energy from it.
>
> (Dutch woman, age 36)

The perception of cheerful, happy and relaxed life makes interviewees critical towards their home society with its materialistic and individualistic values ('In Holland we all are spoilt assholes', Dutch woman, age 35), but, on the other hand, observing poverty is generally conducive to a greater appreciation of life at home.

Much of the experience and learning results from interaction within the group of volunteers. The group can be a source of frustrations and irritations, but participants often mention an increased awareness and appreciation of other people, in terms of feeling less self-centred, more thoughtful and more open.

> A group that consists of women is a source of trouble. Minor problems become bigger and bigger in a group of only women. But I'd like to see that as a challenge.
>
> (Dutch woman, age 18)

> I learned how to live in a very close proximity to other people. I started to feel really close to other people even though they were from different countries.
>
> (Australian female student)

'Confidence' is characterized by a firmer belief in one's self, abilities and skills. Terms such as self-concept (how we define ourselves), self-esteem (satisfaction and confidence in ourselves) and self-efficacy (the strength of our belief in being able to accomplish a task) are all interlinked and relate to confidence (Wearing, 2001, p. 131).

> Personally I think it gives you motivation because you have had a hands-on practical experience that has generally been pretty successful. It gives you confidence and self-esteem.
>
> (Australian male student)

> That is something you forget in a society like ours. It is so easy to just buy something from the shop or get someone in to fix things and whatever else. We made a tent, a kitchen and shelves and we did it all ourselves. Everything we did, we pulled it out of nowhere and created it.
>
> (Australian female student)

Wearing (2001, p. 103) cites several Australian students who were deeply touched by observing family life in Costa Rica.

> I came back with a real sense of what a wonderful thing it is to have a family. It's something that is really basic, and you kind of almost think because we are such consumers, it almost defaults it.
>
> (male student)

> I came back and took off 6 months so I could go and visit my family. I hadn't seen my grandparents for 5 years. I wanted to go and see my grandfather for Christmas this year, it was to get that increased sense of family.
>
> (male student)

> I have three younger brothers and I don't know them very well. . . . I have made the hugest effort to make them a large part of my life again and I have.
>
> (female student)

Perspectives of local stakeholders have not been the object of interest in most studies. A Costa Rican psychologist, who works for ACI (Asociación Cultural de Intercambio), which is the National Committee for Youth Exchange, makes some critical observations about volunteers in Costa Rica. Most volunteers are from the UK, Germany, Switzerland, Scandinavia and Australia. In her view, some feel like missionaries, with all the patronizing connotations. They are participating in projects to help developing countries and derive a good feeling from that. Some even give the impression of making great sacrifices to do something good by renouncing Western comfort temporarily. For others, the main reason to participate is to travel and see something of the world.

### Romance tourism

Sex tourism to the Third World is often associated with the exploitation of local women and children in the context of neocolonial exploitation of developing countries. The term usually evokes the image of men, often older and in less than perfect shape, travelling to developing countries for sexual pleasures generally not available, at least not for the same price, in their home country (Oppermann, 1999, p. 251). According to Oppermann, however, the vast majority of tourists who use prostitutes to satisfy their sexual needs do not travel for that purpose alone. This is often just a by-product or side attraction rather than the main and sole purpose (p. 252). In some cases, both sex 'providers' in the South and tourists from the West will experience sexual encounters as intercultural encounters rather than prostitution or the search for mere sexual gratification. This holds true in particular for encounters between indigenous men and European or North American women. What was exceptional in the 1970s and 1980s has become common practice in recent years. A growing number of studies (e.g. Meisch, 1995; Pruitt and LaFont, 1995; Herold *et al.*, 2002) demonstrate that encounters between indigenous men and female tourists are perceived by both sides as romantic affairs rather than exchange of sex for money. Countries such as the Dominican Republic, Jamaica, Kenya and The Gambia are well-known destinations for romantic interaction between European or North American women and indigenous men. But several other countries in Africa, Asia or South America serve this purpose as well. According to Meisch (1995, p. 451), romanticism between *'gringas'* (foreign women) and *'Otavaleños'* (indigenous men from Otavalo, Ecuador) is basically the latest version of the noble savage trope (trope meaning 'images and ideas'). In Cusco, Peru, *'bricheros'* present themselves as descendants of the Incas to charm Western women who are in search of Andean mysticism (Bosman, 2005, p. 95). In Jamaica, the Rastafarian man represents archetypal masculinity (Pruitt and LaFont, 1995). The anthropologist Trouillot (cited in Meisch, 1995, p. 452) observed that 'one suspects that the savage as wise is more often than not Asiatic, the savage as noble is often a Native American and the savage as barbarian is often African or African-American'. Western women construct the latter – 'black men' – as more passionate, more emotional, more natural, and sexually tempting (Pruitt and LaFont, 1995, p. 430). Moreover, for many Western women, the local man is not merely a sexual object, but rather the woman's cultural broker. 'He serves to ease her experience in the society and provide her with increased access to the local culture' (p. 426). For women who are in search of the exotic and authentic life of indigenous communities local men give access to the back region. In the words of Meisch (1995, p. 452), 'What could be more backstage, and offer a more intimate experience of a culture, than being invited into someone's bedroom and bed?' According to her, the image of the timeless, noble savage is fostered by most guidebooks and by the tourism literature produced abroad and locally, but also by 'the New Age fascination with shamanism and the ecology movement's apotheosis of indigenous people as "natural ecologists"' (p. 452). Because indigenous people in Ecuador historically have been a disparaged and vilified population, many mestizo-whites cannot believe that a foreigner would prefer any *'indígena'* to themselves. Yet the vast majority of *'gringas'* are attracted to *'indígenas'* because of their search for an unspoilt, pre-industrial lifeway (p. 457).

Indigenous men in the Dominican Republic, Jamaica and Otavalo have developed subtle strategies to meet female tourists' romantic and exotic expectations. Typically, they approach women in a manner which is friendly and non-threatening. They don't speak about sex or money. Flattery is one of the main seduction strategies. In discos they will display their dancing skills. Rather than asking for money, they use different strategies to indicate their lack of money to pay for drinks, admission to disco or taxi transportation. 'Reluctantly' admitting to have money problems and allowing the woman to provide some assistance is preferred to asking for money (Herold *et al.*, 2002, p. 992).

The above-mentioned authors agree that there are proportional gender differences on the continuum of romance tourism on one pole and sex tourism on the other. Female tourists tend to be motivated toward the romance end and men more toward the sex end. Local men involved with female tourists are much more accepted in their own communities than local female sex workers. In the Dominican Republic, for example, the latter are stigmatized far more by the local population than the beach boys (Herold *et al.*, 2002, p. 982). They also have clients from the local population whom they charge considerably less than they do the male tourists. The beach boys only receive money from female tourists. Whereas female sex workers are exclusively motivated to make money, beach boys are also motivated by peer group status and perspectives of having their share of Western life.

# The Tourist Unravelled

This chapter presents conceptual conclusions based upon a comparison between the theoretical perspectives discussed in Chapter 2 and the empirical data presented in Chapter 3. First of all, the lines of thought that are outlined in Chapter 2 are evaluated, in order to find out which lines are most fruitful in explaining contemporary travel to the South by citizens from the historically Protestant countries of Europe. Europe's modern consumer culture, as discussed in Chapter 2, turns out to be a key concept in search of such an explanation.

Still, these West–South tourists do not constitute a univocal phenomenon. The present chapter demonstrates that they exhibit a great diversity of life-worlds, lifestyles, and corresponding motivations, interests, preferences and behaviour. An important finding is that considerable discrepancies can be identified between, on the one hand, the value systems of these tourists and their corresponding interests and expectations and, on the other hand, their actual behaviour.

The consequences of this analysis for planning and management of tourism in destination areas in the Third World are far-reaching if these areas want to plan for the 'right' tourists, i.e. want to optimize the desired benefits of tourism and minimize undesired impacts.

## 4.1  Evaluation of the Theoretical Perspectives

Chapter 2 presented several lines of thought, each of which leads to specific views and explanations of the tourism phenomenon. Based upon the empirical studies presented in Chapter 3, these possible explanations will be evaluated here.

## Rationalization

According to this line of thought, the origin and development of the holiday phenomenon should be sought in compensation motives. Deficiencies in our daily existence induce us to travel in order to compensate for these deficiencies. Holidays offer opportunities to re-energize. Having re-created one's physical and mental powers and recharged the batteries, both modern employers and employees are able to contribute fully again to a rational functioning of society.

This structural–functionalist explanation of holidaymaking has been widely adopted by present-day consumers. Respondents commonly refer to compensation motives in terms of hectic and stressful daily lives that prompt them to have a break. Holidays are supposed to restore the individual's physical and mental powers and endow him or her with a general sense of well-being.

Unfortunately, research attesting to whether or not holidays really offer recuperation and refreshment hardly exist. The present chapter seriously questions this effect. Holidays become more and more routinized. One might hardly expect that the average consumer will be able to turn the knob all of a sudden and leave their day-to-day worries behind when going on holiday. Holidays can be as stressful as daily life. As will be explained shortly, the position taken here is that holidays are a symptom of our modern consumer culture rather than an escape from it.

## Alienation

During the 1960s and 1970s, academic discourse in tourism was much about modern individual's alienation from their society as a reason to travel (e.g. MacCannell, 1973, 1976; Erik Cohen, 1979a). No empirical studies on organized or volunteer tourism were reported during these years. Literature was limited to the predecessors of contemporary backpackers. Although respondents among the organized tourists studied in Chapter 3 may be to different degrees critical of Western civilization in general or their own country in particular, virtually none of them refers to any kind of alienation. Life at home is taken for granted.

Present-day backpackers are different from the drifters, nomads or wanderers of the 1960s and 1970s. The drifters Cohen (1972, 1973) observed in the early 1970s were almost exclusively drawn from the countercultures in society and appeared to have made a commitment to an alternative (escapist, anarchist and hedonistic) lifestyle prior to their departure. In Cohen's view, they were severely alienated from their home societies. The long-term travellers of the 1980s, as described by Riley (1988), were no longer primarily recruited from the counterculture, but from a far wider section of Western society. They were no longer hippies, deviants or anarchistic hedonists but were overwhelmingly middle-class, educated, European, single and obsessively budget conscious. Most contemporary backpacker tourism is not a counterculture any more. In 2002, Westerhausen noted:

> Even though a significant proportion of the counterculture continues to engage in subcultural travel abroad, the majority of today's travellers have little commitment to its values before leaving home. Few appear to be substantially alienated by life in the West prior to their departure.
>
> (Westerhausen, 2002, p. 159)

In general, they are (future) pillars of society, on temporary leave from affluence, but with clear and unwavering intentions to return to 'normal' life (Sörensen, 2003, p. 852). Almost all have a fixed return date, typically defined by their flight ticket (p. 852).

Cohen concluded in 2004 that the overall degree of the alienation of backpackers had apparently diminished with time.

> Few see in travel an alternative to a 'normal' career or seek an 'elective centre' abroad. Within this limited period, they primarily desire the achievement of unlimited freedom to do their own thing, which may include the unrestricted hedonistic quest of enjoyment and fun.
>
> (Cohen, 2004, p. 51)

So, ironically, whereas backpackers used to search for 'alternative' life and still want to be alternative to mainstream tourism, they are doomed to be pre-eminently, representatives of modern life in the West.

One might conclude that the materialistic, increasingly affluent society of the 1960s and 1970s took many – students and academics particularly – by surprise and evoked more countercultural movements and escapist behaviour than the fully-fledged consumer culture of recent years, which is taken for granted by many.

## Escape routes

Academic discourse in the 1960s and 1970s also referred to holidays as the archetypical free area, the institutionalized setting for excursions away from the domain of paramount reality (e.g. Stanley Cohen and Taylor, 1976, and see the section 'The disorder of things', in Chapter 2). Holidays offer ways to escape the mundane, routine, boredom of daily life in structurally separated (mostly) legitimate zones, where irrationality and emotion are no longer required to be subdued by Reason and Rationality.

This is apparent among backpackers. A sense of freedom may be seen as one of the major attractions of backpacking (Richards and Wilson, 2004, p. 5). A sense of freedom, or perceived freedom, is rewarding in modern Western society, which on the one hand highly values individuality and self-determination but on the other hand brings along endless obligations and constraints. Feeling free to make one's own choices, determine one's own itinerary, change travel plans at will, etc. are features of travel that are very important for backpackers, irrespective of the question whether they are actually conforming to the norms and codes of conduct of the backpacker subculture.

Respondents among organized tourists and volunteers did not make any reference to travelling as a legitimate zone where emotionality and emotion are less subdued than in their daily lives. Rather, they exhibit controlled and cultivated pleasure, reminding of Wang's (2000) poetic Eros. There is no indication at all that the basic social mores of life at home are temporarily suspended.

### Poetic Eros versus carnivalesque Eros

Wang uses the concept of a 'space of Eros' to refer to the separated zones where irrational factors are licensed and channelled to be released and celebrated (see the section 'The disorder of things', in Chapter 2). He divides Eros into 'poetic Eros' (cultivated emotional and imaginative pleasure, Romanticism, or sublimation of instinctual pleasures in a Freudian sense) and 'carnivalesque Eros' (sensual pleasure and sensation seeking). The latter seeks satisfaction in a direct, crude, primitive way. Pleasure is the only goal. The empirical studies presented in Chapter 3 do not give much evidence for this type of sensual pleasure and sensation seeking. Some backpackers, in particular the ones participating in full-moon dance parties in Thailand, reflect the unrestricted quest of enjoyment and fun mentioned by Cohen in the previous section. In general, however, both organized tourists and volunteers, as well as quite a few backpackers, reflect the *poetic* version of Eros rather than the *carnivalesque* version. They seek decent and respectable cultivated pleasure.

### McDonaldization and 'Fordism'

Ritzer's (2000) concept of 'McDonaldization' (or 'McDisneyization' as far as tourism is concerned) conceives the world as growing increasingly efficient, calculable, predictable and dominated by controlling non-human technologies. It corresponds to the concept of 'Fordism', as opposed to 'post-Fordism' (see section 2.2). The results of Chapter 3 do not give cause to a dichotomy between 'Fordism' and 'post-Fordism' (or even 'post-tourism'), or 'old tourism' and 'new tourism' (e.g. Poon, 1993). They rather demonstrate that 'McDonaldized'/'McDisneyized', 'Fordist' and 'old' practices are much alive in tourism and actually become increasingly popular. Cruise ships, all-inclusive resorts, theme parks, casinos and shopping malls – all booming businesses – are the most obvious examples of growing efficiency, calculability and predictability and, consequently, of rigid standardization.

Package tours from West to South fit into the concepts of McDonaldization and 'Fordism'. They are 'Fordist' rather than 'post-Fordist' products, 'old tourism' rather than 'new'. All kinds of expert systems allow present-day consumers to book efficient, calculable and predictable trips to the most remote areas of the globe, without risks. Trust in aviation systems, tour operating systems, information systems and so on is justified because risks are minimized. Consumers can trust that the tour operator has taken care of eliminating most of the physical, financial and psychological risks.

Much individual travelling is also 'McDonaldized'. It is easier than ever before to travel unorganized, because much of the larger society has been 'McDonaldized' by means of standardized aviation and reservation systems, travel 'bibles', transnational hotel chains, youth hostels, Internet cafés, mobile phones, etc.

Without any doubt, the arrival of expert systems and the subsequent efficiency, safety and predictability have brought the world within attainable reach for many in Western society. They paved the way for modern man or woman to satisfy their generalized curiosity and their restless drive to seek novelty and have interesting experiences. Even backpackers and volunteers, who like to see themselves as alternatives to mainstream tourism, can virtually only exist thanks to expert systems in tourism.

## Romanticism

Romanticism appears to be an extremely important concept in explaining long-haul travel from West to South. The second half of the 20th century, the final decades in particular, witnessed the emergence of a new Romanticism in terms of interest in 'unspoilt' nature and communities, not contaminated by the achievements of the modern consumer state. It is reflected in Urry's (1990, 2002) 'Romantic gaze'. National parks and wildlife, but also the simplicity and 'non-modernism' of exotic communities, have become major selling points for tour operators all over the Western sphere of influence. This new Romanticism is common among both organized tourists, backpackers and volunteers and is the *raison d'être* of romance tourists.

Interest in exotic people and cultures has two contradictory sides, the colonialist and the romantic. Enlightenment thinking in Europe regarded European rational order as a universal value system. Exotic peoples were perceived as primitive, violent, preoccupied with sex, and incapable of self-governance. This perception was at the basis of both colonialism and missionary work and was still dominant in the first half of the 20th century. It generated a lot of tourism in terms of officials, civil servants, teachers, traders, anthropologists, missionaries, etc., rather than leisure-related travellers who wanted to learn about exotic cultures. Along with the new romantic wave of our present times, the perception of 'primitive-ness' has shifted to 'simplicity', 'freedom' and 'naturalness' and, conse-quently, exotic destinations are commonly presented by the tourism and travel industry as paradises or idyllic communities where life is 'unspoilt', simple and natural, reflecting an idealization of Others and difference. Recurring themes are: exotic, timeless, authentic, paradise, unspoilt, mys-tical and erotic (Echtner, 2002, p. 416).

How can idealized romantic images of exotic destinations become so prominent in contemporary West–South tourism?

First, modern Europeans and North Americans live in technological environments – evolved out of 'The roots of order' (see 'The disorder of things' Chapter 2, pp. 24–25), that provide physical protection and sup-port necessary for human survival and the maintenance of well-being. Although life at home is taken for granted by the vast majority of tourists that have been studied in Chapter 3, they are to different degrees critical of Western civilization. Quite a few respondents express feelings of dis-comfort in relation to the dominant consumer culture ('we are spoilt', 'we don't know how to live any more', 'we are too materialistic', etc.). They want to have a glimpse of simplicity and naturalness in the destinations visited. MacCannell's conceptualization of tourism as a pilgrimage in search of authentic life elsewhere was based on alienated life in Western societies. As discussed in the previous section, whether alienation is a dominant feature of present-day Western society can be seriously questioned. Nostalgic romantic images of and feelings towards 'unspoilt' natural life, however, appear to be very much alive. As long as they are far away, exotic people can easily be subject to projections of nostalgia, Utopia, search for 'Otherness' and difference. In the words of Craik:

> In contrast to what is commonly assumed, the cultural experiences offered by tourism are consumed in terms of prior knowledge, expectations, fantasies and mythologies _generated in the tourist's origin culture_ rather than _by the cultural offerings of the destination._
>
> (Craik, 1997, p. 118, emphasis in original)

When they move to the Western world as refugees, asylum seekers or cheap workers, exotic people will lose their appeal.

Second, according to Welk (2004, p. 82), for Western Protestant societies, paradise – the mythological place of origin, of creation itself – serves as the antithesis of modern civilization (i.e. to its negative excesses) and is, in this way, a projection of our own romantic yearning for virgin innocence and originality. The touristic 'return' to paradise is a symbolic 'return' to the origins of mankind, in order to make us feel like being without sin (p. 82).

Third, one of the contemporary features of Romanticism is a movement against Western assimilation of cultural differences. Modern society – as reflected in tourism – generates two opposing cultural tendencies; one is standardization of facilities, the other is celebration of uniqueness and diversity. In the words of Rousseau and Porter (1990, p. 2): 'Romanticism proclaimed the sovereignty of uniqueness and holiness of diversity. And today, it is "difference" that dominates our discourse.' It is a counter-movement against standardization and uniformity, leading to a re-appreciation and consequently re-vitalization of indigenous culture, including language, folklore, craft, art, architecture, i.e. culture in both a broad and narrow sense (van Egmond, 2005, p. 77). All West–South tourists that have been studied in Chapter 3 are in search of difference and diversity. Even when the glances they take at local culture are quick and superficial, the most annoying experiences in exotic destinations are: coming across either familiar standardized Western facilities such as transnational fast-food chains or other groups of Western tourists, let alone compatriots. Running up against compatriots is among the worst possible experiences.

Three additional explanations can be given of the growing popularity of exotic destinations.

First of all, globalization, or even 'McDonaldization', 'McDisneyization', or 'Cocacolaización' of society, contributes to the spread of dominant Western consumption patterns to the most remote edges of the world. This process entails a tendency towards standardization of facilities, lifestyles and behaviours worldwide. Mass tourism in particular contributes to global standardization of facilities and thus has a huge levelling effect. Referring to *The Golden Hordes* of tourists, Turner and Ash as early as 1975 sighed 'The pursuit of the exotic and diverse ends in uniformity' (1975, p. 164). The consequence of this process of globalization and standardization is that 'Others' and difference become rare and threatened with extinction or will be 'lost to modernization'. Indigenous communities, quite a few animal species, rainforests and glaciers become valuable because they are disappearing. They are cultivated for being rare rather than for their intrinsic qualities. The German Magazine *Der Spiegel* called it 'Ansturm auf die letzten Paradiese' (a 'rush on the last paradises'): we have to go there now, before it is too late. This holds particularly true for destinations that are at the basis of the destination hierarchy (see Figures 4.3 and 4.4).

Moreover, some of Europe's historically Protestant countries were colonial powers in the past, many of them sent missionaries to the South to convert the primitive natives, all of them embraced the colonial ideology for some time. The shift in Western countries from 'Materialist' to 'Postmaterialist' values (see the section 'The Protestant ethic' in Chapter 2) brought along a new type of 'political correctness' that condemns racism, discrimination, maltreatment, and promotes equality between peoples, development cooperation, and mutual respect. Postmaterialist attitudes towards the Third World may contain an element of guilt related to previous discrimination and maltreatment of 'primitive' peoples, be they Indians in the United States, Papuans in New Guinea, Herero in Namibia, or Aboriginals in Australia. Visiting indigenous communities may be an unconscious, perhaps even conscious, drive of Westerners to alleviate this guilt by showing respect and demonstrating that they are less prejudiced and politically more correct now. Many respondents are critical of other tourists who 'don't know how to behave'. In the countries of origin of West–South tourists, numerous 'Codes of conduct' for both tourist and tour operator have been formulated that specify how to behave correctly in relation to 'hosts'.

The final reason – for some an effect rather than a reason – corresponds with a perspective put forward by Craik (1997, p. 114). Tourists revel in the 'Otherness' of destinations, peoples and activities because they offer the illusion or fantasy of otherness, of difference and counterpoint to the everyday. At the same time, however, the advantages, comforts and benefits of home are reinforced through the exposure to difference. By visiting exotic cultures one might feel more comfortable at home. This perspective is strongly confirmed by many respondents, organized tourists in particular. The confrontation with poverty, stench, waste, inefficiency, crime, lack of hygiene, disease, etc. generates feelings of satisfaction with the conditions at home. So, on the one hand, the romantic perceptions of 'relaxed' and 'happy' life in exotic destinations make respondents critical of their home society with its materialistic and individualistic values, but, on the other hand, observing poverty is conducive to a greater appreciation of life at home.

Whatever the reasons for romantic images of exotic destinations having become so prominent in contemporary tourism, including tourism-related mass communication, these images are *projections* of Western consciousness, feelings of guilt and Utopia rather than an exploration into the reality of exotic people's existence (Wang, 2000, p. 143). The distinction drawn by Gunn (in Mill and Morrison, 2002) between 'organic' and 'induced' images is relevant here. An 'organic' image is based on non-touristy, non-commercial information provided by mass media in general, education and word-of-mouth. Organic images of Third World countries are often negatively biased. African countries, for example, are often associated with tribal wars, famine, poverty, AIDS, etc.

Induced images are based on both commercial tourism information as presented by tourism-related media and personal experiences of individuals and their social circles. Projections of Western consciousness, feelings of guilt and Utopia relate much more to induced images than to organic. Because images are based on information from either media or social circles, Wang (2000, p. 135) calls an image 'second-hand knowledge of a place, a people, or a culture', as opposed to an impression which is obtained from direct personal visual encounters. Unfortunately, research aiming at measuring the effects of direct visual encounters on images has hardly ever been conducted. Perceptions of indigenous peoples by tourists in terms of 'they are happy', 'they are innocent', 'they are materially poor, but spiritually rich' suggest that visual encounters often reinforce existing images rather than modify them.

## The Protestant ethic

West–South tourism is serious business. The historically Protestant countries of Western, Northern and Central Europe are among the most secularized countries of the world, but the Protestant ethic is still strikingly alive. It deeply affects the value system of West–South tourists and their subsequent interests and motivations. It does so in several ways, both directly, as will be demonstrated in this section, and indirectly, through our modern consumer culture.

First of all, in the Puritan tradition, waste of time was the first and in principle the deadliest of sins. Loss of time through idleness was, in the words of Weber (1976, p. 158), 'worthy of absolute moral condemnation'. In secularized modern times, doing nothing is still 'not done'. Organized tourists in particular don't want to waste time. They want to see a lot and do a lot or even see and do as much as possible. This is tiring, exhausting for some, but they prefer it to being idle. The programmes organized by European tour operators consequently include as many interesting ingredients as possible, leading to tight travel schedules. For many respondents, doing nothing, i.e. being idle on a beach, is allowed only when they have 'deserved' a couple of days on a beach after having 'worked hard'. Some even have to 'motivate themselves' to go and see something before being entitled to relax.

Among the moral obligations to make good use of one's time are educational elements. Visiting temples, churches, monuments and having explanations by tour managers or local guides are essential parts of a trip. Although they feel embarrassed to do so, quite a few interviewees admit that seeing so many temples was boring: 'actually, when you have seen two temples, you have seen them all'. Some respondents don't want to learn something during their trip, because that interferes with their 'holiday feeling', but the vast majority expresses the need to have a lot of educational elements in their programme. 'To learn something', or even 'learn a lot', is definitely highly valued among organized tourists.

Volunteers also want to make good use of their time. They don't want to be 'like tourists' who just watch things and then go. They want to 'do something useful/valuable/worthwhile/constructive/helpful'. They work to 'deserve' a round trip afterwards, in a similar vein as organized tourists 'deserving' a beach extension. After having worked, they are entitled to enjoy their trip. Several European and Australian participants mentioned that they anticipated working hard to be able to contribute to local development and found it difficult to leave behind their work ethic. Some couldn't get used to the slow local pace of work and did not have the patience to sit and wait for any length of time. Others were annoyed by the obvious lack of efficiency by local workers.

Second, part of the traditional Protestant ethic was a deep suspicion of self-indulgence and excessive consumption. In the Puritan version of Protestantism asceticism was the key word. A broad range of attitudes can be found among the respondents concerning luxury and 'big spending', but among the Europeans from the traditionally Protestant countries – rather than French and Belgians – there is a strong tendency towards renouncing luxury temporarily and turning to an ascetic lifestyle. This holds true for many backpackers and volunteers, but also for a considerable portion of organized tourists. Dutch respondents in particular don't want luxurious accommodation and facilities. Among backpackers, low spending patterns, 'hard' living, contracting diseases, 'suffering like local people' contribute to road status. Volunteers want to share local life for some time and renounce Western comfort. Living ascetic lives often has connotations with searching for one's true self, one's existential authenticity, by giving up temporarily technological comfort one is used to at home.

Third, in the Protestant tradition, the ordinary person bears some individual moral responsibility for the fate of the world. Not taking responsibility might result in feelings of guilt. For many respondents, observing poverty in developing countries is a serious issue. Resulting feelings range from embarrassment and helplessness to guilt. While French and Belgian respondents advocate government intervention to reduce poverty, respondents from the Protestant European countries feel prompted to 'do something', to take personal action. A wide range of individual strategies to cope with feelings of embarrassment and guilt towards poverty is identified in Chapter 3. Individual moral responsibility corresponds with the postmaterialist values as described by Inglehart *et al.* (1998). The 'historically Protestant' countries of the world are supporting these values much more than all other countries, the Scandinavian countries and the Netherlands ahead of German- and English-speaking countries (1998, p. 20). The desire to 'do something' is most prominent among organized tourists and volunteers. For many volunteers it is the very essence of their trip.

## Modern consumer culture

Travelling from West to South perfectly reflects our modern consumer culture (see Chapter 2). First, all respondents from the West have learned to want holidays and have come to think of them as essential for their psychological well-being. Holidays offer, in the words of Wang (2002, p. 293), surplus value compared to material consumer goods, because tourist experiences are easy and quick to change. 'This situation makes tourism an exemplary domain to explore and satisfy the generalized consuming needs of modern consumers' (p. 293).

Most respondents among the organized tourists are well-travelled. Many make a long-haul trip every year, in addition to several short-haul trips. They display a common travel career pattern. Europeans start travelling in Europe, mostly unorganized. Going to the South is for well-travelled consumers. Most trips are definitely routinized, in that the decision-making process starts with the question 'Where are we going for the holidays?' rather than 'Are we going anywhere this year?' Whereas the first holiday or long-haul trip might be a source of great excitement and satisfaction, away from everyday life's routine, in a surprising and contrasting holiday world, in the long run seeking novelty becomes routine. In general, respondents do not recall much of previous trips. During the trip, a common subject of conversation is where to go next time, probably next year.

Second, destinations are not places of specific interest, but objects of a generalized curiosity. Although they constitute a hierarchical order in terms of the most popular ones at the top and the least popular at the base, destinations are chosen arbitrarily and are easily interchanged. A generalized curiosity and a restless drive to have ever-new experiences are reasons why destinations are visited only once. Having seen a country, one turns to another, at the same horizontal level or down the hierarchy. This holds true for both organized tourists and backpackers. In explaining 'The global nomad', Richards and Wilson (2004, p. 5) point to the 'experience hunger' of modern backpackers. They seem to be driven into the far corners of the globe by the restless search for ever-new experiences. 'Once they have consumed the experiences offered by one place, they need to move on to find new ones. Just like traditional nomadic peoples, the global nomad constantly moves from place to place' (p. 5).

So, both organized tourists and backpackers display Bauman's 'grazing behaviour' (see Chapter 2): 'the world . . . is a huge collection of grazing grounds, and living in such a world is shaped after the pattern of wandering from one succulent and fragrant meadow to another' (in Franklin, 2003b, p. 208). Ties with place are loose. Tourists do not have a firm commitment to the places and people they visit. Relationships are casual and brief. By their 'grazing behaviour', their loose ties and casual relationships, they are perfectly modelled after modern society, according to Bauman, whereas our role as consumers in liquid modernity can be characterized as rather like tourists.

Third, restlessness is characteristic of modern consumer culture. Rojek (1995, p. 109) even refers to a 'corrosive restlessness' in the psyche of modern man. We are used to more stimuli to reach an optimal level of arousal than ever before. Both work and leisure conditions in Western society are hectic. Reasons respondents mention for travelling to the South have nothing to do with the South, but are based on hectic and stressful daily lives that prompt them to have a break. They need a break to relax and recuperate. Almost none of the interviewees was reflexive upon the seemingly paradoxical situation of having a 'see a lot, do a lot' trip to relax and escape from stressful daily life.

The obvious conclusion is that tourism – even long-haul tourism from West to South – has become an established part of everyday life culture and consumption. Rather than a 'departure' from the routines and practices of everyday life, holidaying is integral to contemporary modern lifestyles.

To sum up, travelling from West to South perfectly reflects our modern consumer culture. This culture has strong roots in both Protestantism and Romanticism. Tourism is a symptom of this consumer culture rather than an escape from it, although respondents commonly refer to escape and compensation motives in terms of hectic and stressful daily lives that prompt them to have a break. West–South tourists are motivated by a generalized curiosity and a restless drive to seek novelty and have interesting experiences rather than by specific interests. They are not mere hedonists in search of sensual pleasure and sensation but seek decent and respectable cultivated pleasure.

Contemporary society, with its modern consumer culture, is taken for granted by most respondents, although they may be critical of the materialistic and individualistic values of Western society. The 20th century witnessed a shift from 'colonial' perceptions of exotic people in the first half towards 'romantic' and 'politically correct' perceptions in the second half, corresponding to the shift from materialist values towards postmaterialist values that is most prominent in Europe's historically Protestant countries.

## 4.2   Life-worlds, Lifestyles and Distinctive Preferences of Tourists

West–South tourists do not constitute a univocal phenomenon. They display a broad range of life-worlds, lifestyles and corresponding preferences.

Section 2.3 explored the concept of 'life-world' according to the explanation given by Schutz and Luckmann (1974). Our everyday life-world is that province of reality that we take for granted and view as self-evidently 'real'. It is fundamentally intersubjective; we share our life-world with other people who are presumed to have the same perception of the world, i.e. who are supposed to share a common frame of interpretation with us. Schutz and Luckmann use the term 'cognitive style' to refer to differences in frames of interpretation. Groups of people who share interpretations of reality share a cognitive style. Cognitive styles are not fixed, but may vary according to the groups one belongs to or refers to.

The organized West–South tourists studied in Chapter 3 display a remarkably homogeneous cognitive style. First of all, virtually all of them represent middle-class citizens, with middle-class values. Consequently, they display a Romantic Gaze rather than a Collective Gaze, in Urry's (1990, 2002) terms, or reflect Wang's poetic Eros rather than his carnivalesque Eros. What these tourists seek is referred to in section 4.1 as 'decent and respectable cultivated pleasure'. Second, they perceive the whole world as a domain within attainable reach, i.e. they see more and more previously unknown parts of the world as domains for exploration and familiarization. In the words of Schutz and Luckmann, the world within actual reach and the world within attainable reach are coinciding to an ever greater degree. Third, as mentioned in the previous section, they share a generalized curiosity and a restless drive to seek novelty and have interesting experiences.

Organized West–South tourists understand each other well, although those tourists participating in 'adventurous trips' often prefer to see themselves as different from those participating in 'conventional package trips', i.e. as 'travellers' rather than 'tourists'. So, while life-worlds are quite similar objectively, subjective definitions of life-worlds can make a great difference.

Backpackers are less homogeneous than organized tourists. Although they share middle-class values with organized tourists and – even more so than organized tourists – perceive the whole world as a domain within attainable reach, they appear to have different definitions of their life-worlds. What ties backpackers together in a shared life-world or backpacker culture is the strongly defended differentiation of their life-world from that of mainstream tourists. In particular they are unified in their dislike of commercial package tours. 'Backpacker' is actually a socially constructed identity rather than a definition. More so than organized tourists, backpackers celebrate Western individualism as a central value in life. Feeling free to make one's own choices and determine one's own itinerary, in addition to the unrestrained permissiveness found in the backpacker enclaves, are features of travel that are very important for backpackers. This freedom results in a broad range of backpacker practices, from full-moon partying on Thai beaches to ascetic lives with the poor.

Consequently, backpackers understand each other quite well when they differentiate themselves from mainstream tourists. Beyond that, however, ascetic long-term travellers and short-term hedonists do not have much in common.

The life-world of long-term travellers who return home might be fundamentally different from the life-worlds of residents back home. Often the transition back to 'ordinary life' is difficult, according to Westerhausen (2002, p. 122), due to 'the profound sense of alienation from a society whose values are now foreign'. The confusion or even desperation these long-term travellers experience when they feel strangers in their own society is commonly referred to as 'reversed culture shock'. This alienation from their own society is the major reason for repeat long-term travelling.

Volunteers represent the postmaterialist values of the historically Protestant countries pre-eminently. They display a mixture of idealism, feelings of guilt towards poverty, a 'politically correct' excuse to make a long-haul trip, and, most of all, the need to 'do something' for a better world. With backpackers they share adverse attitudes towards mainstream organized tourists. By perceiving themselves as different from 'ordinary tourists', quite a few volunteers feel great ambivalence when faced with their roles as tourists during their trips after work is finished.

Literature does not offer a clear-cut distinction between *life-worlds*, as explained by Schutz and Luckmann, and *lifestyles*. The latter will be used here as a 'translation' of life-worlds into 'a more or less integrated set of practices which an individual embraces' (Giddens, 1991, p. 81).

Similarly, whereas Bourdieu's concept of 'habitus' corresponds with the 'cognitive style'of Schutz *et al.*, lifestyles refer to 'systems of classified and classifying practices' (1984, p. 171). Taste is 'the generative formula of lifestyle, a unitary set of distinctive preferences' (p. 173). By means of taste, according to Bourdieu, social classes distinguish themselves from other social classes.

The vast majority of tourists studied in Chapter 3 represent European middle classes. Many want to distinguish themselves from other people, but from other types of middle-class tourists rather than from the working classes. Only incidental (adverse) references were found to the working classes who prefer being on crowded beaches, but reacting against other types of tourists is common practice. Backpackers and volunteers like to perceive themselves as different from mainstream tourists, adventurous tourists prefer to see themselves as 'travellers' rather than 'conventional tourists', organized tourists react against backpackers as 'lazy youngsters, who just hang around and do not know how to behave'. Both backpackers and volunteers correspond with the 'ego-tourists', as identified by Mowforth and Munt (2003, p. 123, see also section 2.3).

Referring to Bourdieu's 'new petit bourgeoisie', they describe ego-tourists as middle-class people who search for a style of travel which is reflective of an 'alternative' lifestyle, as an expression of a 'new ideology founded upon the pursuit of difference, diversity and distinction' (p. 123).

Cohen (2004, p. 51) points to the ironical fact that the quest of the contemporary backpacker to do 'his or her own thing' leads to uniformity. Like conventional tourists, from whom they desire to distinguish themselves, most backpackers actually pursue highly conventional lifestyles, characteristic of their subculture.

The organized tourists studied in Chapter 3 do not show signs of being weighed down with 'the burden of class differentiation', in order to 'differentiate themselves from the working classes below and the high-spending classes above' (Mowforth and Munt, 2003, p. 123). They do differentiate their own travel group from other groups, i.e. they tend to see their own group as more positive and attractive than other groups and try to outdo other groups in terms of having had more interesting experiences. This holds particularly true for Japanese and American groups who represent 'typical tourists' in the eyes of Europeans. Similarly, Israeli, Italian and Japanese backpackers are not 'real' backpackers in the eyes of (Northern) European backpackers, because of their habit of sticking together in their national enclaves.

So, generally speaking, the middle-class tourists studied try to differentiate themselves from other middle-class tourists rather than other classes. This is done 'on the road' rather than back home. To achieve social status at home by travelling is more and more difficult. When travelling abroad becomes routinized, family, friends, colleagues and neighbours at home will be increasingly indifferent to the experiences, stories, photographs and films the travellers bring back home. The travellers Harrison interviewed (Mowforth and Munt, 2003, p. 77) complained that they often found themselves with nobody to listen to their stories. A cursory summary of a trip was all that people wanted to hear. This limited interest contrasted with the enthusiasm shown by friends made on the road.

What distinctive preferences can be identified among West–South tourists?

On the dimension ranging from extreme hedonism on one pole to rigid asceticism on the other (see Chapter 2), West–South tourists display all kinds of preferences. Among organized tourists mere hedonism is not common. The only examples found were British and Australian participants in organized overland trips in Africa who were, according to African tour guides, more interested in partying and getting drunk than in nature or culture. Rigid asceticism is not common either among organized tourists, but many show a clear tendency to renounce luxury and comfort – to a certain extent – during their trip, Europeans from the 'Protestant' countries rather than French and Belgians, Dutch rather than Germans. The distribution of organized tourists on this dimension seems to be normal (see Figure 4.1).

Some backpackers evidently display an extremely hedonistic lifestyle. Full-moon dance parties in Thailand reflect a hedonistic search for exciting

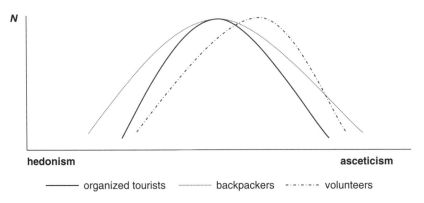

**hedonism**                                                    **asceticism**

———— organized tourists   ·············· backpackers   - · - · - · - volunteers

**Fig. 4.1.**  Hypothetical distribution of tourists on the dimension hedonism vs asceticism.

experiences, including sexual adventures, use of party drugs and a feeling of unrestrained freedom and permissiveness. Quite a few backpackers, on the other hand, aim at living (eating, sleeping, working) with indigenous locals in poor countries and step out of their 'backpacker bubble', at least temporarily. Sometimes they are even prepared to endure malaria, dysentery, typhus and other illnesses, as well as poverty, although they will always be aware that they can return to the developed world from which they originate. These ascetic backpackers are outnumbered by the vast majority who are in search of interesting experiences on a low-budget basis. The distribution of backpackers on the dimension 'extremely hedonistic' versus 'rigidly ascetic' seems to be normal, but is probably a little bit more spread to the extremes poles than the distribution of organized tourists (see Figure 4.1).

Volunteers are prepared to renounce comfort and luxury for some time, in order to be able to live with local families and connect intimately with the people whom they have come to help. The arrangements made by either the tour operator or non-governmental organization that sends them out, however, prevent volunteers from having to live under rigid ascetic conditions. So, the distribution of volunteers on the dimension extremely hedonistic versus rigidly ascetic seems to be clearly skewed to the ascetic pole (see Figure 4.1).

On the 'dimension ranging from an extreme blasé attitude at one pole to an eager desire to learn at the other' (see Chapter 2), West–South tourists also display all kinds of preferences. The vast majority of both organized tourists, backpackers and volunteers are supposed to possess quite a lot of cultural capital, in terms of Bourdieu's embodied and institutionalized state. The latter refers to academic qualifications. The first – more important in the present context – refers to cultivation, *Bildung*. The work on acquisition of embodied cultural capital is work on oneself (self-improvement), 'an effort that presupposes a personal cost, an investment, above all of time, but also of that socially constituted form of libido, *libido sciendi*' (Bourdieu, 1986, p. 247), the desire to learn, to know and understand.

'Learning about other cultures' and 'interacting with local people' are among the central interests of the respondents. These interests are not only found among backpackers, volunteers and organized tourists who make use of local guest houses or one/two-star accommodation, but are also common as well among 'luxury' respondents, staying in four- and five-star hotels with standardized facilities. Learning is highly valued among most tourists. It reflects Western middle-class values, such as the urge of making good use of one's time and the need for self-actualization. The need for interaction is part of the romanticized perception of indigenous communities.

Extreme blasé attitudes are not found. Some do not want to learn anything, because learning resembles work and interferes with a 'holiday feeling', but these respondents are exceptional. In spite of the frequently expressed desire to learn, extreme *libido sciendi* is not found either. In actual practice most respondents did not read any literature about the destination prior to departure. They all have travel books, but these are used as reference books during and after the trip rather than as a source of information prior to the trip. For many, the information provided by either tour manager or local guide will do. For some it is more than enough. The tour managers who have been interviewed are rather negative about the participants' desire to learn.

Respondents only recall minimal facts from their visits. They cannot give many details about previous trips. This underlines the routinization process these holiday-makers are going through.

Obviously, there is a clear discrepancy between what is desirable and what is actually done. The desire to learn represents social desirability rather than social practice. What holds true for organized tourists also holds true for backpackers and volunteers: being in an unfamiliar social and cultural environment all too soon brings a surfeit of information in terms of novelty and strangeness that is too high to be comfortable. Perceived control fades away when this happens. Striving to achieve an agreeable balance between novelty/strangeness and familiarity leads to a limited search for the new. Although unorganized individual travelling offers tremendous opportunities to learn from and about other cultures, actual practice demonstrates that, for many, interacting with fellow-backpackers, being guided by their *Lonely Planet*, and having only distant superficial glimpses of local life represents mainstream backpacker tourism. Cohen's (1972) 'environmental bubble' is still a suitable concept for well-travelled tourists in the 21st century.

    The conclusion is (see Figure 4.2) that there is a broad range of atti-
tudes to learning among tourists, from indifference to eagerness, but for
most tourists the frequently expressed desire to learn is not reflected in
actual behaviour. In spite of their comparatively great cultural capital in
both Bourdieu's embodied and institutionalized state, the majority of
respondents do not exhibit a great eagerness to learn and to know. Only a
minority of 'hard core' tourists display a great *libido sciendi*.

    This conclusion is – to a certain extent – supported by McKercher's
(2002) classification of cultural tourists and Weaver's findings related to
ecotourists. Among cultural tourists (McKercher's model was tested in
Hong Kong), only a small minority represents the 'purposeful cultural
tourism market'. This market is characterized by the desire to learn about
the destination's culture or heritage as a major reason for visiting it.
Instead of being a mainstream market, as is commonly presumed, according to McKercher, the purposeful cultural tourist represents a small niche
market. The vast majority belong to one of the categories 'sightseeing cultural tourists' (learning as part of a more shallow, entertainment-oriented
experience), 'casual cultural tourists' (cultural reasons play a limited role
in the decision to visit a destination), 'incidental cultural tourists' (culture
plays little or no meaningful role in the destination decision-making process, but while at the destination, the person will participate in cultural
tourism activities), or 'serendipitous cultural tourists' (culture plays little
or no role in the decision to visit a destination, but while there this type of
cultural tourist visits cultural attractions and ends up having a deep experience). For Chinese tourists, learning was less a reason to visit a destination than for Europeans, North Americans and Australians.

    McKercher's classification of cultural tourists corresponds with
Lindberg's classification of ecotourists (1991, p. 3): 'hard-core' ecotourists
are scientific researchers such as biologists, archaeologists, geologists, and

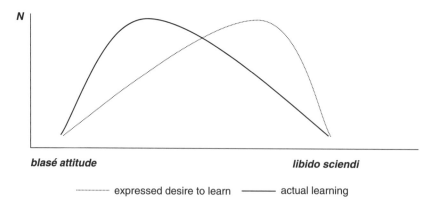

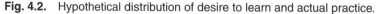

**Fig. 4.2.**   Hypothetical distribution of desire to learn and actual practice.

special interest tourists such as birdwatchers and botanists. They are presumed to have a great *libido sciendi*. 'Dedicated' ecotourists are people who take trips specifically to see protected areas and want to understand local natural and cultural history. For these tourists nature often has spiritual significance in terms of awe and admiration or rebirth.'Mainstream' ecotourists are people who visit specific nature areas primarily to take an interesting trip and have – rather passively – unusual experiences. Finally, 'casual' ecotourists are similar to McKercher's incidental cultural tourists. For these tourists, visits to nature areas are part of an excursion from a beach resort or part of a broader trip. For national parks in Costa Rica and Kenya, the hard-core ecotourist is, according to Weaver (1999, p. 809), seemingly irrelevant, being marginal in numbers. The numbers of dedicated ecotourists are small too. Passive, mainstream and casual ecotourists constitute the biggest group. Their desire to learn is limited, as is the time spent in the area.

Based upon the empirical studies, a third dimension can be identified, ranging from mere observing 'local life' at one pole to intimate connection at the other. Some of the tourists who visit countries in the South just want to watch and observe local life, to 'gaze' in Urry's terms (1990, 2002). Many, however, express a desire to connect with other people, both with fellow-tourists and – even more so – with residents of the destinations visited. From her research among Canadian travellers, Harrison (2003, p. 91) also concluded that 'these tourists in their travels anticipate, and desire, connection'. Sociability and intimacy – or sincerity (Taylor, 2001, p. 23) – are highly valued by many tourists. Similar to learning, interaction between tourists and residents represents social desirability rather than social practice (see Figure 4.3). In spite of this desirability, actual interaction between tourists and residents is extremely limited. This can be partly put down to practical reasons. Most organized visits are brief, visitors do not have time to interact. Moreover, communication and connection are hampered by language problems. Tour guides are needed as intermediaries. Spontaneous and artless interaction is difficult. Beyond practical explanations, there are some social and cultural ones. Not all residents are interested in interaction with tourists. Some 'hosts' boast a long tradition of hospitality, whereas others have a history of isolation or distrust of strangers. Obviously, interest in interaction is more probable when residents are in the phase of 'Euphoria' in Doxey's (1985) 'Irritation Index' or when destinations are in the stage of 'Exploration' of Butler's (1980) 'Tourist Area Cycle of Evolution' than when they are in other phases. In areas where tourism development is in Butler's stage of consolidation or stagnation, harassment of tourists by street vendors, masseuses, prostitutes and begging children might be the main form of interaction between tourists and residents. In these areas, tourists' interest in starting communication with local people might disappear completely. Even in early phases of tourism

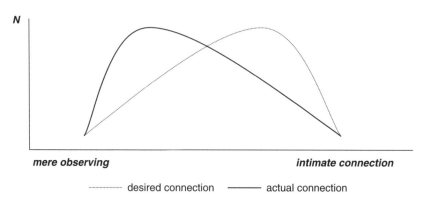

Fig. 4.3.   Hypothetical distribution of the desire to connect and actual practice.

development in destination areas, however, many tourists demonstrate a certain reluctance to interact when they are confronted with local life. Tour guides observe that only small proportions of their customers actually want to mingle with residents. Even when they visit a 'staged' village, many tourists appear to be hesitant or afraid of direct interaction ('They want to see the locals, but when you take them there, it is more like they don't feel comfortable there'). Moscardo and Pearce (1999), who studied tourism to Aboriginal communities in Australia, refer to an approach–avoidance conflict, where the stimulus to interact is strong but some unidentified fears keep the tourists from actual interaction. The nature of these fears has as yet been unexplored. Is it just because interaction is difficult? Is it because tourists feel embarrassed to demonstrate their wealth? Is it because tourists do not know how to bridge the difference between obviously distinct life-worlds? Is it because tourists are afraid that the romantic images they cherish will be affected by direct contact?

So, in spite of their expressed desire to connect with local people, the distribution of tourist behaviour on the dimension from mere observing to intimate connection clearly tends to be skewed to the first pole.

A fourth dimension relates to tolerance of 'staging' of authenticity. The term 'staged authenticity' has been coined by MacCannell (1973) to describe the artful presentation of contrived sites and sights as if they were authentic. The dimension ranges from indifference to staging at one pole to 'allergy' to staging at the other. Tourist attractions range from 'natural' attractions that are completely 'unmarked' (sites and sights which have not yet undergone any physical or symbolic intervention) to 'contrived' attractions, which are specifically created for touristic purposes and are wholly artificial in character (Cohen, 1995, p.15). Most respondents express a desire to see the 'real life', 'taste local culture', 'visit unspoilt places', i.e. they express a preference for 'natural' and

'unmarked' sites. 'Unspoilt' often has the connotation of 'not contaminated by other tourists or tourist facilities'. This desire is most urgent
among visitors of countries that are low in the destination hierarchy.
Moreover, it is more urgent among those who want to see themselves as
'travellers', as compared to conventional tourists. Rather than conventional tourists, 'travellers' tend to be 'allergic' to staging of local life and,
consequently, desire local culture to remain unchanged and in an
untouched state. Travellers with a low tolerance to 'staging', however, are
only a small minority. Although in academia, *authenticity* is a perennial
source of misconceptions, to be cast aside (Aramberri, 2001, p. 740), tourists eagerly engage in authenticity-talk and refer to it as something highly
valuable. Seeing 'authentic family life' is given a higher priority by many
than seeing ruins, museums or buildings. Authenticity, evidently, is not a
univocal concept among tourists. It appears to be 'negotiable' in Cohen's
(1988, p. 374) terms. All tourists are fully aware of their status as tourists.
They can easily cope with the paradoxes in their quest for 'real life' in
'staged' and 'contrived' conditions, as long as they – in the words of
Tucker (2001, p. 886) – 'are free to negotiate them and play with them'.
Playing is hindered when local 'hosts' start trying to sell commodities or
services to tourists or when guides pay the 'hosts' openly. Most of the
tourists studied in Chapter 3 – conventional tourists rather than 'travellers' – confirm Cohen's view (1995, p. 20) that tourists have a predisposition for playfulness, a predisposition to ludically (playfully) accept
'contrived' attractions as if they were real.

As a matter of fact, many aspects of real life in poor countries do not
appeal to most tourists at all. Grinding poverty, disabled beggars and
dirty and smelly streets without sewer systems represent forms of authenticity most tourists are definitely not searching for. For both conventional
and adventurous organized tourists, observing this part of 'authentic life' –
if observed at all – is limited to watching it through the windows of the
coach or minibus. Urry (2002, p. 150) refers to the 'spectatorial gaze'.

By their very nature, all tourist products and facilities (host families,
native shows, museums, craft shops, etc.) are staged or contrived, because
tour operators will arrange every single element of the trip in advance and
backpacker facilities will have been adapted for their target group. Most
tourists appear to be happy catching only incidental glimpses of 'real'
local life. For both organized tourists and backpackers, local markets that
are frequented by residents are popular spots for a stop, allowing the
tourists to smell the *couleur locale* informally. They are popular just
because they are not set up for tourists and allow interaction without
personal involvement or commitment.

So, the majority of respondents are eager to see 'real life' and visit
'unspoilt places', i.e. 'natural' and 'unmarked' sites and sights, not contaminated by other tourists. In practice, however, they visit 'staged' and

'contrived' sites, which are either created for tourists or adapted to tourists' tastes and comprehension. Tourists can easily cope with this paradoxical situation, as long as they are able to frame their own experiences and play-fully accept 'contrived' attractions as if they were real.

## 4.3   Life-worlds of 'Hosts' versus 'Guests' – an Intermezzo

> There was a slight smell of wood-smoke in the air, a smell that tugged at her heart, because it reminded her of her mornings around the fire in Mochudi. She would go back there, she thought, when she had worked long enough to retire. She would buy a house, or build one perhaps, and ask some of her cousins to live with her. They would grow melons on the lands and might even buy a small shop in the village; and every morning she could sit in front of her house and sniff at the wood-smoke and look forward to spending the day talking with her friends. How sorry she felt for white people, who could-n't do any of this, and who were always dashing around and worrying them-selves over things that were going to happen anyway. What use was it having all that money if you could never sit still or just watch your cattle eating grass? None, in her view; none at all, and yet they did not know it. Every so often you met a white person who understood, who realised how things really were; but these people were few and far between and the other white people often treated them with suspicion.
>
> (*The No.1 Ladies' Detective Agency* by Alexander McCall Smith, 1998, p. 160)

> Mma Ramotswe found it difficult to imagine what it would be like to have no people. There were, she knew, those who had no others in this life, who had no uncles, or aunts, or distant cousins of any degree; people who were *just themselves*. Many white people were like that, for some unfathomable reason; they did not seem to want to have people and were happy to be just them-selves. How lonely they must be – like spacemen deep in space, floating in the darkness, but without even that silver, unfurling cord that linked the astronauts to their little metal womb of oxygen and warmth.
>
> (*Tears of the Giraffe* by Alexander McCall Smith, 2000, p. 208)

The life-worlds of Western tourists ('guests') are probably fundamentally different from the life-worlds of residents ('hosts') in most of the areas visited, in rural areas in particular.

As far as organized tourists are concerned, several features of their behaviour might be unfamiliar to residents. Tight travel schedules, rest-less dashing around, voluntarily renouncing Western comfort, feelings of guilt or embarrassment when confronted with poverty, interest in local life, search for authenticity, etc., can be perceived by residents as wholly alien to their nature. For indigenous peoples, who have been disparaged and maltreated in their home countries through the years, European interest in their 'authentic life' might be difficult to understand. This interest, on the other hand, may be conducive to increasing self-respect and cultural awareness among these peoples. A lot of mutual personal investment is required from both 'host' and 'guest' to bridge the gap between their life-worlds. The very nature of organized round trips, however, prevents tourists from making in-depth investment in social interaction with residents.

The life-worlds of any type of backpackers are fundamentally different from the life-worlds of residents in most of the – often collectivistic – areas visited. Both hippies in the 1960s and 1970s and present-day students on temporary leave represent life-worlds that are difficult for local people to understand and that can easily lead to adverse reactions in destination areas. Travelling individually, not having any social or family obligations, renouncing Western comfort and wearing ripped clothes are among the features that can be perceived by residents as wholly alien to their nature. Loose sexual morality, use of drugs and petty theft are among the annoying features.

A lot of mutual personal investment is required for both parties to understand each other. Only a few backpackers are able and/or prepared to do so. Although their average length of stay in any destination area is long, compared to organized trips, most backpackers invest in social interaction with fellow-tourists rather than with residents.

Volunteers really want to connect with the people they have come to help. They are prepared to invest personally in getting close ties with these people, but the gap between the life-worlds of helpers and helped is huge. Not many residents will easily understand why Europeans, Americans or Australians from the developed world are prepared to pay handsome amounts of money to come and work with them, wanting to connect with poor rural people and voluntarily renouncing Western comfort.

Bridging the gap between the life-worlds of 'hosts' and 'guests' appears to be possible only when quite a few conditions are met (van Egmond, 1989, 2005):

- 'Host' and 'guest' must have time for each other. Casting a brief glance at village-dwellers is more like visiting a zoo than an encounter, provoking stereotyping from the people visited. A long stay close to one another, but in separate circuits (e.g. backpacker circuits), might entail 'having time', but not 'having time for each other'.
- Residents must be in control of their own situation. The loss of perceived control might result in helplessness, apathy, depression and adverse reactions towards tourists.
- Visitor and resident must be able to communicate with each other. The more 'exotic' the resident is, the smaller the possibility of verbal communication. Guides can play an important role as interpreters.

- 'Guest' and 'host' must have mutual interests and respect and must consider each other as equals. When tourists perceive the visited population as 'primitive', 'underdeveloped', 'pitiable', 'pathetic', 'innocent', etc., there is no equality. On the contrary, this perception is more conducive to stereotyping and paternalistic or neocolonial sentiments ('don't give them any money, or else they will get lazy', Dutch woman, in her sixties) than mutual understanding.
- Mutual respect and equality exclude partial or mutual exploitation. Abusing children for sexual purposes or using natives as 'camera fodder' are examples of one-sided exploitation, as are robbing or harassing tourists.
- Actual interaction between visitors and residents is only possible on a small scale. In social psychology, a group of 12 persons, visitors and residents together, is presumed to be the maximum for actual interaction.

Obviously, not many tourist–resident encounters meet these conditions.

## 4.4    A Classification of West–South Tourists

The conclusion of sections 4.2 and 4.3 is that tourists from the historically Protestant countries of Europe, who go to the South for holiday purposes, exhibit a great diversity of life-worlds, lifestyles and corresponding motivations, interests, preferences and behaviour. They are all trying to find a balance between the opposite poles on four dimensions.

An important finding is that considerable discrepancies can be identified between, on the one hand, the value systems of many of these tourists and their corresponding interests and expectations and, on the other hand, their actual behaviour.

The life-worlds of these tourists are probably fundamentally different from the life-worlds of residents ('hosts') in most of the areas visited, in rural areas in particular. So, on the one hand, tourists are interested in difference and 'otherness' but, on the other hand, it is difficult to bridge the gap between fundamentally different life-worlds, resulting in approach–avoidance conflicts for quite a few tourists and – perhaps – residents.

Destination areas have to deal with this great diversity of interests among tourists, as well as the discrepancies between social desirability and actual behaviour. In the process of planning and management of tourism, destinations have to cope with questions on which interests they are able to meet, which interests they are prepared to meet and how they can manage tourist behaviour, in order to optimize the desired benefits of tourism and minimize undesired impacts.

Chapter 5 will address the issue of planning for the 'right' tourists. For the sake of convenience tourists are roughly classified according to Table 4.1. Thus, organized tourists and backpackers are classified according

**Table 4.1.** A classification of West–South tourists.

|  | Organized Tourists | | |
|---|---|---|---|
| *'Accidental' Tourists* | *Mainstream Tourists* | *'Dedicated' Adventurers* | *'Hard core' Tourists* |
| • Arrive 'accidentally', e.g. excursion | • Destination is part of the package | • Destination is part of the package | • Purposefully chosen destination |
| • Exhibit a generalized curiosity | • Exhibit a generalized curiosity | • Exhibit a generalized curiosity | • Have specific interests |
| • Seek interesting experiences/ entertainment | • Seek decent and respectable cultivated pleasure | • Seek decent and respectable cultivated pleasure | • Seek gratification of specific interests and needs |
| • Go to tourism highlights | • Go to tourism highlights | • Want to go into 'depth' | • Want to go into 'depth' |
| • Not prepared to renounce comfort | • Some renounce comfort to some extent | • Renounce comfort – to some extent | • Renounce comfort to a large extent |
| • Have limited desire to learn and connect | • Express a great desire to learn and connect | • Express a great desire to learn and connect | • Express a great desire to learn and connect |
| • Are not/hardly interested in interaction | • Actual learning and interaction are very limited | • Actual learning and interaction are rather limited | • Actual learning and interaction are comparatively great |
| • Are indifferent towards 'authenticity' | • 'Authenticity' is important but highly negotiable | • 'Authenticity' is important and is hardly negotiable | • 'Authenticity' is important and is not negotiable |
| • Have shallow experiences | • Have shallow experiences | • Claim to have 'deep' experiences | • Claim to have 'deep' experiences |
| • Volumes are variable | • Biggest volumes | • Small volumes | • Negligible volumes |
| • Visits are short | • Visits are short | • Visits are comparatively long | • Visits are comparatively long |

(*Continued*)

**Table 4.1.** (Continued)

| | Backpackers | | |
|---|---|---|---|
| *'Hedonists'* | *Mainstream Backpackers* | *'Dedicated' Backpackers* | *'Pioneers'* |
| • Seek places 'where the action is' (parties) | • Stay on the beaten backpacker track | • Try to go off the beaten track | • Go outside the backpacker circuit |
| • Seek fun/excitement/drugs/sex | • Exhibit a generalized curiosity | • Exhibit a generalized curiosity | • Exhibit a generalized curiosity |
| • Go to the 'famous' places | • Visit places known from travel literature | • Go beyond 'must see' places | • Avoid 'tourist' places |
| • Not prepared to renounce comfort | • Renounce comfort – to a certain extent | • Renounce comfort – to a certain extent | • Temporarily renounce comfort completely |
| • Have no desire to learn or connect | • Express great desire to learn and connect | • Express a great desire to learn and connect | • Express a great desire to learn and connect |
| • Are not/hardly interested in interaction | • Actual learning and interaction are very limited | • Actual learning and interaction are comparatively great | • Actual learning and interaction greatest of all categories |
| • Are indifferent towards 'authenticity' | • 'Authenticity' is important but highly negotiable | • 'Authenticity' is important and hardly negotiable | • 'Authenticity' is important and not negotiable |
| • Have no experiences of culture or nature | • Have either shallow or 'deep' experiences | • Claim to have 'deep' experiences | • Claim to have 'deep' experiences |
| • Volumes depend upon destination | • Biggest volumes | • Small volumes | • Very small volumes |
| • Short-term backpackers | • Both short- and long-term backpackers | • Long-term backpackers mostly | • Long-term backpackers |

to their interests, their preferences for learning, interaction and connection with residents and authenticity, as well as their desire to renounce luxury and comfort. 'Accidental' versus 'hard core' tourists and 'hedonists' versus 'pioneers' do not have much in common. They have different, often opposite, needs and expectations and, consequently, they define the quality of their experiences in different terms. From left to right in Table 4.1, needs are increasingly specific, willingness to renounce comfort grows, and the desire to learn and connect with local people becomes more urgent. The more tourists tend to be 'dedicated' or even 'hard core' or 'pioneer', the less tolerant they are of staged authenticity, specific 'tourist things', and coming across other tourists. Obviously, 'dedicated' adventurers, 'dedicated' backpackers, 'hard-core' tourists and 'pioneers' consider themselves 'travellers' rather than 'tourists'.

The category 'accidental' is an adaptation of the 'casual' or 'incidental' tourists described by McKercher (2002), Lindberg (1991) and Weaver (1999). They are identified in this classification as visitors making excursions to culture or nature sites from the beach resorts or cities they are staying in. Their numbers vary per destination. For example, many national parks in Costa Rica are within easy reach from quite a few beach resorts, as well as from San José, the capital. Consequently, the majority of visitors can be identified as 'accidental' visitors. Remote sites, i.e. sites that are far away from the major tourist circuits, on the other hand, are not visited by 'accidental' tourists at all.

Adventurous tourists often claim to be 'dedicated' tourists. Many adventurous trips, however, can not be distinguished objectively from mainstream tourism. Consequently, 'dedicated' tourists and adventurous tourists do not coincide. Adventurous tourists are partly ascribed to the category of mainstream tourists and partly to 'dedicated' tourists. The volunteers that have been described in Chapter 3 fit into the latter category.

Concentration of tourists varies greatly per category. In the early 21st century, coastal areas of Thailand were the place to be for 'hedonists' (as this research was conducted in 2004, the impacts of the unprecedented disaster of December 2004 could not be taken into account). By definition, mainstream tourists are concentrated in tourist circuits along the highlights of a destination country. 'Dedicated' tourists prefer to go off the beaten track, but they still visit the highlights. 'Hard-core' tourists and 'pioneers' are the most dispersed tourists, consciously avoiding the tourist circuits. For destination areas their quantities are often negligible.

## 4.5 Towards Cross-cultural Comparative Studies

The findings and conclusions of the previous chapters and sections concern Europeans from the historically Protestant countries who travel to the South. These chapters and sections give an account of the motivations, interests, preferences and behaviour of these tourists. They do not give a decisive answer to the question why other types of tourism (e.g. beach tourism, adventure tourism, camping, winter sports) are popular among these Europeans. Nor do they explain why travel markets – predominantly domestic – are emerging in Southern and Eastern Europe, East and South Asia and other parts of the world. Most probably, tourists who do not stem from countries where a Protestant ethic and a romantic movement have been extremely influential do not exhibit the same life-worlds, lifestyles, distinctive preferences and behaviour as the tourists studied in Chapter 3. In the words of Robinson (1999, p. 22): 'Out of the world's 6000 cultures relatively few are seekers of difference through the tourism process'.

Some selected examples suggest clear differences between 'Western' tourists on the one hand and Japanese, Chinese or Muslim tourists on the other. This is also suggested of domestic tourists in the South.

## Differences between 'Western' and 'non-Western' tourists

- Japanese tourism has certain characteristics which differentiate it from the tourism of the contemporary West. To most Japanese, nature is boring to contemplate, dangerous to enter, and far removed from everyday life, rather than subject to romantic interest and admiration (Graburn, 1995, p. 62). It is only appreciated when it is strictly controlled, and when it is 'naturally' represented and miniaturized (e.g. in bonsai and gardens), and socially approved for perusal (and photography) at the right seasons (p. 62).
- Similarly, Lindberg *et al.* (2003, p. 119) argue that Eastern cultures, including Chinese, tend to favour human manipulation of nature in order to enhance its appeal, in contrast to preservation in a pristine state. The Chinese image of natural landscapes is, according to these authors, nurtured by cultural sources such as poems and paintings rather than the search for 'unspoilt paradise'.
- Although most Western tourists in the South travel in groups, yearning for 'solitude' has been referred to in Chapter 2 as characteristic of Protestant middle-class mental programmes. Being alone in nature – or even 'paradise'– and having personal spiritual nature experiences are highly valued. Individual travellers of the pioneer-type are the role models for many in the West. In collectivistic 'Non-Western' societies individual travel is not highly valued. 'Rarely does anyone [Japanese] go anywhere alone, and loneliness, especially "in nature", is to be feared above almost anything else in life' (Graburn, 1995, p. 64). Enjoyment of nature stems more from sociality than from personal spiritual experiences. According to Kim and Lee (2000, p. 157),

opportunities for unplanned action and freedom from institutional-ized regulations are distinctive characteristics of the Western tourists. On the other hand, people in collectivistic cultures think of them-selves less as individuals and more as being members of some group. A long vacation away from the group means painful separation and a danger to mental well-being. Group interaction, which is closely associated with dependence on others to provide satisfaction in the experience, is also an important component of the tourism experience.

Perceptions of crowding may also vary across cultures. Lindberg *et al.* (2003, p. 119) demonstrate that the level of crowding in nature reserves in China is much more tolerable to Chinese visitors than to Western visitors.

- Japanese nostalgic tradition resembles present Western interest in cul-tural heritage at first sight, but is a tradition as old as Japan itself (Graburn, 1995, p. 67). According to Graburn, this backward looking search reflects a millennia-old search for identity, because Japan, as a peripheral island nation, has had constantly to redefine its identity vis-à-vis China, Korea and the outside world. Japanese cultural and heritage tourism consequently focuses on historical creations such as shrines, temples, castles, gardens, festivals, etc. rather than indige-nous peoples.

- Graburn's findings are consistent with a survey of Japanese outbound tourism by the US Travel and Tourism Administration (in Andersen *et al.*, 2000, p. 132). In this survey, culture and history were ranked as higher *pull* factors than wilderness. A further study by the Japanese Government (p. 132) identified overseas travel as primarily domi-nated by a desire to see aesthetic landscape and historical sites, rather than travel to understand local cultures.

- Muslims share a tradition of ascetic abstinence with Puritans. For Muslims, 'profligate consumption and all forms of excessive indul-gence are prohibited' (Din, 1989, p. 552). While the Puritan ethic is presumed to be at the basis of Western modern consumer culture – characterized by a morality of pleasure as a duty – Islam deemphasizes pleasure and hedonistic pursuits characteristic of modern tourism and enjoins genuine, humane, equitable and reciprocal cross-cultural communication (p. 554). Islamic states – Arab states in particular – take pride in distancing themselves from the hedonism and self-indulgence Western tourism is felt to represent (Aziz, 2001, p. 158). Rather than a relaxing and invigorating experience, travelling in Islam is viewed as '. . . a trying task which subjects individuals to the tests of patience and perseverance' (Din, 1989, p. 552). Because travelling is a task (cul-minating in the *Haj*), Muslims are asked to always assist the traveller and treat him with compassion. Travelling in order to satisfy a generalized curiosity and have interesting personal experiences does not fit into Muslim tradition. Travelling alone does not fit either. Individual female travellers are at odds with Muslim religion, as many European female backpackers have experienced in Muslim countries.

- A study by Ryan (2002) demonstrates that interest in indigenous Maori culture in New Zealand is mainly limited to Northern Europeans and North Americans. The Asian markets – the most important markets for New Zealand in terms of arrivals and expenditures – are not seemingly interested in Maori culture. Nonetheless they seem to appreciate the stage performances which they attend (p. 966). Tourism products based on Maori culture are also unappealing to the domestic *pakeha* (non-Maori New Zealanders) society (p. 964). When non-Maori New Zealanders visit Maori sites, rarely have they been born in New Zealand, and most commonly they are migrants from Northern Europe (p. 965). Natives will lose their romantic appeal when they become part of our day-to-day lives.

- Quite a few studies demonstrate that domestic tourists in developing countries have little interest in nature and ethnic tourism, e.g.: Ghimire, 2001 (general); Barkin, 2001 (Mexico); Diegues, 2001 (Brazil); Rao and Suresh, 2001 (India); Kaosa-ard *et al.*, 2001 (Thailand); Vogels, 2002 (India); Iversen, 2003 (Vietnam); De Groot, 2004 (Namibia); Loman, 2005 (Peru); Kuja, 2005 (Cameroon). In most countries, VFR ('visiting friends and relatives'), religious tourism to sacred sites and (small) business tourism are important types of domestic tourism. VFR tourism is widely dispersed, reflecting the reverse direction of historical migration patterns, and does not coincide with the existing leisure-related tourism circuit. Leisure-related tourism is limited to higher income groups and is much more focused upon leisure facilities – both in the cities and in rural areas – than rural nature and culture. Visits to rural areas are motivated by the desire to escape crowded and polluted city life and picnic with the family rather than the desire to enjoy nature or get in touch with rural communities. Obviously, wilderness and rural communities are places to avoid rather than enjoy.

Asians are not beach-minded. In South Africa and Latin America beach tourism is popular, but among inhabitants of European descent, not among indigenous peoples.

Comparing domestic Chinese tourists to foreigners, Walsh and Swain (2004, p. 66) conclude that (European and North American) foreigners are frequently disappointed by what they perceive as commercialization and development, while Chinese do not categorically dismiss progress as negative. Fewer Chinese seem to expect a completely untouched paradise. According to Walsh and Swain, 'Chinese tourists are "more sophisticated" in that many accept that minority areas, like others, change and that cultural displays at tourist sites are performed for tourists' (p. 66).

North Americans, Australians and New Zealanders are part of the 'Western' world. These countries were influenced by migrants and their Protestant ethic from the historically Protestant countries of Europe. They appear to be part of the Western modern consumer culture, with its concomitant fun morality, generalized curiosity, 'experience hunger' and restless drive to seek novelty. Unfortunately, the research presented in Chapter 3 does not allow any comparison between North Americans, Australians and New Zealanders on the one hand and Northern Europeans on the other. The research among organized tourists included a very limited number of American respondents (nine interviews, 14 interviewees) and no respondents from 'down under'. The tour guides who have been interviewed are quite consistent in their perception of Americans as more demanding, more direct and more 'McDonaldized' than Europeans. The latter are perceived as better prepared while travelling and more eager to learn. According to these guides, Americans are not really interested in indigenous communities, although they all say they want to see 'the real life'. Visitors to community projects are mostly European.

The research among backpackers suggests that the number of North American backpackers is small in comparison to Northern Europeans. Outside the backpacker enclaves, North Americans are uncommon.

The selected examples are far from being conclusive. Rather than ignoring cultural differences between tourists and bringing different cases under the same heading, it appears an interesting challenge to start cross-cultural comparative studies.

A wide field is open for further exploration.

# Planning for the 'Right' Tourists

**5**

## 5.1 Introduction

The findings of the previous chapters lead to far-reaching strategic and practical conclusions concerning the process of tourism planning in developing countries that want to maximize the desired benefits from tourism and minimize the undesired impacts. Destinations must ask themselves which types of tourism are desirable and preferable and which are feasible, given the prevailing conditions. Beyond that, they must decide, in practical terms, how to set about them.

Strategic conclusions relate to macro-level policymaking, planning and promotion in destination countries. Practical conclusions relate to product development, visitor management and marketing at the meso and micro level.

With a few exceptions only, developing countries exert themselves to develop tourism in order to generate foreign exchange earnings, income and employment, to diversify the economy, and raise the standard of living in as many regions as possible. Moreover, tourism is often conceived as a powerful tool for the protection and preservation of nature and culture. Many countries have formulated a Tourism Master Plan, a Strategic Tourism Plan, a National (Eco)Tourism Strategy, or other tourism development plans, that reflect their ambitions. However, virtually none of these plans specifies which types of tourism have to be promoted, in order to achieve the desired goals. Numerous guidebooks are available for national authorities and local planners – e.g. *Tourism and Poverty Alleviation, Recommendations for Action* (WTO, 2004), *Guide for Local Authorities on*

*Developing Sustainable Tourism* (WTO), *Ecotourism Development, A Manual for Conservation Planners and Managers* (Drum and Moore, 2002), but they do not discuss which types of tourism will bring along the desired rather than undesired impacts, nor do they specify how the 'right' tourists should be addressed and attracted. Tourists seem to be taken for granted or 'as broad a range of tourists as possible should be attracted'. The present chapter argues that understanding tourists' motivations, interests, preferences and behaviour, and, subsequently, planning for the most preferred types of tourism and tourists are basic requirements for destination areas to reach their goals. In recent years this position has been supported by several publications:

- 'Sound decisions by Third World governments as to what type of tourism is most conducive to development . . . can only be based on a differentiated analysis' (Theuns, 2002, p. 79).
- 'Positive developmental impact can be enhanced by differentiating between types of tourism, and then assessing and adapting them with respect to local livelihoods' (Ashley, 1998, p. 344).
- 'If ethnic groups seek to use tourism to their advantage, it is important to find out whether they understand how potential markets are likely to respond to the products that they develop' (Moscardo and Pearce, 1999, p. 431).
- 'Knowledge of experiences can be used to make the product suitable for the preferred experiences of the actual visitors' (Elands and Lengkeek, 2000, p. 79).

First, however, this chapter argues that the dominant concepts used in international tourism discourse – such as ecotourism, sustainable tourism, 'dark green' environmentalism, ethnic tourism, and search for authenticity – are actually Western Protestant middle-class concepts. Many tourism development plans of Third World countries are written or supported by Western consultants. The question arises whether or not developing countries can implement these Western concepts and Western tourist practices without reserve.

## 5.2  Understanding Tourism Concepts

The previous chapters discussed tourists from 'Western' countries (i.e. the historically Protestant countries of Europe and, to a lesser extent, North America and Australia), visiting the South (i.e. Latin America, Asia or Africa). The overwhelming majority of backpackers originates from these Western countries (see section 3.3). Organized tourists from the West also constitute a disproportionate amount of international tourists.

Among the common characteristics of tourists from the West is an interest in exotic, 'unspoilt', 'authentic' nature and culture. This interest is presumed to be rooted in their Protestant and romantic tradition. Whether or not such an interest is also characteristic of tourists from other parts of the world has not been an object of study in these chapters. This is consistent with the notion that 'the motivations of many South American, Arab, African, Indian, or non-English-speaking Europeans are hardly known at all internationally' (Prentice, 2004, p. 276). Nevertheless, the selected examples mentioned in section 4.4 demonstrate clear differences between 'Western' and 'non-Western' tourists.

## Ethnic tourism and ecotourism

These examples suggest that Northern Europeans and – perhaps – North Americans and Australians are the most important target groups for both ethnic tourism and ecotourism. They also suggest that 'dedicated' tourists, 'hard-core' tourists and 'pioneers' are exceptional or non-existent in the newly emerging Asian markets. The latter appear to be devoted to mainstream tourism rather than less conventional types of tourism.

Ethnic tourism can be distinguished from cultural tourism in general. The latter involves exposure to a culture in an indirect way (e.g. museums, visitor centres, souvenir shops), while ethnic tourism involves first-hand experiences with the practices of indigenous cultures (Wood, 1984). It presupposes a kind of direct interaction between 'guests' and 'hosts'. It is the Northern European market, rather than Asian, African or Latin American markets, that is interested in direct interaction and having a glimpse of 'real' local life, although – as is demonstrated in the previous chapters – there is a considerable discrepancy between social desirability and social practice. It is this market that is primarily concerned in authenticity issues.

If the interest in indigenous peoples concerns Northern Europeans first and foremost, the implications for the development of tourism to the South are considerable. Whereas the proportion of European tourists is limited, the regions and communities in the South that like to welcome tourists as a means of alleviating prevailing poverty are numerous. 'Fishing from the same limited pond' makes destinations highly competitive. The reality is that quite a number of community-based rural projects, focused on receiving tourists and thus contributing to local poverty alleviation, do not manage to earn back their investments, let alone make profits, considering the fact that domestic tourism in virtually every country in the South can be ignored as a source of visits and income to local indigenous communities. 'Fishing from the same pond of Europeans' requires defining which group or groups are best suited to the local conditions and using the scarce marketing tools effectively to reach and serve these groups.

Although 'ecotourism' is a widely-used concept nowadays, there is a great variety in definitions and, consequently, a lack of consensus on its precise meaning. Moreover, several definitions are value-based rather than operational, as is the case in the frequently cited definition of The International Ecotourism Society (TIES): 'responsible travel to nature areas which conserves the environment and improves the welfare of local people' (www.ecotourism.org). Core criteria of ecotourism which recur in most definitions are: a nature-based element, an educational or learning component, and requirements of sustainability (Weaver, 2001, p. 7). Among these requirements are: contributions to the conservation of nature and welfare of local people in destination areas. Seen like this, ecotourism has a distinctly 'Protestant' connotation, as will be explained shortly, and it goes without saying that the interest in 'unspoilt' nature, nature conservation, learning about nature and contribution to the development of local communities can predominantly be found in Northern European and – perhaps – North American and Australian markets. Nature areas, national parks in particular, which are not far from urban centres in developing countries are frequently visited by a huge flow of domestic visitors. The lack of awareness among these visitors concerning environmental problems, however, results in serious damage to the local ecosystems (e.g. Kaosa-ard *et al.*, 2001, p. 138). Visits like these cannot be regarded as ecotourism according to the core criteria mentioned earlier in this section. Domestic interest in wilderness tourism is of rather limited importance in most countries in the South. Remote nature areas are predominantly dependent on Northern European tourists. In this case again it is true that the proportion of European tourists is limited and that the number of regions and nature areas trying to attract nature-minded tourists in order to either preserve nature or generate income and jobs for their inhabitants has grown overwhelmingly. Again, the pond is too small for all.

## Ecotourism and 'dark green' environmentalism as Protestant concepts

Vogel (2001) draws a distinction between 'dark green' countries and 'light green' countries. In the first type of countries, environmental politics and policies are more likely to express an environmental ethic:

> One which encompasses but goes beyond domestic health, safety and amenity concerns. By contrast, in the latter type of countries, environmental politics and policies tend to be more instrumental; they are more likely to represent responses to clearly defined threats to domestic public health.
>
> (Vogel, 2001, p. 6)

A defining characteristic of dark green countries is that public concern about environmental issues is *not* a response to the environmental problems that affect their daily lives; citizens tend to define their interest more broadly. They are more likely to regard the environment as being in a state of crisis. In light green countries the environmental agenda is more limited and narrowly focused. Public interest in environmental issues tends to be episodic rather than sustained and the salience of these issues varies considerably over time. According to Vogel (p. 8), dark green countries are the historically Protestant countries of Europe (including Austria, a Catholic country with – according to Inglehart *et al.*, 1998 – dominant Protestant values), as well as North America and Australia. Light green countries, on the other hand, are the traditionally Catholic countries in Southern Europe and Confucian countries of Asia.

Vogel points to a number of suggestive affinities between Protestantism and aspects of dark green environmental ethic (2001, pp. 27–30). First, both share an essentially apocalyptic vision: if we continue our present behaviour and values, the world will be doomed. Second, an ascetic discipline finds a contemporary expression in recycling. 'Waste not, want not' becomes 'reduce, reuse, recycle'. Third, modern dark green environmental rhetoric is filled with moral judgements; hence the passion and sense of urgency which is more likely to characterize environmental discourse in dark green countries. By contrast, in non-Protestant cultures citizens talk about the environment less, and in less moralistic terms. Fourth, the Protestant concept of *stewardship* finds its contemporary expression in environmental politics, which hold each individual responsible for 'meeting the needs of the present generations without compromising the ability of future generations to meet their own needs' (Brundtland, 1987). Fifth, the notion that nature has rights is most influential in Protestant, dark green countries. The rights of whales, tigers and rainforests imply a moral obligation for any citizen to protect them. Finally, Protestantism, precisely because it tends to be relatively devoid of rituals and symbols, may be especially conducive to the notion that nature can, or should, have spiritual significance. Here Protestantism and Romanticism meet.

Vogel (2001, p. 32) points to the irony in the assertion that Protestantism has facilitated a dark green mode of environmentalism. Western civilization has been associated with the subjugation of nature.

> By contrast, Asian religions, in particular Shintoism, Buddhism and Hinduism, have frequently been associated with the idea that people are not separate from or superior to nature. They claim that all forms of life – natural as well as human – are or should be revered equally. Yet people in rich countries whose heritage includes the former ethic have proven considerably 'greener' than those whose cultures have been shaped by the latter.
>
> (Vogel, 2001, p. 32)

Vogel finds one possible explanation in the emphasis in Protestant-ism on the very concept of mastery: 'if one believes that control or mas-tery of the world is possible, one can just as readily choose to save or restore nature as dominate or exploit it.' In the words of Giddens (quoted by Vogel): 'Mastery of nature . . . can quite often mean caring for nature as much as treating it in a purely instrumental or indifferent fash-ion'. Whereas local populations in developing countries may have used ecosystems in sustainable ways, with resource-use systems – owing to their complexity – frequently operating beyond Western understanding, conservation is basically a Western concept, based on the notion that many ecosystems can only be sustained in protected areas (Gössling, 2002, p. 548).

Ecotourism, as dealt with in recent tourism literature, reflects this Western Protestant ethic pre-eminently. It celebrates the spiritual signifi-cance of nature and solitude, stresses the personal moral obligation to pro-tect both nature and inhabitants of nature through conservation, and aims at conserving resources for future generations. It is associated with the protection of ecologically valuable habitats, reduction of water and energy use, use of local materials for construction of accommodation ('eco-cabins', 'eco-lodges'), and prevention and reduction of waste. Western ecotourists, as studied in Chapter 3, are very sensitive to deforestation, perceived loss of animal habitat, litter, human waste and vandalism. They fre-quently complain about inhabitants of tourism destinations who do not take care of these matters and do not have the right attitudes towards the environment.

Acott *et al.* (1998) draw a distinction between 'deep ecotourists' and 'shallow ecotourists'. For the latter, nature is valued according to its usefulness to humans. The environment is seen as a resource which can be exploited to maximize the benefits to humans (p. 244). 'Deep eco-tourism' encapsulates a range of ideas which (among other things) include the importance of intrinsic value in nature, emphasis on small-scale travel, participation of local communities in tourism devel-opment, and (temporarily) renouncing luxury (p. 245). Deep eco-tourists are first and foremost found among Westerners who are strongly influenced by the Protestant ethic, particularly among Western 'dedicated' tourists.

## Sustainable tourism development as a Protestant concept

The 'Brundtland Report' *Our Common Future* (1987) reflects Protestant values such as stewardship, individual moral responsibility for the fate of future generations, the need to protect and preserve the resources of the earth, etc. Sustainable development in these terms is a Western concept.

The definition of sustainable tourism development that is adopted by the World Tourism Organization is based on the 'Brundtland' definition:

> Sustainable tourism development meets the needs of present tourists and host regions while protecting and enhancing opportunity for the future. It is envisaged as leading to management of all resources in such a way that economic, social and aesthetic needs can be fulfilled while maintaining cultural integrity, essential ecological processes, biological diversity and life support systems.
>
> (www.world-tourism.org)

According to the WTO, sustainable tourism should:

> Operate in harmony with the local environment, communities and cultures, so that these become permanent beneficiaries and not victims of tourism development.
>
> (www.world-tourism.org)

The WTO definition is commonly translated into finding a balance between the three Ps of People, Planet and Profit.

Virtually all tourism development plans in developing countries (as well as developed countries!) refer to sustainable tourism development as something highly desirable or self-evident. Rarely is the Western bias of this concept the subject of discussion or debate. Literature on tourism is dominated by academics working essentially to 'Western' discourses (Prentice, 2004, p. 276). Through the World Tourism Organization, United Nations Development Programme, United Nations Environment Programme, European Union, World Bank, regional development banks, NGOs for nature protection, NGOs for development aid, national ministries, etc., Western authors, consultants, trainers, teachers and development-aid workers are implementing essentially Western concepts such as sustainable tourism and ecotourism in non-Western countries. Thus Third World tourism has created a huge range of job opportunities for the new middle classes in the First World (Mowforth and Munt, 2nd edition, 2003, p. 127). To be effective, these concepts should at least be applied practically in the local conditions (see the case study of Bali). Tourism trainers and consultants should be able to take national and local destination perspectives as a starting point of their professional activities. They should be able to distance themselves from the moral debate concerning the most appropriate way of holidaying, which is primarily a Western, First World debate. This debate is, according to Mowforth and Munt (p. 26), highly polarized and simplified, equating to 'tourists = mass tourism = bad' and 'travellers = appropriate travelling = good'. The following section will argue that this simplistic view from a First World perspective is not effective.

**Bali**

In 2004, Dutch consultants, sponsored by the Dutch Ministry of Environment, cooperated with stakeholders from both public and private sector in the Indonesian island of Bali to create 'a toolkit to develop and promote sustainable tourism in Asia' (CREM, 2004). They used to employ the Western People–Planet–Profit concept of sustainable tourism development that aims at finding a balance between these three elements. The Balinese, however, have a different concept of sustainable tourism development, *Tri Hita Karana* (THK), that aims at finding a balance between the social environment ('*pawongan*'), the spiritual environment ('*parhyangan*'), and the natural environment ('*palemahan*') (van Aart, 2004, p. 62). This concept is deeply rooted in Balinese Hinduism. In recent years, a 'THK Award and Certification Programme' has been launched to promote sustainable practice in the Balinese accommodation sector. Comparison of the THK criteria with the checklist of the European tour operator TUI revealed a great difference, THK stressing the social and spiritual elements, TUI stressing the environmental ('planet') elements. Discussing sustainable tourism development appeared to be effective only from the Balinese THK perspective.

## Challenges for tourism education

Universities and other institutions – both in the West and South – that aim at educating and training consultants, teachers and trainers, face the challenge of taking national and local destination perspectives as a starting point of their educational activities. Students should be enabled to conduct fieldwork in destination areas to learn about local perspectives and put tourism concepts and tools into practice in the local conditions. Competencies to make destination analyses in terms of a stakeholder analysis, resource analysis, demand analysis and impact analysis, as well as competencies to develop visions, goals and strategies to bring about tourism that meets the needs of both host regions and selected types of tourists are essential ingredients of any programme. If anything, consultants, teachers and trainers should learn how to assess the tourism potential of a destination area, not only in terms of institutional development and availability of resources but even more so in terms of market potential.

To sum up, concepts such as sustainable tourism development, ethnic tourism, ecotourism, conservation of ecosystems in protected areas – although used in tourism development plans all over the world – are essentially Western Protestant concepts. Rarely is the Western bias of these concepts the subject of discussion or debate. These concepts are distributed by Western consultants through a multitude of international organizations, as well as national ministries and NGOs. For these concepts to be effective, tourism consultants and trainers should be able to take national and local destination perspectives as a starting point of their professional activities and put tourism concepts and tools into practice under local conditions.

## 5.3    Planning for the 'Right' Tourists

### Planning for desired economic benefits

For sustainable tourism development to 'meet the needs of host regions', these needs should be identifiable and unequivocal. Unfortunately, not much is known about them. Commonly they are defined in general economic terms such as (additional) income and employment, without any specification. According to Theuns (2002, p. 79), the traditional economic impact assessment concentrates on the tourism sector as if tourism were monolitic and not differentiated into several types. What is needed instead is a differential economic impact assessment for each relevant type of tourism. A contribution from tourism to a country's GDP does not necessarily imply a contribution to local or regional economic development. For tourism to be a tool for the latter, specification of the impacts of tourist expenditures, in terms of additional local income and employment, is necessary per type of tourism. Planning for tourism should start with the following questions: What economic benefits are desirable? For whom (Treasury, the poor, domestic entrepreneurs, transnational companies)? Who/what types of tourists are supposed to provide these benefits? Is it feasible to plan for these types of tourists? If so, how?

The economic revenues for the destination country or area may vary substantially per type of tourism. The hypothetical cases in Boxes 1 to 8 in Appendix B suggest that the net income for destination countries is highest from organized adventurous tourism ('dedicated' adventurers), followed by mainstream backpacker tourism. When the comparatively long stay of 'dedicated' backpackers and 'pioneers' (several months to more than 1 year) is taken into account, the net income is highest from these types of tourism.

The luxury segment of mainstream organized tourism yields the highest tax revenues for the Treasury. Backpacker tourism, particularly the 'dedicated' and 'pioneer' types, yields the lowest tax revenues, as much backpacker money is spent in the informal economic sector, including unregistered accommodation. This is one of the possible explanations of the popularity of 'big spenders' among governments, as opposed to low-spending backpackers.

Organized adventurous tourism ('dedicated' adventurers) still yields the highest net income revenues for local and regional economies in destination countries, followed by mainstream backpacker tourism. Boxes 1 to 8 in Appendix B suggest that there is a more or less ex aequo ranking for 'accidental' tourism, mainstream low-priced package tourism, mainstream luxury tourism and 'dedicated' backpacker tourism. 'Hedonist' and 'pioneer' tourism generates the lowest income, but – once more – when the comparatively long stay of 'dedicated' backpackers and 'pioneers' is taken into account, these three types of tourism produce the highest net income. Luxury tourists spend handsome amounts of money, but leakage mechanisms mounting up to an estimated 80 per cent are responsible for limited net revenues in regional economies. 'Dedicated' types of tourists and 'pioneers', as well as – to a lesser extent – mainstream backpackers, prefer (cheap) local goods to imported goods and locally-owned facilities with some specific *couleur locale*, to foreign-owned standardized facilities. Their expenditures, consequently, do not leak away much from the region and bring along greater economic dynamics in terms of income multiplier effects than other types of tourism. The most lucrative type of tourists are students who stay with local families for several weeks or months to study the local language (often Spanish) or conduct their field research. Their expenditures are hardly subject to leakage. When the days spent with the family add up to several months, these students turn out to be the most lucrative tourists (see Box 9, Appendix B).

These findings confirm that lower multipliers are associated with highly concentrated large-scale, foreign-owned tourism complexes, while higher multipliers are connected to more dispersed, smaller-scale – often unclassified – locally-owned operations that tend to be better linked to the local economy (Brohman, 1996, p. 56; Hampton, 1998, p. 652).

The relatively low daily expenditure of backpackers is not only compensated for by a long average length of stay, but also by a distribution of their spending over a wider geographical area. To a somewhat lesser extent, this holds also true for adventurous organized tourists, including volunteers. Outside the circuit of tourism highlights, these types of tourists may provide much more local income than the mainstream types, including luxury tourists, 'hedonists' and 'accidental' tourists. For communities in rural areas outside the established tourism circuit, these types of tourists may be the only possible options. Remote rural areas, that are far from both backpacker and organized adventurous tourist circuits and are not recommended as 'must see' attractions in tourism literature, do not have any options, except for some 'pioneers'.

During the off-season, i.e. outside the holiday season in the generating countries, long-term backpackers, not being bound by the seasonality of tourism, may provide the only relatively steady source of income.

'Dedicated' tourists, rather than mainstream, can be served by small local entrepreneurs with little investment capital or training and without formal qualifications. These types of tourists, rather than other types, are conducive to local ownership of facilities and local control, and, in the end, to empowerment of local communities in upholding their interests and negotiating with outside bodies (Scheyvens, 2002, p. 152). Stimulating local entrepreneurship in tourism by national and regional authorities, as well as NGOs, can be considered a low-cost strategy of economic and social development. 'The payback is very large relative to each unit of government [or NGO] assistance, whether such assistance is in the form of training entrepreneurs or the provision of low interest loans' (Echtner, 1995, p. 123). Activities that require low initial investment are small-scale accommodation (homestay, bed and breakfast, guesthouse), food and beverage service (small cafes, bars, tea stalls, food stalls, restaurants), selling handicraft (either from home or a small shop), short distance shuttle/ transportation service, tours of the local area, rentals (sporting equipment, bicycles), souvenir stalls or shops, folk entertainment, opportunities for tourists to observe local activities (production of handicraft, pottery, baskets, etc.) and opportunities for tourists to participate in local festivals and activities (id).

Mainstream tourism, on the other hand – luxury tourism more than lower-priced tourism – requires big investment of both public and private sector in infrastructure, accommodation and facilities that meet international standards. These investments increase the country's dependency upon foreign capital and are conducive to growth of leakage (see Appendix B for sources of leakage).

Employment impacts per type of tourism are an unexplored field. Rodenburg's research in Bali (1980) is still the most frequently cited source. According to him, employees in large-scale tourism properties receive higher average salaries than those in small operations, but the benefits are highly concentrated in the enclave rather than dispersed throughout the local economy. Increasing size of industrial tourism actually employs more labour per room than smaller operations. In Bali, the largest hotels employed 2 per room, 'homestay' accommodation 0.47 per room. In the small-scale informal accommodation sector, however, quite a few unpaid family members should also be taken into account. Many employees in large-scale accommodation are from other parts of the country. Small-scale tourism does not result in the employment of large numbers of people.

This raises the question of the type of job opportunities created by tourism, such as the difference between a cleaner in a large international hotel compared with being the owner of a small *losmen*, cooking and serving at tables in their own place (Hampton, 1998, p. 650). Labour recruited from elsewhere is presumed to contribute more to diminishing local control than local ownership.

To conclude, both independently travelling tourists and organized adventurous tourists are often overlooked by governments and tourism bodies because the income they bring is usually not taken as seriously as that derived from mainstream mass groups. However, organized adventurous tourism and backpacker tourism, it is argued in this section, bring along the highest net income revenues for local and regional economies as far as spending per person is concerned. This holds particularly true when the average length of stay is taken into account. Moreover, expenditures of organized adventurous tourists – including volunteers – and backpackers are distributed over a wider geographical area than those of mainstream organized tourists, 'accidental' tourists or 'hedonists'. Outside the circuit of tourism highlights, these types of tourists may provide much more local income than the mainstream types. For communities in remote rural areas outside the established tourism circuit these types may be the only possible options. They are more conducive to local ownership of facilities and local control than mainstream types of tourism. Stimulating local entrepreneurship by authorities or NGOs as a low-cost strategy of economic and social development should go hand in hand with stimulating these types of tourism.

## The competitiveness of destinations in the South

The competitive position of developing countries on the European market differs per type of tourism. Northern, Western and Central Europeans tend to visit destinations only once. Having seen one country, they easily turn to another. Destinations constitute a hierarchical order per type of tourism. Individual travel careers commonly develop top-down. Among organized European tourists who are preparing for their first long-haul trip to the South, Thailand is the most preferred country, at least in the early 21st century. Its neighbour Laos is much lower in the destination hierarchy. Competition between destinations takes place on the horizontal level rather than the vertical one. This competition is worldwide. Consumers who are making decisions where to go can take destinations in all three continents in the South into consideration. Thailand is not a competitor to its neighbouring countries but rather an opportunity. The popularity of Vietnam, Cambodia, Laos and – to a certain extent – Myanmar/ Burma is rising due to the fact that, by now, many people appreciate Thailand and want to see more of South–east Asia.

On the mainstream backpacker market, the hierarchy is slightly different, although Thailand is also the top destination in the developing world on this market. 'Dedicated' tourists, both organized and unorganized, prefer destinations that are low in the destination hierarchy. They commonly constitute well-travelled tourists who have already visited the 'must see' countries. 'Pioneers' prefer unexplored countries and areas. They have been the first to appear in Vietnam, Cambodia, Ethiopia, Guatemala and Mozambique after the end of the wars in these countries. They are destined to pave the way for 'dedicated' tourists, who, in their turn, pave the way for mainstream tourists.

When planning for the 'right' tourists, one should take the competitive position of the destination on the desired market into consideration. Given the prevailing conditions, Laos, Cambodia, Angola, Cameroon, Ethiopia, Mozambique, Bolivia, Nicaragua and many other countries can only aim at the 'dedicated' types of tourists, as well as some 'hard-core' tourists and 'pioneers'. Destinations that are high in the hierarchy might aim at the whole range of tourists. They might consider concentrating on mainstream tourists, 'accidental' tourists and 'hedonists' in specific tourist areas in order to manage the big flows of visitors effectively and spread the other types to more remote areas in order to contribute to regional economic development.

Tourists from the West who visit destinations in the South generally first did some travelling within their own continent. Many respondents visit the South as long as they are in a physical and mental condition to do so. They anticipate 'returning' to their own continent when travelling to long-haul destinations becomes too exhausting. Oppermann (1995) refers to a 'travel life cycle'.

His research on the German market (1995) reveals that successive generations have different travel patterns. The younger generation appears to be travelling more frequently and farther than previous generations at the same age. Through their travelling the youth gain different travel experiences, which makes it unlikely that they will select the same destinations as previous generations in later stages of their life-span. This could have an enormous impact on tourism destinations. Oppermann advocates a longitudinal analysis of travel patterns with respect to individual travel life cycles and changing destination choices of successive generations to provide destinations with valuable insights into their markets.

## Planning for desired social and cultural impacts

Much the same as the economic impacts, social and cultural (as well as ecological) impacts may vary substantially per type of tourism. Paradoxically, positive economic impacts do not have to go hand in hand with positive social and cultural impacts. As discussed in the previous section, 'dedicated' or 'pioneer' tourism that is going beyond the mainstream tourism circuit may be positively valued from a local or regional economic development point of view. However, as these tourists exhibit a great desire to interact with residents of the areas visited and are in search of 'authenticity' that is hardly negotiable, they run the risk of invading the residents' privacy. The more tourists are interested in going 'backstage' and getting in touch with 'real' local life, the more hazardous their interests are of intruding into local life. Harrison (2003, p. 136) refers to the 'penetrative actions of their arrival in foreign communities' and 'an implicit aggressive assumption' of their right to intrude, to be welcomed, and take photographs (p. 137). Munt (in Tucker, 2001, p. 870) has argued that – behind their disguise as socially and environmentally sensitive travellers – these tourists are in fact strong proponents of ethnocentric imperialist values. In these views tourism is all but a vital force for peace (see box 'Tourism, a vital force for peace?'). According to Craik (1995, p. 88), new forms of tourism – such as ecotourism, rural tourism and ethnic tourism – are increasingly intrusive and dependent upon the destination community. This holds particularly true for the most vulnerable and endangered people: 'the "Fourth World" ethnic minorities, tribal groups and remnants of hunter-gatherer bands whose "real" life is threatened to become a show for organized touristic visits' (Cohen, 1995, p. 17).

Just like the Canadian travellers studied by Harrison, the respondents in the present research all seem to assume a desire on behalf of the local people to have strangers around and connect with foreigners. They all consider a place for themselves in the Other's world something self-evident. Their arrival is almost exclusively imagined in positive terms rather than anything reminiscent of an act of rape.

Harrison (2003, p. 210) raises the question of how it is possible – recognizing the economic realities of the tourism business for many communities – to keep the fascination with difference alive among travellers, 'while maintaining, or in some cases restoring, the dignity and integrity of the lives of those who live in tourist destinations around the globe?' She finds the answer in changing tourist attitudes (p. 212). 'Those who arrive at the metaphorical global table in the posture of a tourist should not assume their right to be seated. They are there by invitation only' (p. 212). She admits, however, that 'making this journey is going to be one of the most difficult that these tourists . . . have ever undertaken.'

Rather than waiting for tourists to be able to undertake this difficult journey, destinations should take the initiative to 'develop means to *shape* tourism development, *anticipate changes and impacts*, and *manage consequences and conflicts*' (Craik, 1995, p. 88). References to 'penetrative', 'intrusive' or even 'imperialistic' actions support the general notion in tourism-related literature that 'local communities, while becoming socially disrupted, are rendered passive to the tourism process' (Tucker, 2001, p. 869). Communities, however, are agents in the process of modernization and globalization, not just recipients (Erb, 2000, p. 710). They can develop all kinds of strategies to cope with intrusion by tourists. Two related key phrases are relevant here: understanding tourists and perceived control. When local agents – be they

**Tourism, a vital force for peace?**
In its *Manila Declaration on World Tourism* (1980), the World Tourism Organization claims that tourism is 'a vital force for peace'. Leaders of the world, such as Mahatma Gandhi, John F. Kennedy, Ronald Reagan, Mikhail Gorbachev and Pope John Paul II, were united in proclaiming tourism a powerful tool for understanding between peoples and, consequently, a powerful tool for peace.

Presently, the World Tourism Organization – through its Secretary-General (2004) – contends that 'tourism and peace are inseparable' and 'tourism is a harbinger of peace'. For the time being, these claims are out of step with on-the-ground development in West–South tourism. Robinson (1999, p. 2) refers to 'a residual attitude derived from the romantic (and élitist) traditions of travel in the 18th and 19th centuries' and a 'Eurocentric, moralistic tradition' that 'has developed into political advocacy' (p. 3). According to him, tourism is an activity increasingly characterized by conflict. As a matter of fact, interaction between tourists from the West and residents of the South is extremely limited. Consequently, understanding between 'guest' and 'host' can only arise indirectly. Understanding is hampered by mutual romantic perceptions – or even stereotyping, tourists seeing locals as 'unspoilt', 'innocent', 'poor but happy', etc., locals seeing tourists as living in times of plenty. Bridging the gap between the life-worlds of 'hosts' and 'guests' appears to be possible only when quite a few conditions – specified in section 4.3 – are met. They cannot be met by mainstream tourists, 'hedonists' or 'accidental' tourists. 'Dedicated' tourists exhibit a desire to learn about local life and interact with locals. Mostly, however, the life-worlds of tourists and residents are fundamentally different, as is argued in section 4.3. A lot of mutual personal investment is required for both parties to understand each other. 'Pioneers', as well as some 'dedicated' organized tourists and backpackers, on the one hand, run the risk of invading the residents' privacy but, on the other hand, are the only ones that are able to meet the conditions of section 4.3 and invest in bridging the gap. Respectful 'pioneers' and 'dedicated' tourists arriving in a destination area where residents are in a phase of Euphoria rather than Apathy or Irritation, have the best chance of bringing about mutual understanding with residents who are in control of the situation.

communities, authorities, NGOs or entrepreneurs – understand the tourist phenomenon, this might contribute to the development of perceived control, i.e. the feeling that they are in control of tourism development. In the words of Erb (p. 711): 'Those who understand are in a position of power over those who do not.'

Fortunately, the great majority of tourists are relatively easy to manage. In spite of the frequently mentioned desire to meet local people, actual search for interaction with residents is generally extremely limited. Most tours, mainstream tours in particular, avoid local villages and communities.

The more tourists are 'dedicated' to being 'travellers' or even 'pioneers', the more they are interested in interaction with locals. This holds true for both organized tourists and backpackers. Still, quite a few 'travellers' were straightforward in stating that they do not want contact with local people, they just like to 'observe' local life. They feel safer and more comfortable then. Consequently, it is a minority among the 'travellers' that actually has some kind of direct interaction with residents.

The broad range of tourist preferences requires an 'orchestrated approach', as Pearce (1995) advocates. 'In offering a range of contact opportunities (particularly where the visited cultures are sub-groups within larger societies), the use of guides; boundary/buffer zones; and structured approaches to visiting the communities in terms of time, behaviours on display and set locations are all useful control features for tourism planners' (p. 149). The list that follows presents an elaboration of such an 'orchestrated approach'.

- 'Accidental' tourists are relatively easy to manage. They make excursions from urban areas or beach resorts to visit tourism highlights, e.g. from Cancún, Yucatán, Mexico, to the archaeological sites of ancient Maya culture or from Pacific beach resorts in Costa Rica to national parks, such as Manuel Antonio or Monteverde. They seek entertainment and 'doing something interesting' rather than interaction with local communities. Their visits are short, 1 or 2 hours on the average. They can be served satisfactorily within Turner and Ash's (1975) 'pleasure periphery'. Among the tools for destinations to manage 'accidental' visitor flows are: dissemination of information in the generating resorts, arrangements with excursion operators in the generating resorts, zoning of the site by concentrating facilities such as parking, toilets, visitor centre, shops, etc. in the arrival area, and developing products that can be consumed within 1 or 2 hours. By paying an entrance fee, buying souvenirs, having some food or drinks, 'accidental' tourists contribute to the regional economy. As this type of tourism is confined within a specific tourist periphery, interference in local life is minimized.
- Just like 'accidental' tourists, 'hedonists' are confined to a specific 'pleasure periphery'. They seek places 'where the action is' in order to have fun and find excitement. When partying, they might spend handsome amounts of money. The flow of 'hedonists' is dependent upon the party facilities. These tourists are densely concentrated in the party enclaves and, consequently, are easy to manage. Among the tools destination managers can employ – in addition to concentration of facilities – are: the quality of the entertainment facilities, such as type of music and an exotic entourage, permissiveness as far as free sex and alcohol and drug use are concerned, as well as the general

price level. The economic benefits 'hedonists' generate, too, are highly concentrated in these enclaves. As they are confined within a specific tourist periphery, their interference in local life is minimal.

- Flows of mainstream round-trip tourists (both organized and unorganized) can be managed by developing tourist facilities in designated tourist realms. In these realms 'local life' is represented by means of museums, visitor centres, cultural villages, 'native shows', souvenir shops, etc., that offer tourists an opportunity to learn about local culture and satisfy their generalized curiosity. Specific tourist realms allow authorities and managers to control the visitor flows. As long as these products are attractive and efficient (i.e. allow a short visit), they will be able to satisfy most mainstream tourists – Asians perhaps more than Europeans. Still, quite a few visitors might want a glimpse of 'real' local life. Visits to local markets, shops, factories, etc. will do, allowing these visitors to have some interaction with locals. As Tucker (2001, p. 886) notes, regardless of whether the products are perceived as authentically traditional by the tourists, the encounters with locals in themselves satisfy the quest for the 'authentically social' precisely because the experience is not blatantly staged.

- 'Dedicated' tourists are more demanding as far as interaction with locals and authenticity issues are concerned. Although they might visit specific tourist attractions, they want, in addition to that, to go more into 'depth' and have 'deep' experiences, as opposed to 'shallow' common tourist experiences. 'Deep' experiences are closely associated with interacting with locals outside the specific tourism realm and getting in touch with 'real' local life. More than mainstream tourists, 'dedicated' tourists are conservative in that they desire the cultures and nature areas they visit to remain unchanged and in a primitive and untouched state. They are easily disappointed when elements they perceive as 'authentic' turn out to be contrived. In other words, they are less able to playfully negotiate 'authenticity' than mainstream tourists are. Consequently, 'dedicated' tourists are the most difficult to manage. Suppliers should understand the desires of these tourists, in order to offer good quality to them in terms of supplying elements that enable them to negotiate the 'realness' of the products. Souvenirs should be (at least appear to be) locally produced, folkloric singers or dancers should not perform for tourists specifically – let alone be paid openly – sites and products should not be commercialized and commoditized explicitly, the residents visited should not be openly after the tourists' money. Organized 'dedicated' tourists visit selected local families and workplaces. Although they are fully aware that these families and workplaces are carefully selected by the tour operator and/or the local agent, they still want to be able to perceive them as 'real', i.e. not made for tourists and not visited by mainstream tourists. If the experience or encounter is already decided upon and packaged as a touristic event, then these tourists lose their interest or might get disappointed.

• 'Pioneers' are the most dispersed type of tourists. Their numbers are small. They want to go beyond 'tourist places' and avoid tourists and tourist facilities. They penetrate deepest into local life of all tourist categories. Because 'pioneers' are the first tourists to arrive in an area, most residents will not be 'apathetic' or 'irritated' in terms of Doxey's Irritation Index (1985), but rather 'euphoric'. When the first 'pioneers' arrive, residents will be able to perform the roles of hosts and welcome them into their private realm. When 'pioneers' are satisfied with the 'realness' of local life and the depth of their experiences, they might stay in the area for quite a few days. Their per-day expenditures are modest, but – once more – by staying for a long time and living with locals these spendings may be quite significant for the local economy. 'Pioneers', however, are difficult to manage. They come and go whenever they want and are fairly elusive for destination managers.

A similar 'orchestrated approach' can be developed where preventing or reducing environmental impacts upon nature areas are concerned. As Weaver puts forward (1999, p. 810), if properly managed, large numbers of visitors within a restricted space can still meet criteria of sustainability and in doing so perhaps even ensure that more sensitive extensive areas are less impacted. Fortunately, most visitors to nature areas prefer staying in touch with the social world rather than going 'deep' into the wilderness. This holds true for non-Europeans, but also for quite a few Europeans. Although taste and regard for 'unspoilt' and well-preserved nature is characteristic of many Western tourists – 'dedicated', 'hard-core' and 'pioneers' rather than others – fear for nature has never completely disappeared. For many, ambivalence remains. Aversive feelings towards nature, such as fear, disgust and discomfort have received little attention in environmental psychology. However, the available evidence (e.g. Bixler and Floyd, 1997) suggests that fear and other negative feelings towards nature continue to exist among quite a few people and are easily activated by external stimuli. Moreover, increasing psychological distance from nature in our technological societies may have diminished people's capacity to cope with uncontrollable and threatening aspects of nature. So, in spite of the frequently expressed desire to enjoy untouched nature, celebrate solitude and have spiritual experiences, the overwhelming majority of tourists prefers to stay in touch with other people, as well as tourist facilities. 'Hard-core' tourists, as well as some 'dedicated' tourists and 'pioneers', are the obvious exceptions. Ambivalence is solved by having guided safaris and trekkings in groups, visiting famous panoramas, and having brief glimpses of rainforests, swamps, wetlands and wildlife in designated tourist areas. Both tour operators who offer nature trips and destination managers should understand this ambivalence and find the right balance between preventing feelings of fear and discomfort on the one hand and avoiding crowding on the other. According to Iso-Ahola (1980, p. 300), crowding is felt when people experience more social interaction than is desired. Europeans are presumed to be less tolerant towards crowding than non-Europeans. The more Europeans perceive themselves as 'travellers' rather than 'tourists', the lower their tolerance towards crowding.

Concentrated flows of 'accidental' and mainstream visitors are easier to manage than scattered small-scale special interest tourists. Furthermore, large volumes of users justify making investments in appropriate services such as sewage treatment, as much as concentration of accommodation and facilities pays where conventional beach tourism is concerned (van Egmond, 2005, p. 138). Thus the issue is not one of incompatibility of sustainable tourism or ecotourism with mass tourism per se, but of incompatibility with *unsustainable* mass tourism (Weaver, 1999, pp. 810–811).

Promotion of destination areas on the Western markets requires the use of differential channels. 'Accidental' tourists can be addressed in their temporary place of residence through excursion operators. All organized tourists are 'hidden' behind tour operators in the generating countries. The holiday fairs in Europe, such as ITB, Berlin, World Travel Market, London, and Vakantiebeurs, Utrecht, provide an opportunity for developing countries to get in touch with both tour operators and consumers. Two major channels to reach 'hedonists' and mainstream backpackers are the Internet and travel guides, *Lonely Planet* first. 'Hard-core' tourists can only be addressed through specific magazines, journals or websites. 'Dedicated' backpackers and – even more so – 'pioneers' are difficult to reach. They have left both *Lonely Planet* and popular backpacker websites behind. Inviting writers of travel reports, travel stories and travel guides is a possible option.

Promotion should reflect the 'orchestrated approach' that offers a spectrum of cultural and natural opportunities at the destination area. Websites should therefore be constructed with great care.

If anything, Western tourism consultants should be able to assist destinations in both identifying their target groups in the West and introducing them to the markets.

### 'Alternative' tourism or not?

The notion 'tourists = mass tourism = bad' and 'travellers = appropriate travelling = good' (see Mowforth and Munt, 2003, p. 26) can be dismissed now as a simplistic view. Quite a few authors equate appropriate tourism with *alternative* tourism (for an overview, see Wearing, 2001, p. 6). Alternative tourism is conceptualized as opposed to conventional, institutionalized or mainstream tourism (van Egmond and Ars, 1993). Wearing (2001, p. 30) distinguishes alternative tourism from mass tourism (conventional, standard, large-scale tourism). The previous section demonstrates that, as far as West–South round trip tourism is concerned, there is no institutionalized or standard tourism as opposed to alternative forms. All tourists are searching for a balance between hedonism and asceticism, a blasé attitude and the desire to learn, between observing and connecting and between indifference to staging and 'allergy' to staging. The economic impacts vary greatly per type of tourism, as do the social and cultural impacts. Types of tourism that can be valued positively from a regional economic development point of view cannot by definition be assessed positively from a social and cultural perspective. Moreover, all types of West–South tourism have a long-haul flight in common, which cannot be labelled 'appropriate' or 'alternative' according to any standard.

Rather than aiming at 'standard' or 'alternative' tourism, destination areas should exert themselves to specify what types of tourism and tourism impacts are desired and develop products and management systems accordingly.

## Conclusion

To 'meet the needs of . . . host regions' and operate 'in harmony with the local environment, community and cultures, so that these become the permanent beneficiaries and not victims' (WTO's definition of sustainable tourism), tourism development requires local control, i.e. the opportunity for residents to decide what types of tourism and interaction are desirable and plan and manage tourism consequently. For authorities, communities, NGOs and entrepreneurs to be able to control tourism, understanding the tourist phenomenon is a prerequisite. Generally, in Third World countries, research in order to understand tourists is either lacking or limited to quantifying travel flows in terms of number of arrivals and bednights, use of accommodation, length of stay, generating countries and general expenditures. To understand tourists' interest, preferences and subsequent behaviour additional qualitative research is needed. The broad range of interests, preferences and behaviour that Western tourists exhibit requires an 'orchestrated approach' on behalf of destination managers in terms of offering a spectrum of contact opportunities and themes, ranging from a 'pleasure periphery' or specific tourism circuit ('frontstage') to daily local life that is less suitable for public access ('backstage'). Which elements of the spectrum are actually exposed to tourists is for destination authorities and communities to decide.

# References

Acott, T.G., La Trobe, H.L. and Howard, S.H. (1998) An evaluation of deep ecotourism and shallow ecotourism. *Journal of Sustainable Tourism* 6(1), 238–253.

Adler, Judith (1985) Youth on the road: reflection on the history of trampling. *Annals of Tourism Research* 12, 335–354.

Andersen, Vivien, Prentice, Richard and Watanabe, Kazumasa (2000) Journeys for experiences: Japanese independent travelers in Scotland. *Journal of Travel and Tourism Marketing* 9(1/2), 129–151.

Apostolopoulos, Yiorgos, Leivadi, Stella and Yiannakis, Andrew (1996) *The Sociology of Tourism: Theoretical and Empirical Investigations.* London: Routledge.

Aramberri, Julio (2001) The host should get lost. *Annals of Tourism Research* 28(3), 738–761.

Ashley, Caroline (1998) Tourism, communities and national policy: Namibia's experience. *Development Policy Review* 16(4), 323–352.

Ateljevic, Irena and Doorne, Stephen (2004) Theoretical encounters: a review of backpacker literature. In: Richards, Greg and Wilson, Julie (eds) *The Global Nomad. Backpacker Travel in Theory and Practice.* Clevedon: Channel View Publications, pp. 60–76.

Aziz, Heba (2001) The journey: an overview of tourism and travel in the Arab/Islamic context. In: Harrison, David (ed.) *Tourism and the Less Developed World: Issues and Case Studies.* Wallingford: CABI Publishing, pp. 151–159, CAB International, Wallingford, Oxon.

Bargeman, Bertine (2001) Kieskeurig Nederland. Routines in de vakantiekeuze van Nederlandse toeristen. PhD Thesis, Amsterdam Thela.

Barkin, David (2001) Strengthening domestic tourism in Mexico: challenges and opportunities. In: Ghimire, Krishna B. (ed.) *The Native Tourist. Mass Tourism within Developing Countries.* pp. 30–54, Earthscan, London.

Baudrillard, Jean (1988) *Selected Writings*. Edited and Introduced by Mark Poster, Polity Press, Cambridge.

Bauman, Zygmunt (2000) *Liquid Modernity*. Polity Press, Cambridge.

Bauman, Zygmunt (2002) *Society Under Siege*. Polity Press, Cambridge.

Berlyne, D.E. (1960) *Conflict, Arousal, and Curiosity*. New York: McGraw-Hill.

Bixler, R.D. and Floyd, M.F. (1997) Nature is scary, disgusting and uncomfortable. *Environment and Behavior* 29, 443–467.

Boorstin, Daniel J. (1961, 1980) *The Image. A Guide to Pseudo-Events in America*. Atheneum, New York.

Bosman, Karin (2005) De Laatste Inca. Master's thesis, University of Amsterdam.

Both, Katja (2004) Through the eyes of the experience. BA thesis NHTV Breda University of Professional Education.

Bourdieu, Pierre (1984) *Distinction: a Social Critique of the Judgement of Taste*. Routledge, London.

Bourdieu, Pierre (1986) The forms of capital. In: Richardson, John (ed.) *Handbook of Theory and Research for the Sociology of Education*. pp. 241–258, Greenwood Press, New York.

Bradford de Long, James (1989) *The 'Protestant Ethic' revisited: a twentieth-century look*. Harvard University and NBER.

Brohman, John (1996) New directions in tourism for Third World development. *Annals of Tourism Research* 23(1), 49–70.

Brundtland, Gro Harlem (1987) *Our Common Future*. World Commission on Environment and Development (WCED), Oxford University Press.

Butler, R.W. (1980) The concept of a tourism area cycle of evolution. Implications for the management of resources. *Canadian Geographer* 24, 5–12.

Campbell, Colin (1983) Romanticism and the consumer ethic. Intimations of a Weber-style thesis. *Sociological Analysis* 44(4), 279–296.

Campbell, Colin (1987) *The Romantic Ethic and the Spirit of Modern Consumerism*. Blackwell, Oxford.

Cohen, Erik (1972) Towards a sociology of international tourism. *Social Research* 39(1), 164–182.

Cohen, Erik (1973) Nomads from affluence: Notes on the phenomenon of drifter tourism. *International Journal of Comparative Sociology* 14, 89–103.

Cohen, Erik (1979a, 1996) A phenomenology of tourist experiences. *Sociology* 13(2), 179- 201; reprinted in Apostolopoulos, Y. (ed.) (1996) *The Sociology of Tourism*. Routledge, London.

Cohen, Erik (1979b) Rethinking the sociology of tourism. *Annals of Tourism Research* 6(1), 18–35.

Cohen, Erik (1988) Traditions in the Qualitative Sociology of Tourism. *Annals of Tourism Research* 15, 29–46.

Cohen, Erik (1988) Authenticity and commoditization in tourism. *Annals of Tourism Research* 15, 371–386.

Cohen, Erik (1995) Contemporary tourism – trends and challenges: sustainable authenticity or contrived post-modernity? In: Butler, Richard and Pearce, Douglas (eds) *Change in Tourism: People, Places, Progresses*. pp. 12–29, Routledge, London.

Cohen, Erik (2004) Backpacking: Diversity and Change. In: Richards, Greg and Wilson, Julie (eds) *The Global Nomad. Backpacker Travel in Theory and Practice.* Clevedon: Channel View Publications, pp. 43–59.

Cohen, Stanley and Taylor, Laurie (1976, 1992) *Escape Attempts. The Theory and Practice of Resistance to Everyday Life.* Routledge, London.

Corrigan, Peter (1997) *The Sociology of Consumption.* Sage, London.

Craik, Jennifer (1995) Are there cultural limits to tourism? *Journal of Sustainable Tourism* 3(2), 87–98.

Craik, Jennifer (1997) The culture of tourism. In: Rojek, Chris and Urry, John (eds) *Touring Cultures. Transformations of Travel and Theory.* pp. 113–136, Routledge, London.

Crawshaw, C. and Urry, J. (1997) Tourismand the photographic eye. In: Rojek, C. and Urry, J. (eds) *Touring Cultures. Transformations of Travel and Theory.* Routledge, London, pp. 176–195.

CREM, Consultancy and Research for Environmental Management BV (2004) *A toolkit to develop and promote sustainable tourism in Asia.* Amsterdam.

Csikszentmihalyi, M. (1975) *Beyond Boredom and Anxiety.* Jossey-Bass, San Francisco.

Dann, Graham (1999) Writing out the tourist in space and time. *Annals of Tourism Research* 26(1), 159–183.

Dann, Graham M.S. (ed.) (2002) *The Tourist as a Metaphor of the Social World.* CAB International, Wallingford.

Dann, Graham, Nash, Dennison and Pearce, Philip (1988) Methodology in tourism research. *Annals of Tourism Research* 15, 1–28.

De Groot, Ellen (2004) Hulle het karre en geld. Social representations of Tourism in Spitzkoppe. MA Thesis Cultural Anthropology, University of Amsterdam.

Denzin, Norman and Lincoln, Yvonna (1994) *Handbook of Qualitative Research.* Sage, California.

Diegues, Antonio Carlos (2001) Regional and domestic mass tourism in Brazil: an overview. In: Ghimire, Krishna B. (ed.) *The Native Tourist. Mass Tourism within Developing Countries.* pp. 55–85, Earthscan, London.

Din, Kadir H. (1989) Islam and tourism, patterns, issues, and options. *Annals of Tourism Research* 16, 542–563.

Doxey, G.V. (1985) A causation theory of visitor–resident irritants; methodology and research inferences. In: Peter E. Murphy (ed.) *Tourism, A Community Approach.* Methuen, New York.

Drum, Andy and Moore, Alan (2002) *Ecotourism Development. A Manual for Conservation Planners and Managers.* Volume I, *An Introduction to Ecotourism Planning.* Nature Conservancy, Arlington, Virginia, USA.

Echtner, Charlotte M. (1995) Entrepreneurial training in developing countries. *Annals of Tourism Research* 22(1), 119–134.

Echtner, Charlotte M. (2002) The content of Third World tourism marketing: a 4A approach. *International Journal of Tourism Research* 4, 413–434.

Edensor, T. (1998) Tourists at the Taj: performance and meaning at a symbolic site. Routledge, London.

Elands, Birgit and Lengkeek, Jaap (2000) Typical tourists. Research into the theoretical and methodological foundations of a typology of tourism and recreation experiences. Mansholt Graduate School, Wageningen.

Elias, Norbert and Dunning, Eric (1986) *Quest for Excitement: Sport and Leisure in the Civilizing Process.* Blackwell, Oxford.

Elsrud, Torun (2001) Risk creation in travelling. Backpacker adventure narration. *Annals of Tourism Research* 28(3), 597–617.

Erb, Maribeth (2000) Understanding Tourists: Interpretations from Indonesia. *Annals of Tourism Research* 21(3), 709–736.

Ewert, A. and Hollenhorst, S. (1989) Testing the adventure model: empirical support for a model of risk recreation participation. *Journal of Leisure Research* 21, 124–139.

Franklin, Adrian (2003a) *Tourism. An Introduction.* Sage, London.

Franklin, Adrian (2003b) The tourist syndrome. An interview with Zygmunt Bauman. *Tourist Studies,* 3(2), 205–217.

Fromm, Erich (1957) *The Art of Loving.* Unwin Books, London.

Gaus, Helmut (2001) *Why Yesterday Tells of Tomorrow.* Garant, Leuven, Belgium.

Ghimire, Krishna B. (ed.) (2001) *The Native Tourist. Mass Tourism within Developing Countries.* Earthscan, London.

Ghimire, Krishna B. (2001) The growth of national and regional tourism in developing countries: an overview. In: Ghimire, Krishna B. (ed.) *The Native Tourist. Mass Tourism within Developing Countries.* pp. 1–29, Earthscan, London.

Giddens, Anthony (1990) *The Consequences of Modernity.* Polity Press, Cambridge.

Giddens, Anthony (1991) *Modernity and Self-identity: Self and Society in the Late Modern Age.* Polity Press, Cambridge.

Goffman, Erving (1959) *The Presentation of Self in Everyday Life.* Penguin, Harmondsworth.

Gössling, Stefan (2002) Human–environmental relations with tourism. *Annals of Tourism Research* 29(2), 539–556.

Graburn, Nelson H.H. (1995) The past in the present in Japan. Nostalgia and neo-traditionalism in contemporary Japanese domestic tourism. In: Butler, Richard and Pearce, Douglas (eds) *Change in Tourism: People, Places, Progresses.* pp. 47–70, Routledge, London.

Hampton, Mark P. (1998) Backpacker tourism and economic development. *Annals of Tourism Research* 25(3), 639–659.

Harrison, Julia (2003) *Being a Tourist. Finding Meaning in Pleasure Travel.* UBC Press, Vancouver.

Herold, Edward, Garcia, Rafael and DeMoya, Tony (2002) Female tourists and beach boys. Romance or sex tourism? *Annals of Tourism Research* 29(4), 978–997.

Hessels, A. (1973) *Vakantie en vakantiebesteding sinds de eeuwwisseling.* van Gorcum, Assen.

Hill, Roger B. (1996) *History of Work Ethic.* http://www.coe.uga.edu/~rhill/workethic/hist.htm

Hofstede, Geert (1991) *Cultures and Organizations. Software of the Mind.* McGraw-Hill International.

Inglehart, Ronald, Basañez, Miguel and Moreno, Alejandro (1998) *Human Values and Beliefs. A Cross-Cultural Sourcebook.* Ann Arbor: University of Michigan Press.

Inglis, Fred (2000) *The Delicious History of The Holiday.* Routledge, London.

International Student Travel Confederation (ISTC) and Association of Leisure and Tourism Education (ATLAS) (2002) *Young Independent Travel Survey.*

Iso-Ahola, Seppo E. (1980) *The Social Psychology of Leisure and Recreation.* WCB Company Publishers.

Iversen, Nina (2003) Tourism development of U Minh Thuong National Park, Vietnam. BA thesis NHTV Breda University of Professional Education.

Jamal, Tazim and Lee, Jin-Hyung (2003) Integrating micro and macro approaches to tourist motivations: towards an interdisciplinary theory. *Tourism Analysis* 8(1), 47–59.

Kaosa-ard, Mingsarn, Bezic, David and White, Suzanne (2001) Domestic tourism in Thailand: supply and demand. In: Ghimire, Krishna B. (ed.) *The Native Tourist. Mass Tourism within Developing Countries.* pp. 109–141, Earthscan, London.

Kardes, Frank R. (2001) *Consumer Behavior and Managerial Decision Making.* Prentice Hall.

Kim, Chulwon and Lee, Seokho (2000) Understanding the cultural differences in tourist motivation between Anglo-American and Japanese tourists. *Journal of Travel and Tourism Marketing* 9(1/2), 153–170.

Kuja, Beatrice (2005) Tourism potentials in Cameroon. BA thesis NHTV Breda University of Professional Education.

Lash, Scott (1999) *Another Modernity A Different Rationality.* Blackwell, Oxford.

Lee, Tae-Hee and Crompton, John (1992) Measuring novelty seeking in tourism. *Annals of Tourism Research* 19(4), 732–751.

Lemaire, Ton (1988) *Binnenwegen. Essays en excursies.* Ambo.

Lengkeek, Jaap (1996) *Vakantie van het leven. Over het belang van toerisme en recreatie.* Meppel: Boom.

Lengkeek, Jaap (2002) A love affair with elsewhere: love as a metaphor and paradigm for tourist longing. In: Dann, Graham M.S. (ed.) *The Tourist as a Metaphor of the Social World.* Wallingford: CABI Publishing, pp. 189–208.

Lindberg, Kreg (1991) *Policies for maximizing nature tourism's ecological and economic benefits.* World Resources Institute, Washington DC.

Lindberg, Kreg, Tisdell, Clem and Xue, Dayuan (2003) Ecotourism in China's nature reserves. In: Lew, Alan A., Yu, Lawrence, Ap, John and Guangrui, Zhang (eds) *Tourism in China.* Haworth Hospitality Press, pp. 103–122.

Löfgren, Orvar (1999) *On Holiday. A History of Vacationing.* University of California Press.

Loker-Murphy, Laurie and Pearce, Philip (1995) Young budget travelers: backpackers in Australia. *Annals of Tourism Research* 22, 819–843.

Loman, Inge (2005) A Tough Mountain to Climb. Towards competitiveness in community-based mountain tourism. BA thesis NHTV Breda University of Professional Education.

MacCannell, Dean (1973) Staged authenticity: arrangements of social space in tourist settings. *American Journal of Sociology* 79(3), 589–603.

MacCannell, Dean (1976) *The Tourist. A New Theory of the Leisure Class.* Schocken Books, New York.

Macnaghten, P. and Urry, John (1998) *Contested Natures.* Sage, London.

Mager, Daniël (2005) Backpackers and Package Tourists in Cusco, Peru. Master's thesis, CEDLA Masters Programme, University of Amsterdam.

Mannell, Roger C. and Iso-Ahola, Seppo E. (1987) Psychological nature of leisure and tourism experience. *Annals of Tourism Research* 14(3), 314–331.

Maslow, Abraham (1970) *Motivation and Personality.* 2nd edn. New York: Harper.

McCabe, Scott (2002) The tourist experience and everyday life. In: Dann, Graham M.S. (ed.) *The Tourist as a Metaphor of the Social World.* pp. 61–75, CAB International, Wallingford, Oxon.

McCall Smith, Alexander (1998) *The No.1 Ladies' Detective Agency.* Polygon.

McCall Smith, Alexander (2000) *Tears of the Giraffe.* Polygon.

McKercher, Bob (2002) Towards a classification of cultural tourists. *International Journal of Tourism Research* 4, 29–38.

Meisch, Lynn A. (1995) *Gringas* and *Otavaleños.* Changing tourist relations. *Annals of Tourism Research* 22(2), 441–462.

Mill, Robert Christie and Morrison, Alastair M. (2002) *The Tourism System.* 4th edn, Kendall/Hunt Publishing Company.

Miller, Dr Graham A., University of Westminster, London (2002) Presentation at the annual 'Groeneveldconferentie', NHTV, Breda, The Netherlands.

Mintel International Group Limited (2003) *Youth Travel and Backpacking – International – December 2003.* http://reports.mintel.com

Moore, Kevin (2002) The discursive tourist. In: Dann, Graham M.S. (ed.) *The Tourist as a Metaphor of the Social World.* pp. 41–59, CAB International, Wallingford, Oxon.

Moscardo, Gianna and Pearce, Philip L. (1999) Understanding ethnic tourists. *Annals of Tourism Research* 26(2), 416–435.

Mowforth, Martin and Munt, Ian (1998) *Tourism and Sustainability. Development and New Tourism in the Third World.* 2nd edn. 2003. Routledge, London.

Murphy, Laurie (2001) Exploring social interaction of backpackers. *Annals of Tourism Research* 28(1), 50–67.

Noy, Chaim (2004) This trip really changed me. Backpackers' narratives of self-change. *Annals of Tourism Research* 31(1), 78–102.

Oppermann, Martin (1995) Travel life cycle. *Annals of Tourism Research* 22(3), 535–552.

Oppermann, Martin (1999) Sex tourism. *Annals of Tourism Research* 26(2), 251–266.

Pearce, Philip L. (1988) *The Ulysses Factor: Evaluating Visitors in Tourist Settings.* Springer-Verlag, New York.

Pearce, Philip L. (1990) *The Backpacker Phenomenon: Preliminary Answers to Basic Questions.* James Cook University of North Queeensland, Townsville, Australia.

Pearce, Philip L. (1995) From culture shock and culture arrogance to culture exchange: ideas towards sustainable socio-cultural tourism. *Journal of Sustainable Tourism* 3(3).

Pimlott, J.A.R. (1976) *The Englishman's Holiday: A Social History.* Harvester Press, Brighton.

Plog, Stanley C. (1998) Why destination preservation makes economic sense. In: Theobald, William F., (ed.) *Global Tourism*. 2nd edn. pp. 251–266, Butterworth-Heinemann, Oxford.

Poon, Auliana (1993) *Tourism, Technology and Competitive Strategies*. CAB International, Wallingford, Oxon.

Porter, Roy (2003) *Flesh in the Age of Reason*. Penguin, London.

Poster, Mark (1988) *Jean Baudrillard. Selected Writings*. Polity Press, Cambridge.

Prentice, Richard (2004) Tourist motivation and typologies In: Lew, Alan A., Hall, C. Michael, and Williams, Allan M. (eds) *A Companion to Tourism*. pp. 261–278, Blackwell Publishing, Oxford.

Pruitt, Deborah and LaFont, Suzanne (1995) For love and money. Romance tourism in Jamaica. *Annals of Tourism Research* 22(2), 422–440.

Rao, Nina and Suresh, K.T. (2001) Domestic tourism in India. In: Ghimire, Krishna B. (ed.) *The Native Tourist. Mass Tourism within Developing Countries*. pp. 198–228, Earthscan, London.

Richards, Greg and Wilson, Julie (2004) *The Global Nomad. Backpacker Travel in Theory and Practice*. Channel View Publications, Clevedon.

Richards, Greg and Wilson, Julie (2004) Drifting towards the global nomad. In: Richards, Greg and Wilson, Julie (eds) *The Global Nomad. Backpacker Travel in Theory and Practice*. pp. 3–13, Channel View Publications, Clevedon.

Riley, Pamela J. (1988) Road culture of long-term budget travellers. *Annals of Tourism Research* 15, 313–328.

Riley, Roger W. and Love, Lisa L. (2000) The state of qualitative tourism research. *Annals of Tourism Research* 27(1), 164–187.

Ritzer, George (2000) *The MacDonaldization of Society*. Pine Forge Press, Thousand Oaks, California.

Ritzer, George and Liska, Allan (1997) 'McDisneyization' and 'Post-Tourism'. Complementary perspectives on contemporary tourism. In: Rojek, Chris and Urry, John (eds) *Touring Cultures. Transformations of Travel and Theory*. Routledge, London.

Robinson, Mike (1999) Cultural conflicts in tourism: inevitability and inequality. In: Robinson, Mike and Boniface, Priscilla (eds) *Tourism and Cultural Conflicts*. pp. 1–32, CAB International, Wallingford, Oxon.

Robinson, Mike and Boniface, Priscilla (eds) (1999) *Tourism and Cultural Conflicts*. CAB International, Wallingford, Oxon.

Rodenburg, Eric E. (1980) The effects of scale in economic development: tourism in Bali. *Annals of Tourism Research* 7(2), 177–196.

Rodgers, D.T. (1978) *The Work Ethic in Industrial America, 1850–1920*. University of Chicago Press, Chicago.

Rojek, Chris (1995) *Decentring Leisure. Rethinking Leisure Theory*. Sage, London.

Rojek, Chris and Urry, John (eds) (1997) *Touring Cultures. Transformations of Travel and Theory*. Routledge, London, pp. 1–19.

Rousseau G.S. and Porter, Roy (eds) (1990) *Exoticism in the Enlightenment*. Manchester University Press, Manchester.

Ryan, Chris (1998) The travel career ladder: an appraisal. *Annals of Tourism Research* 25(4), 936–957.

Ryan, Chris (2002) Tourism and cultural proximity. Examples from New Zealand. *Annals of Tourism Research* 29(4), 952–971.

Scheyvens, Regina (2002) Backpacker tourism and Third World development. *Annals of Tourism Research* 29(1), 144–162.

Schiffman, Leon G. and Kanuk, Leslie Lazar (2004) *Consumer Behavior.* Prentice Hall, Pearson.

Schutz, Alfred and Luckmann, Thomas (1974) *The Structures of the Life-World.* Heinemann, London.

Sharpley, R. and Sharpley, J. (1997) Sustainability and the consumption of tourism. In: Stabler, M.J. (ed.) *Tourism and Sustainability. Principles and Practice.* CAB International, Wallingford, Oxon.

Slaughter, Lee (2004) Profiling the international backpacker market in Australia. In: Richards, Greg and Wilson, Julie (eds) *The Global Nomad. Backpacker Travel in Theory and Practice.* pp. 168–179, Channel View Publications, Clevedon.

Smith, Christine and Jenner, Paul (1992) *The Tourism Industry and the Environment.* EIU Special Report No 2453.

Solomon, Michael R. (2001) *Consumer Behavior. Buying, Having, and Being.* Prentice Hall.

Solomon, Michael, Bamossy, Gary and Askegaard, Sören (2002) *Consumer Behaviour. A European Perspective.* Prentice Hall.

Sörensen, Anders (2003) Backpacker ethnography. *Annals of Tourism Research* 30(4), 847–867.

Spreitzhofer, Guenther (1998) Backpacking tourism in South-East Asia. *Annals of Tourism Research* 25(4), 979–983.

Stabler, M.J. (ed.) (1997) *Tourism and Sustainability. Principles and Practice.* CAB International, Wallingford, Oxon.

Taylor, Gordon D. (1998) Styles of travel. In: Theobald, William F. (ed.) *Global Tourism.* 2nd edn. pp. 267–277, Butterworth-Heinemann, Oxford.

Taylor, John P. (2001) Authenticity and sincerity in tourism. *Annals of Tourism Research* 28(1), 7–27.

Theobald, William F. (ed.) (1998) *Global Tourism.* 2nd edn. Butterworth-Heinemann, Oxford.

Theuns, H. Leo (2002) Tourism and development: economic dimensions. *Tourism Recreation Research* 27(1), 69–81.

Tribe, John (1997) The indiscipline of tourism. *Annals of Tourism Research* 24(3), 638–657.

Tucker, Hazel (2001) Tourists and troglodytes. Negotiating for sustainability. *Annals of Tourism Research* 28(4), 868–891.

Turner, Louis and Ash, John (1975) *The Golden Hordes: International Tourism and the Pleasure Periphery.* Constable, London.

Uriely, Natan, Yonay, Yuval and Simchai, Dalit (2002) Backpacking experiences. A type and form analysis. *Annals of Tourism Research* 29(2), 520–538.

Urry, John (1990, 2002) *The Tourist Gaze.* Sage, London.

Van Aart, Nina (2004) Bali. Balancing culture, community and the environment. BA thesis NHTV Breda University of Professional Education.

Van Egmond, Ton (1989) *Toerisme: verbroedering of verloedering?* Breda: DTV uitgeverij.

Van Egmond, Ton (1996) *Vakantiepreferenties. Een consumentenonderzoek.* Interne publicatie NHTV, Breda.

Van Egmond, Paul (2004) Gebakken Cavia of Pizza. Diversiteit onder backpackers. MA thesis Cultural Anthropology, University of Amsterdam.

Van Egmond, Ton (2005) *The Tourism Phenomenon: Past, Present, Future*, 2nd edn. ToerBoek, Leiden.

Van Egmond, Ton and Ars, Brigitte (1993) *Toerisme naar de Derde Wereld*. Garant, Leuven, Belgium.

Vogel, David (2001) The Protestant ethic and the spirit of environmentalism: the cultural roots of green politics and policies. Unpublished manuscript, Haas School of Business, University of California, Berkeley.

Vogels, Charlotte Jacaranda (2002) Tourism as a tool for empowerment of local communities in Kerala, India. BA thesis NHTV Breda University of Professional Education.

Vogt, Jay W. (1976) Wandering: youth and travel behaviour. *Annals of Tourism Research* 4, 25–41.

Walle, Alf (1997a) Pursuing risk or insight: marketing adventures. *Annals of Tourism Research* 24, 265–282.

Walle, Alf (1997b) Quantitative versus qualitative tourism research. *Annals of Tourism Research* 24(3), 524–536.

Walsh, Eileen Rose and Swain, Margaret Byrne (2004) Creating modernity by touring paradise: domestic ethnic tourism in Yunnan, China. *Tourism Recreation Research* 29(2), 59–68.

Wang, Ning (2000) *Tourism and Modernity. A Sociological Analysis*. Pergamon, Oxford.

Wang, Ning (2002) The tourist as peak consumer. In: Dann, Graham M.S. (ed.) *The Tourist as a Metaphor of the Social World*. Wallingford: CABI Publishing, pp. 281–295.

Wanhill, Steven (1994) The measurement of tourist income multipliers. *Tourism Management* 15, 281–283.

Wearing, Stephen (2001) *Volunteer Tourism. Experiences that Make a Difference*.

Wearing, Stephen (2002) Re-centring the self in volunteer tourism. In: Dann, Graham M.S. (ed.) *The Tourist as a Metaphor of the Social World*. pp. 237–262, CAB International, Wallingford, Oxon.

Weaver, David (1999) Magnitude of ecotourism in Costa Rica and Kenya. *Annals of Tourism Research* 29(4), 792–815.

Weaver, David (2001) *Ecotourism*. Wiley, Australia.

Weber, Karin (2001) Outdoor adventure tourism. A review of research approaches. *Annals of Tourism Research* 28(2), 360–377.

Weber, Max (1970) *From Max Weber*, ed. by H. Gerth and C. Wright Mills, Routledge & Kegan Paul, London.

Weber, Max (1976) *The Protestant Ethic and the Spirit of Capitalism*. George Allen & Unwin, London.

Welk, Peter (2004) The beaten track: anti-tourism as an element of backpacker identity construction. In: Richards, Greg and Wilson, Julie (eds) *The Global Nomad. Backpacker Travel in Theory and Practice*. pp. 77–91, Channel View Publications, Clevedon.

Westerhausen, Klaus (2002) *Beyond the Beach. An Ethnography of Modern Travellers in Asia*. Studies in Asian Tourism No. 2, Bangkok.

Whimster, Sam and Lash, Scott (eds) (1987) *Max Weber, Rationality and Modernity.* Allen & Unwin, London.

Wilson, Julie and Richards, Greg (2004) Backpacker icons: influential literary 'nomads' in the formation of backpacker identities. In: Richards, Greg and Wilson, Julie (eds) *The Global Nomad. Backpacker Travel in Theory and Practice.* pp. 123–145, Channel View Publications, Clevedon.

Wood, R.E. (1984) Ethnic tourism, the state, and cultural change in Southeast Asia. *Annals of Tourism Research* 11, 353–374.

World Tourism Organization (2004b) *Tourism and Poverty Alleviation; Recommendations for Action.* WTO, Madrid.

World Tourism Organization (2004a) *WTO Members' Update,* 4 March 2004.

World Tourism Organization (various years) *Guide for Local Authorities on Developing Sustainable Tourism.* WTO, Madrid.

Wyllie, Robert W. (2000) *Tourism and Society. A Guide to Problems and Issues.* Venture Publishing, State College, Pennsylvania.

# Appendix A.   Theoretical Understanding of Tourist Preferences

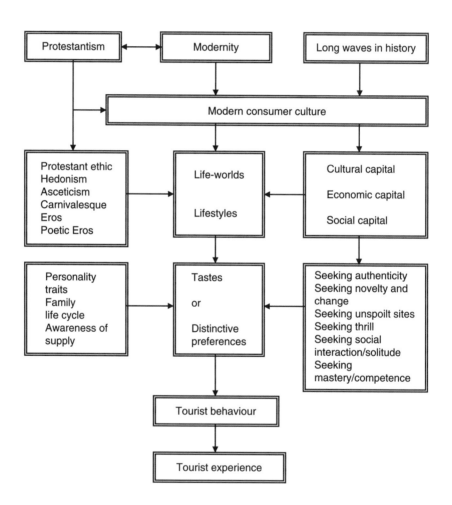

# Appendix B

Net economic results per type of tourism; some
hypothetical cases

Sources: European travel programmes, Mager (2005), Smith and Jenner
(1992), personal data collection

## Notes

There are no data available about organized 'hard core' tourists.

Mainstream organized trips are split up into lower-priced package
tours and luxury trips. 'Accidental' tourists are presumed to have booked
a conventional beach holiday package. Incidentally, they book excursions
from their beach resort to nature or culture sites in the hinterland.

Sixteen-day trips are taken as a starting point for both organized tourists
and 'hedonists'. For the other types of unorganized tourists a length of
stay of 30 days is taken as a starting point. This stay may be part of a longer
international journey.

## Explanation

*Cost of the trip* is the price of a package tour tourists pay to a tour operator
(directly or indirectly via a travel agent).

*Pre-leakage* consists of airfare, tour operator's overhead costs, tour operator's profit, travel agent's commission, etc. Total pre-leakage is the percentage of the cost of the trip that does not arrive in the destination area.

*Gross foreign exchange earnings* of a destination country consist of the cost of the trip minus pre-leakage.

*Leakage* concerns the import factor of tourism and the export of salaries, interest, return on investment and profit. The money spent leaks from the destination's economy and must be subtracted from gross foreign exchange earnings to determine the true economic impact.

*Net foreign exchange earnings* of a destination country consist of gross foreign exchange earnings minus leakage.

*Taxes* are presumed to be levied by the central government ('Treasury'). Taxes constitute leakage from the regional economy.

*Airport tax* is paid by the tourists at the airport. It is not included in the cost of the package.

*Savings* constitute money that is extracted from the regional economy.

*Economic result for destination area* is net foreign exchange earnings minus taxes and savings. It is the amount of local income generated per unit of visitor expenditure (income multiplier) (Wanhill, 1994).

*Economic result for Treasury* is the sum of taxes levied on tourism and tourism expenditures.

Literature provides estimates of the percentages of tourism expenditures that leak away from destination countries as a whole. For example, according to *The Encyclopedia of Ecotourism* (Weaver, 2001, p. 167) leakage for the average Caribbean country is 70 per cent, for Nepal 70 per cent, for Thailand 60 per cent, for The Gambia 55 per cent, etc. Literature that specifies leakage per type of tourism is almost entirely missing. Consequently, the assumptions related to leakage per type of tourism in Boxes 1 to 9 constitute 'intelligent guesses' rather than empirical data.

## Assumptions

The proportion of cost of the trip that is received by the destination country is 45 to 50 per cent. Individual travellers do not pay the cost of their trip to tour operators in their country of origin. Consequently, there is no pre-leakage.

Among the organized tourists, luxury tourists generate the highest leakage, mainly due to their propensity to consume imported goods and services and stay in foreign-owned, and managed, accommodation. Conversely, 'dedicated' adventurous tourists generate the lowest leakage. Similar to 'dedicated' adventurous tourists, backpackers do not generate high leakage; leakage of 'pioneers' expenditure is negligible.

## Sources of leakage

- Foreign debt servicing
- Import of foodstuffs and beverages
- Miscellaneous imports of tourism consumables
- Import of construction materials
- Import of fuel/energy
- Import of tourism infrastructure and capital goods
- Employment of foreign staff
- Foreign ownership and/or financing
- Overseas promotion by tourist boards and individual companies

---

**Box 1. *'Accidental' Tourists***

***Sixteen-day conventional beach holiday from Western Europe to Latin America, July***
*(Package tour, lunch not included, conventional 3\* accommodation; incidental excursions to sites in the hinterland, organized by either Western or local tour operator)*

|  | (€) |
|---|---|
| Cost of the trip, per person | 1290 |
| Pre-leakage (50%) | 645 |
| Gross foreign exchange earnings | 645 |
| Leakage (60%) | 387 |
| Net foreign exchange earnings | 258 |
| (Airport tax) | (25) |
| Taxes, excluding airport tax | 20 |
| Savings | 20 |
| Economic result for destination area (258 − 40) | 218 |
| Economic result for Treasury (25 + 20) | 45 |
| Meals (Lunch 14 × 8) | 112 |
| Bars, drinks | 120 |
| Souvenirs | 60 |
| Shopping | 150 |
| Excursions | 160 |
| Tipping (including guides) | 20 |
| Total expenditures in destination areas | 622 |
| Leakage (40%) | 249 |
| Taxes | 20 |

*(Continued)*

**Box 1.** *Continued*

| | |
|---|---:|
| Savings | 20 |
| Economic result for destination areas (622 – 289) | 333 |
| *Total economic result for destination areas (218 + 333)* | *551* |
| *Total economic result for Treasury (45 + 20)* | *65* |
| *Total economic result for destination country (incl. savings)* | *656* |

**Box 2.** *Mainstream Tourists*

*Sixteen-day mainstream organized round trip from Western Europe to Latin America, July*
*(Lower priced package tour, lunch and dinner not included, conventional 3\* accommodation)*

| | (€) |
|---|---:|
| Cost of the trip, per person | 1180 |
| Pre-leakage (50%) | 590 |
| Gross foreign exchange earnings | 590 |
| Leakage (48%) | 283 |
| Net foreign exchange earnings | 307 |
| (Airport tax) | (25) |
| Taxes, excluding airport tax | 20 |
| Savings | 20 |
| Economic result for destination area (307 – 40) | 267 |
| Economic result for Treasury (25 + 20) | 45 |
| Meals (Lunch $14 \times 6$, dinner/supper $14 \times 8$) | 196 |
| Bars, drinks | 90 |
| Souvenirs | 50 |
| Shopping | 50 |
| Local transport | 5 |
| Tipping (including guides) | 20 |
| Total expenditures in destination area | 411 |
| Leakage (20%) | 82 |
| Taxes | 10 |
| Savings | 10 |
| Economic result for destination area (411 – 102) | 309 |
| *Total economic result for destination area (267 + 309)* | *576* |
| *Total economic result for treasury (45 + 10)* | *55* |
| *Total economic result for destination country (incl. savings)* | *661* |

**Box 3.  *Luxury Organized Tourists***

*Sixteen-day luxury organized round trip from Western Europe to Latin America, July*
*(4\* and 5\* accommodation, breakfast and dinner/supper included)*

|  | (€) |
|---|---|
| Cost of the trip, per person | 3000 |
| Pre-leakage (50%) | 1500 |
| Gross foreign exchange earnings | 1500 |
| Leakage (79%) | 1185 |
| Net foreign exchange earnings | 315 |
| (Airport tax) | (25) |
| Taxes, excluding airport tax | 20 |
| Savings | 20 |
| Economic result for destination area (315 – 40) | 275 |
| Economic result for Treasury (25 + 20) | 45 |
| Meals (Lunch 14 × 10) | 140 |
| Bars, drinks | 130 |
| Souvenirs | 100 |
| Shopping | 150 |
| Local transport | — |
| Tipping (including guides) | 80 |
| Total expenditures in destination area | 600 |
| Leakage (40%) | 240 |
| Taxes | 30 |
| Savings | 20 |
| Economic result for destination area (600 – 290) | 310 |
| *Total economic result for destination area (275 + 310)* | *585* |
| *Total economic result for Treasury (45 + 30)* | *75* |
| *Total economic result for destination country (incl. savings)* | *700* |

**Box 4.**   *'Dedicated' Adventurous Tourists*

*Sixteen-day 'dedicated' adventurous round trip from Western Europe to Latin America, July*
*(1\* or 2\* accommodation, 3 nights in tents, 2 nights in local guest house, during excursions (5 days) meals included, other meals excluded)*

|  | (€) |
|---|---|
| Cost of the trip, per person | 1450 |
| Pre-leakage (45%) | 650 |
| Gross foreign exchange earnings | 800 |
| Leakage (25%) | 200 |
| Net foreign exchange earnings | 600 |
| (Airport tax) | (25) |
| Taxes, excluding airport tax | 30 |
| Savings | 20 |
| Economic result for destination area (600 − 50) | 550 |
| Economic result for Treasury (25 + 30) | 55 |
| Meals (Lunch 9 × 4, dinner/supper 9 × 6) | 90 |
| Bars, drinks | 50 |
| Souvenirs | 50 |
| Shopping | 60 |
| Local transport | 20 |
| Tipping (including guides) | 30 |
| Total expenditures in destination area | 300 |
| Leakage (15%) | 45 |
| Taxes | 8 |
| Savings | 10 |
| Economic result for destination area (300 − 63) | 237 |
| *Total economic result for destination area (550 + 237)* | *787* |
| *Total economic result for Treasury (55 + 8)* | *63* |
| *Total economic result for destination country (incl. savings)* | *880* |

**Box 5.  'Hedonists'**

*Sixteen-day backpacker 'party' trip from Western Europe to*
*Latin America, July*
(use of local guest houses and youth hostels, use of local public transport,
use of local tour operators for excursions)

|  | (€) |
|---|---|
| (Airport tax) | (25) |
| Accommodation (15 × 8) | 120 |
| Meals (brunch 14 × 4, dinner/supper 14 × 6) | 140 |
| Bars, drinks | 140 |
| Souvenirs | 30 |
| Shopping | 60 |
| Local transport | 20 |
| Tipping | 10 |
| Excursions | 80 |
| Total expenditures in destination area | 600 |
| Leakage (20%) | 120 |
| Taxes | 8 |
| Savings | 8 |
| Economic result for destination area (600 – 136) | 464 |
| *Total economic result for destination area* | *464* |
| *Total economic result for Treasury (25 + 8)* | *33* |
| *Total economic result for destination country (incl. savings)* | *505* |

**Box 6.   Mainstream Backpackers**

*Thirty-day mainstream backpacker trip from Western Europe to*
*Latin America (part of 3-month journey), July*
(Use of local guest houses and youth hostels, use of local public transport,
use of local tour operators for excursions)

|  | (€) |
|---|---|
| (Airport tax) | (25) |
| Accommodation (30 × 8) | 240 |
| Meals (breakfast 30 × 2, lunch 30 × 4, dinner/supper 30 × 6) | 360 |
| Bars, drinks | 120 |
| Souvenirs | 20 |
| Shopping | 40 |
| Local transport | 20 |
| Tipping | 5 |
| Excursions | 80 |
| Total expenditures in destination area | 885 |
| Leakage (15%) | 133 |
| Taxes | 6 |
| Savings | 6 |
| Economic result for destination area (885 – 145) | 740 |
| *Total economic result for destination area* | *740* |
| *Total economic result for treasury (25 + 6)* | *31* |
| *Total economic result for destination country (incl. savings)* | *777* |

**Box 7. 'Dedicated' Backpackers**

***Thirty-day 'dedicated' backpacker trip from Western Europe to
Latin America (part of 3-month journey), July***
(Use of local guest houses and youth hostels, partly off the mainstream
circuit; use of local public transport, use of local tour operators for
excursions)

|  | (€) |
|---|---|
| (Airport tax) | (25) |
| Accommodation (30 × 6) | 180 |
| Meals (breakfast 30 × 1, lunch 30 × 2, dinner/supper 30 × 4) | 210 |
| Bars, drinks | 60 |
| Souvenirs | 15 |
| Shopping | 40 |
| Local transport | 20 |
| Tipping | 5 |
| Excursions | 80 |
| Total expenditures in destination area | 610 |
| Leakage (10%) | 61 |
| Taxes | 4 |
| Savings | 4 |
| Economic result for destination area (610 – 69) | 541 |
| *Total economic result for destination area* | *541* |
| *Total economic result for treasury (25 + 4)* | *29* |
| *Total economic result for destination country (incl. savings)* | *574* |

**Box 8. 'Pioneers'**

***Thirty-day trip from Western Europe to Latin America, outside the tourist circuits (part of a long-term journey)***
(Partial use of local guest houses and partly staying with local families, eating 'streetsmart' in food-stalls and in local restaurants, use of public transport)

|  | (€) |
|---|---|
| (Airport tax) | (25) |
| Accommodation (20 × 6) | 120 |
| Meals (breakfast 20 × 1, lunch 20 × 2, dinner/supper 20 × 4) | 140 |
| Bars, drinks | 30 |
| Souvenirs | 15 |
| Shopping | 20 |
| Local transport | 20 |
| Tipping | 5 |
| Excursions | 30 |
| Gifts/payments to local families | 60 |
| Total expenditures in destination area | 440 |
| Leakage (2%) | 9 |
| Taxes | 2 |
| Savings | 2 |
| Economic result for destination area (440 – 13) | 427 |
| *Total economic result for destination area* | *427* |
| *Total economic result for Treasury (25 + 2)* | *27* |
| *Total economic result for destination country (incl. savings)* | *456* |

## Box 9.  Students

### *Three-month stay of Western European students in Latin America*
(Staying in local guest houses or with local families)

|                                                              | (€)   |
| ------------------------------------------------------------ | ----- |
| (Airport tax)                                                | (25)  |
| Accommodation, incl. meals                                   | 1080  |
| Bars, drinks                                                 | 150   |
| Souvenirs                                                    | 30    |
| Shopping                                                     | 60    |
| Local transport                                              | 110   |
| Tipping                                                      | 5     |
| Excursions                                                   | 80    |
| Total expenditures in destination area                       | 1515  |
| Leakage (5%)                                                 | 76    |
| Taxes                                                        | 15    |
| Savings                                                      | 8     |
| Economic result for destination area  (1515 – 99)            | 1416  |
| *Total economic result for destination area*                | *1416* |
| *Total economic result for Treasury  (25 + 15)*             | *40*  |
| *Total economic result for destination country (incl. savings)* | *1464* |

# Index